Washington Nature Weekends

Fifty-two Adventures in Nature

Sunny Walter and Janet O'Mara

FALCON®

Guilford, Connecticut
An imprint of The Globe Pequot Press

Dedication

To Samantha Erler, my daughter, in the hope that her love of
nature will nourish her through the years.
—Sunny

To Peter O'Mara, my husband and best friend, and our
shared delight in the great outdoors.
—Janet

Front and back cover photos: © Sunny Walter
Text design: Lisa Reneson
Maps: Trapper Badinovac
Photo credits: All photos © Sunny Walter, except: p. 38 and p. 218 © Gary Luhm; p. 66
© Gary Lentz; p. 73 © Earthbound Productions; p. 119 © Janet O'Mara; p. 146 © Terry
Wahl; pp. 161 and 237 © Jamie and Judy Wild; p. 176 © Stuart Westmorland; and pp. 148,
207, 227, and 241 © Len Steiner.

Library of Congress Cataloging-in-Publication Data
Walter, Sunny.
    Washington nature weekends: fifty-two adventures in nature / Sunny Walter and Janet
O'Mara.—1st ed.
    p. cm.
    ISBN 1-56044-644-7
1. Natural history—Washington (State)—Guidebooks. 2. Wildlife watching—Washington
(State)—Guidebooks. 3. Washington (State)—Guidebooks. I. O'Mara, Janet. II. Title.

QH105.W2 W26 2001
508.797—dc21   2001033401

Manufactured in the United States of America
First Edition/First Printing

Acknowledgments

A comprehensive guidebook cannot be written without the help of many people. Many thanks to:

Joe La Tourrette, for shared, successful projects and opportunities and for introducing Sunny to the joys and rewards of helping environmental causes through photography.

Janet's family for their constant support and encouragement: my husband, Peter; my parents, Ray and Audrey Peck, who encouraged my passion for writing from early childhood; and to my daughters, Laura and Erin; my son-in-law, Jeff; and my grandchildren, Ashley, Brendan, Amanda, and Caitlin—all of whom helped "keep my enthusiasm fresh."

Sunny's friends, who accompanied her on several explorations and even took notes: Gary Luhm, Anne Seager, Julian Sayers, Sue Cockrell, and other members of the Mountaineers Photography Group.

Janet's longtime friend and colleague, Doug Zimmer, of the U.S. Fish and Wildlife Service, for his wildlife expertise, editing, excursions, and encouragement; and writers/editors/friends Georganne O'Connor and Michaela Mann.

Mike and MerryLynn Denny, of the Blue Mountain Audubon Society, and Len Steiner, of the East Lake Washington Audubon Society, who spent many hours showing Sunny birding locations.

Birding experts and teachers Kraig Kemper and Bob Kuntz.

The many professionals at the Washington Department of Fish and Wildlife, USFWS, National Park Service, USDA Forest Service, and Bureau of Land Management, including but not limited to Mike Davison, WDFW regional biologist; Jon Almack, WDFW senior research biologist; Steve Jeffries, WDFW research scientist; John Garrrett, manager of Skagit Wildlife Area; Gary Lentz, area manager of Lewis and Clark Trail State Park and Camp Wooten; Kent Woodruff, USFS wildlife biologist, Methow Ranger District; Mark Stafford, U.S. Geological Survey biologist, Ozette Ranger Station; Randy Hill, USFWS wildlife biologist, Columbia National Wildlife Refuge; Pam Camp, BLM district botanist; and Mike Judge and Madonna Luers, WDFW Weekender Report authors.

Pat Ness, U.S. Geological Survey volunteer, for her sea otter expertise and enthusiasm; Priscilla Dauble for her Blue Mountains wildflower knowledge; Darlene and Barry Bidwell, The Nature Conservancy stewards at Glacial Creek and Rocky Prairie, for their butterfly expertise; Lorna Ellestad, Ducks Unlimited; Martha Jordan, The Trumpeter Swan Society; Denise Daily and

Bobby Rose of the Makah Nation for their raptor knowledge; Welden and Virginia Clark for their excellent raptor report and assistance; Terry Wahl for his pelagic bird expertise; Andrew Emlen for his kayak tours through, and knowledge of, the Julia Butler Hansen National Wildlife Refuge for the Columbian White-tailed Deer.

Friends and associates who loaned photographs for the book: Gary Lentz, Gary Luhm, Len Steiner, Terry Wahl, Stuart Westmorland, Judy and Jamie Wild, and Earthbound Productions.

The many people both authors have met through the years who have freely shared their knowledge and enthusiasm.

We owe you all our gratitude.

Contents

Foreword

Most of us who live in the Pacific Northwest have a genuine appreciation for the natural beauty of the region and the opportunities to explore some of the most beautiful seacoasts and mountains in the world. What many of us do not have is the time or, in some cases, the inclination to become really knowledgeable or proficient in any particular outdoor pursuit—whether it is bird-watching, sea kayaking, or knowing when and where wildflower displays will appear each spring. Many of us also have a tendency to save up our vacation time and natural experiences for summertime (whenever that is), when the kids are out of school and we can be reasonably assured of good weather.

The reality is that there are wonderful natural events occurring all over Washington State in every season of the year. And you don't always need a week's vacation to enjoy them. In many cases, a weekend is plenty of time to immerse yourself in a remarkable seasonal event somewhere in the state, as long as you are willing to get out of the house and find your way to the event—and as long as you have some idea of when and where you should go for the experience, whether it is a bird migration, major wildflower display, or the Perseid meteor shower.

Well, you came to the right place, so to speak, when you purchased *Washington Nature Weekends*. This is a rich, and in many ways unique, publication. It is not a wildlife field guide, and it is certainly not a travel guide—although it does capture some of the elements of both in a format that is informal, entertaining, readable, and often very personal. It combines the talents and substantial experiences of two remarkable authors, long-time friends and colleagues of mine, into a seasonal compendium of Washington's best natural events. This is a book that you will want to keep for yourself as well as give to friends as gifts.

Washington Nature Weekends should not be read and stored on a bookshelf with your other reference books, travel guides, and novels. Nor should it be stuffed into a daypack with your field maps and bird identification books. Instead, it should be kept in a conspicuous place so that you may consult it year-round, whenever you have a free weekend and the inclination to get outside, even in wet or cold weather, and experience Washington's very best natural events.

Joe La Tourrette
Author and Wildlife Biologist and Consultant
Olympia, Washington

Introduction

Share the Joy

We have included a wide variety of outdoor adventures in this guidebook so that whatever your abilities and interests, you will be inspired to explore. There's no need to be a super athlete to get out there; no need to mortgage the homestead to finance your excursions. With this book, you just look at the calendar, find the appropriate activity, and go!

Along with providing ideas for enjoyable weekends, our goal is to educate and inspire as many people as possible to enjoy all of nature's delights— birds, lizards, wildflowers, otters, whales, stars, geology—and to care about them. We encourage you to develop an appreciation for nature's partnerships and diversity.

Active involvement often follows appreciation. Among ourselves and our friends, we've noticed a natural progression: using, noticing, caring, acting. At first we use a hiking trail and simply enjoy a good day. Our enthusiasm sooner or later leads us to seek more information—a bird book, a mushroom class—and that leads to a heightened awareness of nature's rich surroundings and the constant changes to the colorful palette brought about by seasonal events. Caring deeply about preserving and protecting the environment and its inhabitants usually follows. Then comes action: We join others in contributing energy and time to caring for the natural world.

If you've already developed some knowledge and appreciation of Washington's natural treasures, share them with a friend, a child, a neighbor— share the joy. Can there be greater delight than a seven-year-old boy, grinning from ear to ear, who has just seen his first harlequin duck ("It's beautiful!"). Or a friend, always too busy to spend much time outdoors before, who sees her first bald eagle through a telescope and smiles with pleasure.

Our enduring and shared philosophy, which has become our way of life, is that nature enriches our lives and transforms our spirits. We're pleased to share our knowledge and joy with you.

We hope *Washington Nature Weekends* will inspire you to experience seasonal events across the state and throughout the year. We hope you will discover new places and interests and enrich your appreciation for nature. We also hope you will take some time to "take a deep breath," and, as often as possible, completely immerse yourself in the experience to benefit from the soul-refreshing peace.

How to Use This Guide

We are all busy—working or retired; married or single; no kids, young kids, grandkids—busy, busy. Too often, the outdoor recreation we crave and the serenity we need seem too difficult to achieve.

We need a game plan! The first step is this guidebook. We have assembled all the information you will need to plan an entire year of outdoor activities. All the legwork has been done for you. This book is organized by weekend, January through December, with an outing for every weekend. Each chapter features scheduled nature events or seasonal wildlife opportunities unique to that time of year, along with detailed maps and trip-planning information.

Mother Nature doesn't always cooperate with the timing of natural events. Heavy snow pack in the mountains forces deer, elk, and bighorn sheep to move to lower elevations to find food. It may also delay mountain wildflower blooming and huckleberry ripening, just as a warmer winter, along with adequate moisture, usually brings early wildflower blooming. Drought or early frosts can spoil fall color.

Bird numbers can also vary. Cyclic crashes of subarctic tundra and grassland rodent populations send snowy owls and rough-legged hawks south in greater numbers in winter. Fall irruptions of northern catkin- and seed-eating birds are triggered by the periodic failure of seed crops in the north. Warm weather may convince shorebirds and waterfowl to delay their southward fall migration.

But you can work with Mother Nature by learning to anticipate variations. Getting in tune with Mother Nature lets you see more and do more, and the resulting harmony of nature's music in your life can be a symphony of pleasure.

In the appendices at the end of this book, we've provided contact information—including Web sites—for a number of agencies and organizations that can give you the latest seasonal information. It's a good idea to check with the appropriate agency before hitting the road. We've also provided references for further reading.

If you have children or friends with disabilities, look in the "Best Bet" appendix for trips best suited to them. If you love kayaking, hiking, or photography, look in the same appendix for trips that include these activities. If wildflowers, butterflies, mammals, or geology interest you, look for trips that focus on these subjects.

Use a Calendar

We suggest using an "activities calendar," separate from the one you use to schedule dentist appointments and the like. Note all the events and seasonal opportunities in this book that appeal to you. If you need to make reservations or confirm details in advance, write that on your activities calendar, too, in a contrasting ink, a couple months or so ahead of the event. Check your calendar frequently—always at the first of every month. Soon planning ahead will be routine, and recreation and emotional refreshment will no longer take second place in the rat race of your life.

Plan Your Equipment

Have your outdoor equipment ready and waiting so that you can respond promptly when the urge to commune with nature strikes you. A designated closet or corner in the garage works great. Gather your hiking boots, packs, binoculars, photography equipment, rain gear, and cold-weather gear there. Don't forget the bird book, hand lens, map, and insect repellent. Invest in the appropriate bags to keep all your camera equipment together and to protect field guides and maps.

More complicated trips such as overnight camping or backpacking trips, especially if they involve several people, will benefit from ongoing lists kept on your computer or in a notebook. After each trip, add to that list the items you wish you'd remembered to bring; pretty soon packing will be routine and efficient. Don't forget seasonal emergency supplies, such as chains, a shovel, and blankets for winter driving.

For safety, fun, and comfort, here are ten essential items you should take on every hike—and keep in the car.

1. Extra clothes
2. Extra food
3. Sunglasses
4. Knife
5. Fire starter
6. First-aid kit
7. Matches in a waterproof container
8. Flashlight
9. Map
10. Compass (practice using it before you go)

Don't Forget Your Manners

Two more things to "pack": safety and courtesy! Good manners are as important outdoors as inside. When we enjoy the outdoors, wherever that may be, we are in the homes of wildlife. Be aware of the impact that "just watching" has on wildlife and habitat. Please don't flush or disturb wild animals deliberately. Keep your distance. Stay in a vehicle or watch from a blind when practical. Respect private property. Pull off public roadways to look. Stay on trails and paths. Try not to trample plants; collect them only when it is allowed, and then sparingly. Keep pets in control. Don't litter. Tread lightly and maintain silence as much as possible. Leave an area as pretty as you found it—or better.

Be Safe

Safety and fun go together! Acknowledge your limitations. There are risks inherent in every activity. Plan ahead and make good decisions. Be prepared to change your plans if the weather becomes hazardous. You probably know some of the more obvious things by now, like "hike with a buddy." Take a minute to consult an information center or ranger station and heed any warnings, such as signs alerting you to WATCH FOR BEARS ON THIS TRAIL. No guidebook can anticipate all the dangers you might encounter. Just be sensible, be safe, be smart, and enjoy.

Okay, you're organized. And now the fun begins!

> *Every effort has been made by the authors and editors to make this guide as accurate and useful as possible. However, many things can change after a guide is published—trails are rerouted, phone numbers change, etc. We recommend that you call before traveling to obtain current information.*

Map Legend

Interstate Highway	(5)	National Park; Wildlife Refuge	
U.S. Highway	(26) (101)	Point of Interest	□
State Highway	(220)	Camping	△
County Road	(21)	Parking	P
Forest Road	(220)	Site Number	❸
Unpaved Road		Site/Area Locator	○ □
Boundary		Town	○ TACOMA
Trail		Peak	
Creek		Butte	
River		Visitor Center	
Lake			
Glacier		Location	
State Boundary	WASHINGTON		
		Compass	N

Trip Locator Map

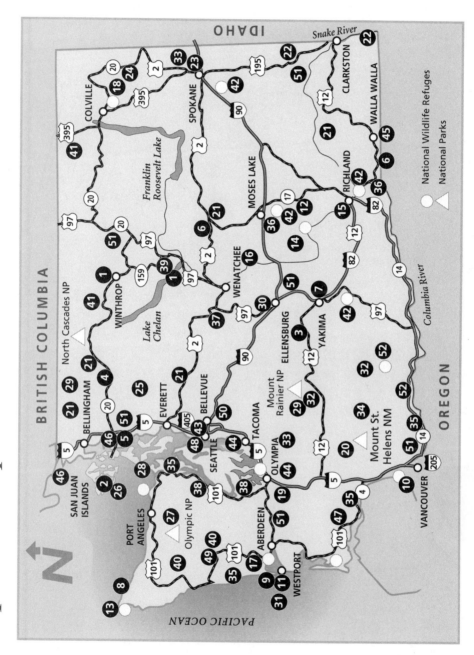

1

Adventure on a Long, Long Lake

Take a boat ride on Lake Chelan, deepest gorge in North America. Soak up the solitude and alpine scenery. See mule deer, mountain goats, and maybe even a cougar.

Site: Stehekin, at the end of Lake Chelan.

Recommended time: January or February.

Minimum time commitment: Day trip or stay the weekend at Stehekin Lodge at the head of the lake.

What to bring: Binoculars, camera, warm clothing, winter boots.

Directions: Chelan is 37 miles north of Wenatchee on SR 97. Lake Chelan Boat Company is 1 mile south of downtown Chelan on SR 97A.

The background: Lake Chelan is an internationally known destination for summer trips; people crowd the boats with luggage and backpacks, eager to explore the beautiful Stehekin wilderness. Winter trips are also popular, but less crowded, and are markedly less expensive.

Lake Chelan is a narrow, deep gorge—one of Washington's largest inland bodies of fresh water. It extends 55 miles into the Cascade Mountains and averages only 2 miles across; breathtaking scenery is all around. The lake is fed by twenty-seven glaciers and fifty-nine streams, and spring brings wildflowers and waterfalls. In winter, snow sharply defines the high mountain peaks, crisps the air, and brings mountain goats and mule deer within easier view.

The fun: To make it an easy day trip, stay overnight in either Wenatchee or Chelan. After breakfast, catch the boat at the Lake Chelan Boat Company dock midmorning. If you don't want to spend your brief layover in Stehekin

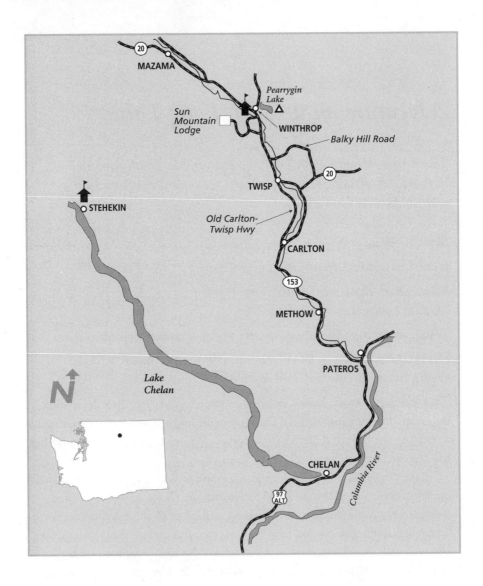

eating, take a lunch to eat on the way or buy light fare on the boat.

Settle in and enjoy the two-and-a-half-hour ride up the lake to Stehekin. Comforts include a heated cabin with lots of windows, coffee and muffins, and rest rooms. An experienced guide provides informative narration and points out wildlife along the way. The captain stops the boat for photographs whenever he sees mountain goats, mule deer, or any other interesting wildlife.

Buy low-priced tickets on the boat for the forty-five-minute bus tour to the 312-foot Rainbow Falls in Stehekin—a good way to spend the ninety-minute layover—or eat lunch, stroll around the tiny mountain community, and enjoy the

Rugged, snowy peaks surrounding Lake Chelan make a striking winter contrast with the deep blue skies of the eastern Cascades.

scenery. The return trip offers more opportunities for wildlife sightings; you will arrive back at the dock in Chelan at about 4:20 P.M.

For the best chance to see mule deer up close, stay overnight in Stehekin (reserve early for the weekends). The restaurant is open and there are special programs every Friday. A "snowshoe weekend package for two" includes boat trip, lodging, breakfast, snowshoes, transportation to trails, and a moonlight snowshoe walk on Saturday night.

If you like solitude and don't mind cooking, rent a housekeeping unit during the week (the restaurant and snack bar are closed). The town shuts down early during the week, but the lodge has a reading and game room. Take a flashlight for the occasional power outage. Rent a pair of snowshoes and travel through a "winter wonderland of frozen waterfalls and snow-frosted pines." There are seven trails varying from easy to advanced; transportation is provided to the trailheads by bus or van. Try the easy Buckner

Mule Deer in the Methow

If you prefer a mule deer site with more amenities and a less-remote location, travel to the Methow Valley (Winthrop, Twisp, Mazama) to see large herds of mule deer when they migrate out of their high-mountain meadows down to the valleys below. Mule deer are so named for their large, mulelike, black-fringed ears. They are commonly seen any time between December and March, depending on the severity of the winter. The recreation bonus is that in these same areas, there are numerous activities to expand the fun—eagle watching, snowshoeing, cross-country skiing, hot air balloon rides, sleigh rides, and much more. Late afternoon and early morning usually are the best times to find deer, but you may see them any time of day in a plentiful year.

Look for mule deer along the river and up on the hills anywhere from Carlton to Winthrop. A huge number of deer migrate to the Methow Valley during a severe winter; when the winter is mild,

A bold and curious mule deer fawn, mother nearby, watches hikers on the lakeshore trail at Stehekin.

more of them stay up in the hills. Even in a mild winter, however, it is not unusual to see herds of sixty or more along the river, sometimes right in Winthrop. Mule deer can often be seen on the Bear Creek Road around Pearrygin Lake and up into the Methow Wildlife Area.

For another good mule deer drive, take the Eastside Winthrop–Twisp Road toward Twisp, then turn left on the Balky Hill Road and follow it to Beaver Creek Road, then right to SR 20, and back to SR 153. Mule deer frequent these hills, and the Tace Ranch (just north of milepost 205 on SR 20) is the site of a feeding station where deer congregate in late afternoon. You can also view mule deer on the old Carlton Twisp Highway (west of the river)—on the hills and at two private feeding stations.

White-tailed deer also winter in the Methow Valley, mixing with mule deer in some areas. Bald eagles are common along the Methow River at all times of day. Look for eagles in the trees at the turnouts about 3.5 miles west of Winthrop; on snags along the two side roads between Twisp and Winthrop that run near to the river; and on pilings in the river on the stretch between Carlton and Pateros. If you spend some time at the turnouts, you should have good success.

For a special treat, take a one-hour balloon ride high over Winthrop to look for mule deer and view the gorgeous mountain valley from above. To explore nature on snowshoes or cross-country skis, join a "Nature of Winter" guided walk. These are offered each Saturday morning, with snowshoes provided free of charge. Call (509) 996–4036 for more information.

The Methow Valley has nearly 100 miles of public, groomed, cross-country ski trails for all levels and abilities. For a map contact the Methow Valley Sport Trails Association at (509) 996–3287; www.mvsta.com/. Several lodges offer snowshoe and cross-country ski rentals and trips as well as sleigh rides.

For more information:
Methow Wildlife Area
(509) 996-2559
Winthrop Chamber of Commerce
(888) 463-8469;
www.winthropwashington.com

Orchard loop for a three-hour snowshoe trip, starting with the frozen Rainbow Falls and then following an easy route through the woods and down along the river.

You most assuredly will see mule deer up close, feeding all along the lakeshore; best times are in late afternoon and early morning. Mule deer migrate down from the higher mountains in December and stay until March. Small family groups of does and fawns often come right down behind the lodge and the ranger station in the afternoon and are easily approachable to within 10 feet. Just getting out and quietly walking along the road and on the Lakeshore Trail is pleasant—deer are often seen here. Rangers advise that cougars are occasionally in the area, scouting out the deer. The ranger station has a brochure telling you how to act if you see a cougar: Basically, don't run, and make yourself look as big as possible.

Be sure to take your binoculars to watch the trumpeter swans, loons, grebes, and other waterfowl on the lake.

Food and lodging: Stehekin Lodge; limited meals during the week.

For more information:

Lake Chelan Boat Company
(509) 682–4584; www.LadyoftheLake.com
Stehekin Lodge
(509) 682–4494
Chelan Chamber of Commerce
(800) 424–3526; www.LakeChelan.com
Lake Chelan National Recreation Area
www.nps.gov/lach/index.htm

2

Life from the Ferry Lane

During the stormy days of winter, enjoy a cozy ferryboat ride and driving tour to view wildlife of the San Juan Islands.

Site: Washington State Ferry and San Juan Islands.

Recommended time: January; though all winter is good.

Minimum time commitment: A day to ride the ferry; a weekend to tour the islands.

What to bring: Warm clothing, windbreaker, rain gear, binoculars.

Directions: From I–5 take Anacortes exit 230, SR 20, and travel 13 miles west, then north at the "Y" into downtown Anacortes. To reach the San Juan ferry terminal, turn left on Twelfth Street and follow the signs. Take the ferry to San Juan Island and follow the map. Winter brings a nice bonus—ferries are only partly filled, so no long waiting lines.

The background: The waters of the San Juan Islands, relatively empty of seabirds during the summer, teem with birds in late fall and early winter. Pick up a copy of *Birding in the San Juan Islands* by Mark Lewis and Fred Sharpe before you go. The good news is that it describes all the best locations in the islands to see birds and marine mammals; the sad news is that the huge numbers of migrating and wintering birds present when the book was written in 1987 just aren't there anymore. So don't expect large numbers, do enjoy what you see, and, if you feel bad enough, volunteer to work on a habitat-protection campaign. When we asked one longtime islander about the lower numbers, she replied that the diversity is still incredible. She sees something wonderful with her scope every time she goes out.

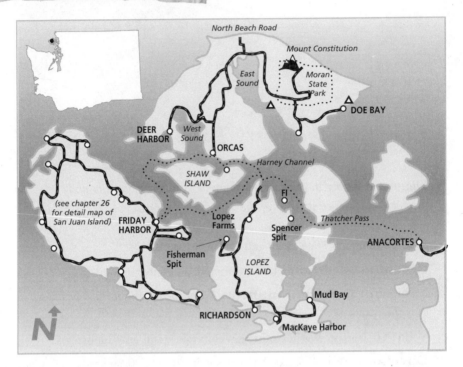

The fun: All along the ferry route you will see birds feeding in the quiet bays and in the swirling waters where currents converge. You have a good chance of seeing loons (Pacific, common); grebes (horned, western); cormorants (Brandt's, double-crested); sea ducks (harlequin ducks, oldsquaw or "long-tailed duck," white-winged scoter, common and Barrow's goldeneye, bufflehead); mergansers (hooded, common, red-breasted); alcids (common murre, pigeon guillemot, marbled murrelet); and gulls (mew, Thayer's, Bonaparte's). Common bay ducks include ring-necked ducks and scaups.

Thatcher Pass north of Decatur Island is excellent for seabirds. As you near Lopez Island, watch for harbor seals sunning themselves on Flower Island and Leo Reef (low tide only). The protected waters of Harney Channel, between Orcas and Shaw islands, are another favorite spot for birds. Watch for bald eagles on all the islands.

At high tide you may be treated to a trip through narrow Wasp Passage as you leave Orcas Island. As you exit this passage, you sometimes see large rafts of cormorants taking off in formation, their dragging feet making glittering patterns on the water. If you travel south around Shaw Island, watch for seals on the rocks as you come into San Juan Channel and large numbers of seabirds feeding in the riptides.

On San Juan Island start your tour by taking Roche Harbor Road north out of Friday Harbor. Highlights of this leg are waterfowl (green-winged teal and northern pintail are the most common) and red-winged blackbirds at Three Meadows marsh and trumpeter swans at Egg Lake. After checking out Roche Harbor, drive down the west side of the island on West Valley Road and stop at English Camp. See several species of sea ducks, great blue herons, and rabbits. At San Juan

Many bald eagles, like this one at Pear Point, can be seen on San Juan Island year-round.

County Park look for cormorants and herons on the rocks. Everywhere you look, the scenery is gorgeous—rocky shores, sand-filled lagoons, madrona trees, fields with muted winter colors, and raptors flying above (northern harriers and sharp-shinned, Cooper's, red-tailed, and rough-legged hawks are common). See Eurasian skylarks year-round.

On the southern part of the island, plan to arrive at False Bay between medium and low tides so that the foraging birds aren't too far away. See lots of gulls, herons, ducks, shorebirds, and a few bald eagles. Then proceed to American Camp, a very special place. The churning waters of Cattle Pass teem with feeding birds; seals haul out on Goose Island at low tide; deer and rabbits are seen in the fields in early morning; and bald eagles soar overhead.

On your way north stop at Pear Point, just south of Friday Harbor. A bald eagle often roosts on its favorite tree east of the gravel pit—you can get quite close if you are quiet. The Friday Harbor docks are a great place to see harbor seals waiting for fish remains and curious river otters swimming and climbing on the docks.

*Black oystercatchers have bright red, stout bills
designed for hammering and prying open mollusks.*

Next best: If you want to do a two-island tour this weekend, stop at either
Lopez or Orcas Island on the return ferry trip. Lopez is a good choice if you
want a quiet rural environment with pretty coves and lots of birds; Orcas is a
good choice for spectacular sunrises/sunsets from Mount Constitution.

Lopez Island: Fisherman Spit, partway down the west side, is a favorite
birding location and a nice place to walk. See marine birds both inside the
spit on Fisherman Bay and outside on San Juan Channel. We saw a flock of
northern pintails on a pond; they are usually skittish, but we were able to
watch them from our car for a long time. On the southwest side of the
island, Richardson dock offers views of beautiful scenery, islands, and coves.
Look for marine birds, bald eagles, and otters. Farther east at MacKaye
Harbor are more views of seabirds, gorgeous little islands, and lots of wave
action, plus ponds with ducks, killdeer, and yellowlegs.

On the east side, Mud Bay's mudflats and salt marshes are very picturesque and productive, but the crescent-shaped beach at the end of Sperry
Road is even prettier. See lots of marine birds and ducks on both the bay and
Rosario Strait. You may see turkey vultures soaring overhead (some stay the
winter instead of migrating south). Other birding locations mentioned in

Birding in the San Juans include Swifts Bay, Lopez Village, and Odlin Park.

Orcas Island: For incredible views, drive to the end of North Beach Road (just east of the airport on the north side of the island) to see open waters dotted with little islands to the north and the Cascades Mountains on the mainland. At Crescent Beach on the north end of East Sound, see marine birds and the occasional black oystercatchers with red bills—a special treat.

For a beautiful sunset or sunrise, follow Horseshoe Highway down the east shore of East Sound to Moran State Park, and turn left (east) up the road to Mount Constitution. Starting at 2.5 miles, stop at any pullout for incredible views of the Puget Trough. A variety of birds may be seen in the woodlands and meadows all the way up the mountain.

The 6-mile road is sometimes closed partway up in winter because of snow; there are good turnarounds for cars (no trailers).

Food and lodging: All three islands have many charming restaurants, shops, and accommodations—only partly filled in winter. Camping is available at San Juan County Park. On Lopez Island, Spencer Spit State Park is closed in winter, but Odlin County Park is open. On Orcas Island, Moran State Park has partial campground service plus Camp Moran Vacation House.

For more information:
San Juan Islands Tourism and Accommodations
www.guidetosanjuans.com
Washington State Ferries
(206) 464–6400 or (888) 808–7977; www.wsdot.wa.gov/ferries/

3

Meet Me at the Feeding Station

Winter feeding stations attract otherwise elusive elk and bighorn sheep for guaranteed close-up viewing. At Oak Creek Wildlife Area, near Yakima, as many as 2,000 Rocky Mountain elk dine each day.

Site: Oak Creek Wildlife Area, 22 miles west of Yakima.

Recommended time: December through February. The bull elk, with their spectacular racks, wait until the snow is deep before coming down. If the snowpack is heavy, January is best. If it is light, January brings mostly elk cows and young, and February is better for viewing bull elk. Feeding is at 1:30 P.M.

Minimum time commitment: At least a couple of hours at Oak Creek plus winter traveling time. Make it a weekend to get to additional sites at the best viewing times.

What to bring: Camera, warm clothing, gloves, boots (WDFW Access Stewardship Decal is waived from December 1 to March 15).

Directions: From Yakima drive 20 miles west on US 12 (through Naches) to the SR 410 junction. Turn left on US 12 and drive 2 miles to Oak Creek Headquarters.

The background: In winter, food for all animals is diminished in the higher elevations. Getting around in deep snow uses valuable energy, there-fore, elk and bighorn sheep migrate down to lower elevations. Before people took over most of the animals' lowland habitat, these large mammals grazed on wild vegetation. Survival in a fenced, plowed, modern world soon dictated another solution. In the 1940s the Washington Department of Wildlife built

In winter, Rocky Mountain bighorn sheep travel down the hillside each morning to the Clemen Mountain feeding station near Naches.

almost 100 miles of 8-foot-high fencing to keep the elk from damaging apple orchards in the Tieton, Naches, and Wenas river valleys, then started supplemental feeding so that the elk wouldn't starve. Today feeding programs help them make it through the winter and ensure adequate populations for hunting. These programs also alter their behavior, making it easier for us to see them. Normally shy, nocturnal animals may be easily seen during the day, and otherwise separate herds of cows and bulls feed together. At Oak Creek the WDFW has put up fencing, an interpretive center, and viewing facilities for the public.

There are two species of elk in Washington, Rocky Mountain and Roosevelt, and two species of bighorn sheep, California and Rocky Mountain. Rocky Mountain elk are found mainly east of the Cascade Crest in Washington, with a smaller herd in the Blue Mountains and a few in the Pend Oreille. They make up about 54 percent of Washington's elk population. Roosevelt elk live on the Olympic Peninsula (see chapter 40) and parts of the

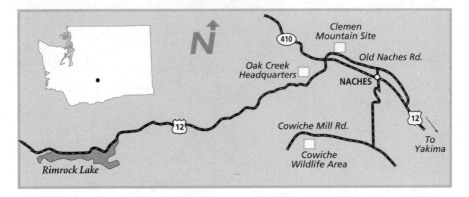

western slopes of the Cascades and Mount Rainier, about 46 percent of the state's elk population. They are slightly larger than Rocky Mountain elk and darker. You will see Rocky Mountain elk and California bighorns at Oak Creek.

The fun: At Oak Creek Wildlife Area, approximately 2,000 elk are fed daily at 1:30 P.M. In a severe winter as many as 5,000 elk may use the feeding areas. Facilities include a large parking lot, covered viewing area, and rest rooms. The interpretive center is open from 9:00 A.M. to 4:00 P.M. during most weekends—less often midweek. The center has a slide program, exhibits, a special kid's corner, and volunteers to answer questions. There is no charge.

If you arrive at the site an hour or so early, you will see groups of elk coming down out of the hills where many of them spend the night. It's a thrilling sight to see a line of bull elk winding their way single file down through the rocks and scrub. Bulls don't lose their antlers until March or April, and it's interesting to watch the younger ones make way for the majestic large bulls with their seven- or eight-point racks.

You will also see thousands of elk at close range just inside the fence: bulls sparring, cows nursing, calves playing, and even a tiny late-born calf once in a while. The fences are low enough so that you get a good view and can take pictures. You can make reservations to ride the hay truck through the area and help throw out hay bales for the long lines of waiting elk. For more natural elk scenes, park on the north side of the road east of headquarters towards the junction and look up the hill. Elk often graze here.

Next best: Around 60 California bighorn sheep and 200 elk are fed between 10:00 and 11:00 A.M. at the Oak Creek Wildlife Area's Clemen Mountain site north of the junction of US 12 and SR 410, just off Old Naches Road. Be there by 9:00 A.M. to see them walking or running down from the higher slopes. You may see sheep rut behavior (head butting, etc.), although the breeding season starts in early November. Bighorn sheep behavior varies. Sometimes they come down right on time, but in a year with more-abundant natural food, they may wait until they're hungry. Sometimes they go straight back up into the hills after eating; sometimes they stay around.

You may notice that both ewes and rams have horns, not antlers, which they never lose. The ewes' horns are small and pointed, while the rams' are curled—the older rams are the ones with the largest curl. The young sheep chase one another around and playfully spar; the older rams will spar for real—butting horns with a loud crack. It's quite a sight. California bighorn sheep rams weigh between 180 and 200 pounds, while Rocky Mountain rams (the largest sheep in North America) reach over 300 pounds. Rams live ten to twelve years, ewes slightly longer.

The best place to see wintering Rocky Mountain bighorn sheep is Pend Oreille County in the extreme northeast corner of Washington, where the terrain is more like the Rocky Mountains than the Cascades. WDFW operates the Sullivan Lake Bighorn Sheep Winter Feeding Station, located on the Noisy Creek campground road, south end of Sullivan Lake. Eighteen sheep were transplanted to Hall Mountain in 1972, and the herd now numbers more than forty. The sheep come down to the site after feeding begins in mid-December and usually remain in the area until feeding ends in late February. Wear warm clothes and warm traction boots for the short walk. Contact the WDFW at (509) 456–4082; www.wa.gov/wdfw/wlm/region1/wildview.htm for directions.

Food and lodging: Naches offers all services. Cabins featuring frequent sightings of black-tailed deer are located about 10 miles west on US 12. See beautiful early-morning vistas of snowy mountains across Rimrock Lake farther up the pass.

For more information:
Oak Creek and Cowiche Wildlife Areas
(509) 653–2390; www.wa.gov/wdfw/lands/r3oakcrk.htm

4

January

Bald Eagles, Surviving and Thriving

*See dozens of bald eagles soar overhead or feast on salmon carcasses
on a gravel bar in the Skagit River. Then attend a festival
celebrating these magnificent birds.*

Site: Along the Skagit River and SR 20, starting 40 miles east of
Burlington. Eagle observation points, festival activities, and parking areas are
in the towns and along the highway.

Recommended time: Eagle watching in the Skagit River Bald Eagle
Natural Area starts in December, but peaks in mid-January, when 300 or
more birds often gather. Sightings usually continue into mid-February. The
Upper Skagit Bald Eagle Festival is held on the last weekend of January or
the first weekend in February. The Bald Eagle Interpretive Center is open
weekends in January and February.

Minimum time commitment: Plan to spend the day. Start early—the
best time of day to look for eagles feeding is in the morning, 8:00 to 11:00
A.M. They leave the river in late afternoon to roost in forested areas.

What to bring: Binoculars and warm clothing.

Directions: From I–5, take exit 230, Burlington, and head east on SR 20
(North Cascades Scenic Highway). Concrete is about 40 miles; Rockport and
Marblemount are a few minutes farther. Watch for signboards to the Bald
Eagle Interpretive Center in Rockport, 1 block off SR 20. Two good eagle
viewing/parking areas are farther east on SR 20: mileposts 99 and 100.
Another good site is the Howard Miller Steelhead County Park at Rockport,
which also has rest rooms, picnic tables, and a playground.

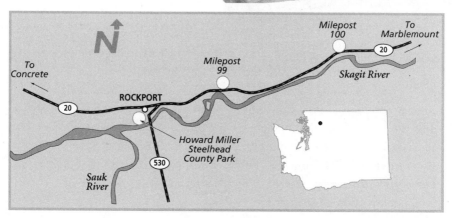

The background: Most of us never lose our sense of wonder and admiration when we spot a mature bald eagle soaring overhead, sweeping dark brown wings fringed with long feathers, white tail and head in bold contrast. Just as special is seeing these giant birds standing on gravel bars along the river, feasting on salmon carcasses. The bald eagle is such an impressive bird and so easily seen in the Pacific Northwest that it is often what first entices people into a lifetime of nature study.

The largest winter concentration of bald eagles, 300 to 500 birds, in Washington is in the northwestern part of the state, a primary winter feeding and roosting area. Here you may see as many as 50 or 60 of these magnificent birds at one time.

Eagle-watching etiquette demands that visitors disturb the birds as little as possible while they are feeding. Please park only in designated parking spots, stay off gravel bars, avoid loud noises, and keep those pets on leashes.

The fun: The Upper Skagit Bald Eagle Festival, held during the peak eagle-watching season, is a good time to go. There are enough free activities to interest everyone, including children. Highlights have included a real eagle nest exhibit; wildlife, history, and ecology presentations; music; Native American storytelling and history; arts and crafts; and food booths. Rockport's free environmental interpretive center is open Friday through Sunday, January and February only.

Bald Eagles, Salmon, and the Rivers

ald eagles, for a time in danger of disappearing from the lower forty-eight states, are now as common as crows in some areas of Washington. The slowly increasing population is the result of a process called "listing" by the U.S. Fish and Wildlife Service, which allows fierce protection of vulnerable species. Eagles were listed as "threatened" in Washington and as the more serious classification, "endangered," in the rest of the United States. At this writing, the birds have recovered enough to be at least considered for "delisting," or removed from such extreme protection. Winter is an appropriate season to celebrate their survival, because they are visible in many parts of the state.

It takes five to six years for the birds to achieve the familiar adult coloration—dark brown bodies and wings, white heads and tails, massive yellow bills, yellow feet with powerful talons. "Immature" or

Bald eagles are protective of their salmon carcasses, loudly screeching at others to stay away.

"juvenile" birds are mostly dusky brown, with no white markings. The birds typically live about twenty-five years.

Nests are huge—6 to 7 feet across and almost as deep, built from large branches and sticks, lined with grass and other soft materials. When they're born, usually early August, eagles are covered with down, helpless for about three months. They "fledge" or fly from the nest at about ten to twelve weeks of age.

Their preferred food is dead or dying fish, but they also eat shellfish, such as abalone, as well as small waterfowl, pigeon guillemots, grebes, and brant. They also can snatch live fish from the surface of the water with their feet, but do not dive into the water after prey. Bald eagles are social birds—they like to flock together, fly together, roost together, and eat together. That is why eagles are usually spotted in groups, whatever they are doing at the time. They often night roost together, too, as many as one hundred eagles in one grove of trees. They even occasionally hunt cooperatively to corner waterfowl.

The fall run of chum salmon is the key to why we can watch eagles along the Skagit River in the winter. Salmon start their lives in fresh water and then journey to salt water to live for a few years (the amount of time varies from species to species and sometimes even within species). This part of the Skagit is an especially healthy and navigable river with no dams in the way of the fish in their journey back from the salt water to spawn, about three to four years later, in the same freshwater stream where they were born. The salmon lay their eggs in shaped areas called "redds" in the river bottom. After the female lays eggs in these indentations and the male fertilizes them, both adults die and become part of the food chain.

The salmon carcasses wash up on gravel bars where eagles eat their fill; the leftovers, including bones, are consumed by rodents. Nothing is wasted.

On weekends watch for Eagle Watcher Volunteers with binoculars and spotting scopes at pullouts along the highway ready to point out the birds. On sunny days groups of eagles may soar overhead, riding the thermals during the middle of the day. Every visitor should be able to see eagles sitting on trees along the river or standing on gravel bars—many of these sightings are possible without leaving the car.

For the adventurous there are guided hikes and float trips. The Seattle Aquarium and several private outfitters schedule float trips between Marblemount and Rockport ($50 to $70), or you can take your own boat. Since this area is within the Skagit River Bald Eagle Natural Area, boaters are asked to stay off the river until 11:00 A.M. and to get off again by 3:00 P.M. (call the USDA Forest Service for river restrictions and current conditions). The Skagit River is part of the Wild and Scenic River System.

Food and lodging: Cities along the route are all full service.

Next best: If you can't make it during the festival, go as close to mid-January as possible and spot eagles on your own. Up to 150 eagles also winter on the Nooksack River east of Bellingham. Welcome Bridge, east of SR 542 on Mosquito Lake Road, is a good viewing site. When the chum salmon run ends, eagles fly to the Padilla Bay National Estuarine Reserve and other bays farther north (see chapter 46).

For more information:
Upper Skagit Bald Eagle Festival
(360) 853–7009; www.skagiteagle.org
USDA Forest Service, Sedro-Woolley
(360) 856–5700

5

February

Big White Birds Flock Together

You may hear them before you see them, squawking, cackling, honking, chattering. When you do see them—flocks of swans and snow geese feeding in the fields and wetlands of the Skagit Valley or flying overhead—you'll be glad you came.

Site: Skagit Valley, near Conway, about 25 miles north of Everett.

Recommended time: Swans and geese begin arriving in the Skagit Valley in mid- to late October and can be seen throughout the valley. Waterfowl season runs through the third week in January, so best birding may be after that time. The swans leave the area by mid-March; snow geese often stay until mid-April. Other waterfowl, shorebirds, and raptors also are abundant in winter (see chapter 46).

Minimum time commitment: A few hours or a day.

What to bring: Binoculars, spotting scope, rain gear, warm clothing, sturdy shoes, WDFW Access Stewardship Decal.

Directions: From I–5, take exit 221, Conway, and drive west—turning right on Fir Island Road, left on Wylie Road, then left again into Washington Department of Fish and Wildlife's Skagit Wildlife Area headquarters. See the map for directions to the Hayton/Fir Island Farms Reserve; Johnson/DeBay Swan Reserve; and Jensen, North Fork, and Big Ditch accesses.

The background: The snow geese that winter in the Skagit Valley nest and raise their young on Wrangel Island, off the northern coast of Siberia. In normal years 40,000 to 60,000 birds nest in the Russian colony, with up to 50,000 wintering in Skagit Valley. Two huge protected areas in British

Snow geese fatten up in the Skagit each winter for the long flight north and also to sustain them at their nesting grounds until food becomes plentiful.

Columbia also attract the Wrangel Island snow goose flocks—the George C. Reifel Migratory Bird Sanctuary and Alakeen National Wildlife Area.

More than 4,000 swans join these thousands of snow geese, all here for the same reason, to rest and eat before they return north. All together, their presence is quite a sight.

The fun: Begin looking in the fields as you drive along I–5, then visit the wildlife areas mentioned above. When you see white birds on the ground here in the winter, they are one or more of three species—gulls, snow geese, or swans. Of course it's pretty easy to tell if the birds are gulls by their smaller size. Snow geese are all white, except for black wing tips that are most visible when they fly. The birds have a 3-foot wing span and weigh about six pounds; bills and feet are pink. Swans are much larger than geese and have longer necks.

At dawn Jensen Access and the new Hayton/Fir Island Farms Reserve are the most reliable places to view snow geese. Both have good parking. The new reserve has a wheelchair-accessible path and viewing area at the mouth

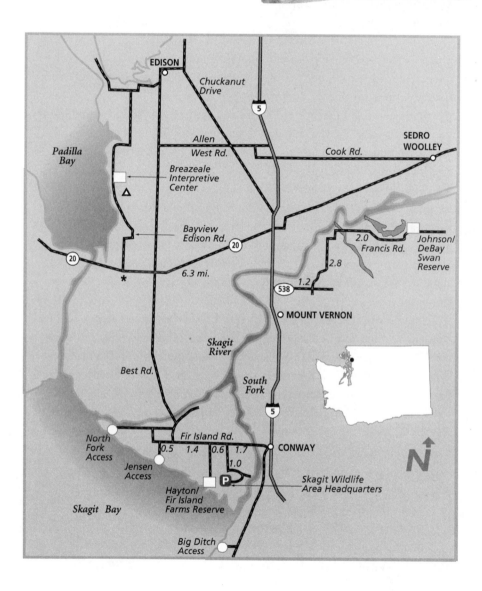

of Brown Slough. (*Note:* the Hayton grain fields are cut in November to provide food for the snow geese and hunting is not allowed on the reserve, so this is an excellent early viewing location. We saw thousands of snow geese in the fields in mid-November.)

Flocks of snow geese fly in from their nighttime roosts on the waters of Skagit Bay to their daytime feeding areas in the Fir Island agricultural fields. One morning before dawn, several photographers were getting their equipment ready at Jensen Access when thousands of geese passed right over their heads. No time for photos, but what a sight to see—and hear!

Snow geese also fly back out to the bay in the evening, and if the tide is low, you can go up on the dike and watch them feeding in the mudflats. Watch the tides and bird accordingly: Low tide, look in the mudflats; high tide, look in the fields.

Walk the paths at Skagit WA headquarters and drive the Fir Island roads for more views of both geese and swans. Kayak the South Fork Skagit River to see snow geese, ducks, and raptors—especially bald eagles. Use the headquarters boat launch and plan around the tides to avoid mud at low tide. Drive west on Rawlins Road to the North Fork Access, then walk up and along the dike to look for trumpeter swans, short-eared owls, and hawks. Watch for snow geese on their evening flight.

Please show courtesy to the birds and the landowners. Swan/snow goose etiquette requires that you stay in your car or on designated trails and quietly observe from a distance. Keep pets in the car and do not flush the birds to "get a better picture." Flushing uses up the birds' critical winter energy. Stay on public roads and do not trespass on farmers' private lands or block driveways. Please don't stop on the roadways—it's dangerous and, in some areas, illegal.

Next best: Every winter about 4,000 trumpeter and tundra swans are drawn to Skagit Valley fields. They dine on what is left of various crops after harvest, such as corn, carrots, and potatoes, or what has been specifically planted for them, such as barley and winter cover crops. In early to mid-March, rested and fortified, the birds begin their journey north to nest and raise their young.

The two native swans in North America are sometimes difficult to distinguish. Tundra swans are the smaller of the two, weighing fifteen to twenty pounds, with a wingspan of 6 to 7 feet. The bill is black, smaller than a trumpeter's, usually with a small yellow spot in front of the eye. Trumpeter swans are larger, heavier-looking birds with a heavy, all-black bill. The trumpeters weigh twenty-five to thirty pounds, with a wingspan of 7 to 8 feet. Males and females look alike, at least to humans; they can live twenty years, and they mate for life. The swans that winter in Skagit Valley breed in Alaska.

The Johnson/DeBay Swan Reserve is owned and operated by the Washington Department of Fish and Wildlife. It has interpretive signs and plenty of parking, including some barrier-free spots. After hunting season ends, WDFW knocks down the grain and there is good viewing of hundreds of swans feeding in the fields, plus tens of thousands of ducks and an abundance of raptors, including bald eagles. Geese also visit the area. Plans are to add trails and an elevated viewing platform. Gates close on March 31.

This wildlife area represents an innovative, partnered approach to wildlife conservation. Part is a reserve habitat for swans; the other part is for seasonal waterfowl hunting and off-season bird-watching. The property was purchased using Pacific Coast Joint Venture funding for swan habitat management. Stewardship partners include Ducks Unlimited, Washington Waterfowl Association, The Trumpeter Swan Society, and Skagit Audubon Society.

Directions: From I–5 take Mount Vernon exit 227 (College Road, SR 538), drive 1.2 miles east and turn left on LaVenture Road. Drive 4.8 miles on LaVenture, which becomes Francis Road, then turn left on DeBay Island Road. Also look for swans in the fields north of SR 20—occasionally near Cook Road to the east of I–5; more often west of I–5 in fields anywhere from SR 20 to Edison. If you spend the weekend, look for raptors in the Samish Flats (see chapter 46).

If you are exploring the area north of SR 20, stop at the Breazeale Interpretive Center at 10441 Bayview-Edison Road (360–428–1558) to pick up a birding location map. To receive a swan identification pamphlet, send a self-addressed, stamped envelope to the Trumpeter Swan Society, MBO 272, Mill Creek, WA 98012.

Food and lodging: Mount Vernon and LaConnor offer all services.

For more information:
Skagit Wildlife Area
(360) 445–4441; www.wa.gov/wdfw/r4skagit.htm
Washington Swan Coalition (Swan Watching in Washington)
(425) 787–0258; www.SwanSociety.org/

6

February

Winter Raptor Central

See lots of raptors from your car this weekend. Large birds of prey concentrate in eastern Washington in the winter, and it's easy to see them in the sky, in trees, on fences, on the ground.

Site: Eastern Washington loop drive; begin in Walla Walla.

Recommended time: February.

Minimum time commitment: A day for each part of the drive—or do the whole loop over the three-day President's Day weekend.

What to bring: Highway map, binoculars, spotting scope, bird field guide.

Directions: See tour below.

The background: It doesn't seem possible to "make appointments" with birds, but birds are more predictable than most people think they are, tending to congregate in certain areas at specific times of the year. Experienced birders cherish their lists of reliable locations where they have the best chances to see their favorite birds. This loop drive is a compilation of some of those locations, gleaned from expert birders Mike and MerryLynn Denny.

The fun: All along your drive, watch for hawks sitting on telephone and power poles and crossbars. Red-tailed hawks and northern harriers are common residents of Washington; rough-legged hawks are here only in winter. Watch for short-eared owls on fence posts, signposts, farm implements, and tussocks or hammocks on the ground. Watch for long-eared and great horned owls in trees and kestrels on telephone or power lines.

■ *Walla Walla to Pasco:* Drive west on US 12, loop through raptor country

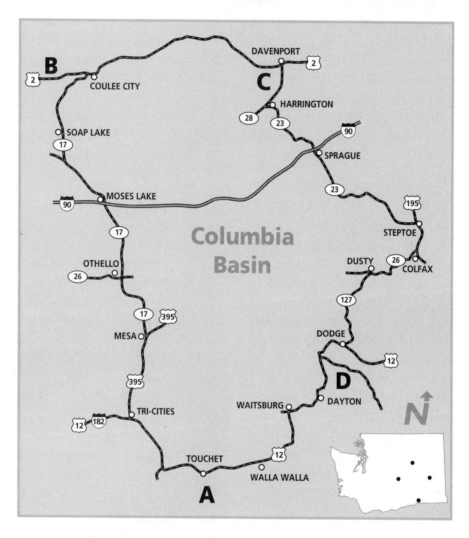

south of Touchet (Hot Spot A), then head west again on US 12 to the Columbia River. Stop at Madame Dorion Park (milepost 307) to see and hear white-throated sparrows. Then scout the Walla Walla River Delta across the road (see chapter 36) to see American white pelicans, gulls,

Winter Raptor Hot Spots

Mike and MerryLynn Denny, Walla Walla expert birders, recommend these spots for raptor, owl, and turkey viewing.

Touchet (Hot Spot A): This drive begins 8.5 miles west of Walla Walla on US 12; turn left (south) on Detour Road and follow the map to see 150 to 200 raptors when the rodent population is good. In early morning, flocks of gulls fly in from the Walla Walla River Delta. See great blue herons in the fields on Detour Road (colony to the north). Watch for nesting great horned owls in a tree on the left after you turn south on Jacobs. In late afternoon (or very early morning), drive down Lovers Lane to see hawks roosting in the maples. Along with more common raptors, watch for long-eared owls on Watson and prairie falcons on Riggs.

At Touchet, turn west on US 12, left on Brynes, and left again on Byerly (past the railroad bridge) to see more raptors. A pair of ferruginous hawks (threatened in Washington) nests in the Horse Heaven Hills to the south (private land). Watch for them on a pole near the 90-degree turn, looking for Great Basin pocket gophers. Cross over the Walla Walla River bridge and drive up on the bluff. Habitat is outstanding for sparrows all along the river; you sometimes see hundreds. Return to Byrnes and head west; watch for deer on your way back to US 12.

Waterville Plateau (Hot Spot B): Drive west on US 2 from Coulee City onto a high, snow-covered plateau to see a rare treat, the gyrfalcon. The gyrfalcon is the world's largest falcon and is circumpolar (breeds all around the Arctic Circle). You will see a high percentage of immature gyrfalcons; they travel as far south as northern Washington in the winter while many adults stay farther north. Here

Snowy owl

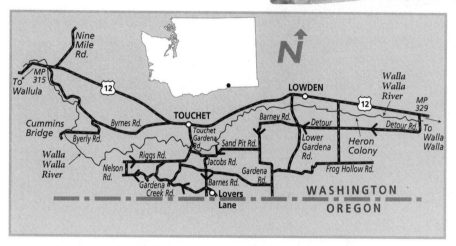

gyrfalcons prey mainly on gray partridges, pheasants, and ducks—occasionally on horned larks and snow buntings. Their level flight is faster than a peregrine falcon, and they can reach 200 mph in a dive.

Explore side roads off US 2 from St. Andrews to Highland School roads for gyrfalcons, rough-legged hawks, and other raptors. Also look for other arctic nesting birds that spend their winters here—snow buntings, Lapland longspurs, and large flocks of horned larks.

Davenport Cemetery (Hot Spot C): Cemeteries are islands of trees that are relatively undisturbed and have a good prey base (grass is green and well watered; gravestones protect burrows and nests). They attract lots of birds, especially during migration. A pair of great horned owls is established in the Davenport Cemetery (0.5 mile south of Davenport on SR 28, then west on the cemetery road).

If you visit at dusk you can hear the owls calling; they are very vocal during this season. Look for regurgitated pellets under the trees to locate the nest, but do not disturb them; they are incubating eggs in February and can be aggressive.

Tucannon River (Hot Spot D): The 19-mile drive up Tucannon River Road to the hatchery is a great place to see wild turkeys. Watch for raptors, great blue heron colonies, wild turkeys in the fields, and both white-tailed and mule deer. If you miss the turkeys here, drive up Mill Creek Road east of Walla Walla and see flocks at the Allen home (8.1 miles from the Isaacs Road turnoff).

waterfowl, and hundreds of dunlin, plus bald eagles looking for injured ducks.

Drive north on US 12, watching for large flocks of waterfowl in ponds north of milepost 300—and peregrine falcons looking for dinner. North of milepost 297, turn right (east) on Maple Road to McNary National Wildlife Refuge to see raptors, waterfowl, red-winged blackbirds, and more.

■ *Pasco to Davenport:* Drive north on US 395, exiting to SR 17 at Mesa. Barn owls are numerous in the cut bank 2 miles north of Mesa (see white droppings in the day; owls in the evening). Explore the side roads southeast of the SR 17/SR 26 junction for short-eared owls, gyrfalcons, Cooper's hawks, and sharp-shinned hawks.

Continue north past the O'Sullivan Dam turnoff and turn left on Route 3 SE to look for snowy owls. One or two always winter here; more in years when food is scarce farther north. Curve south on Route L SE, east on 5 SE, and north on M SE. Snowys usually watch for prey from atop cement drainage ditches or farm implements.

Follow Route M north to SR 17, driving through Moses Lake and past Soap Lake (waterfowl and eagles). Watch for common loons on Blue Lake, along with common goldeneye, hooded mergansers, pied-billed grebes, and raptors. Turn left (west) at US 2 to visit the Waterville Plateau (Hot Spot B).

Drive back east through Coulee City to Davenport; visit the Davenport Cemetery in the evening to see nesting great horned owls (Hot Spot C).

■ *Davenport to Walla Walla:* Drive south on SR 23 through Harrington (trumpeter swans in late February), then southeast through short-eared owl country. Look for red-tailed hawks nesting in old magpie nests in early February—also long-eared and great horned owls in the small wooded areas.

Cross I–90 at Sprague into the channeled scablands, stopping at wetlands to enjoy waterfowl, raptors, and other birds. At St. John, enter Palouse country with its rolling hills—good hawk and falcon populations. Drive through Steptoe and Colfax, then west on SR 26 to Dusty (rest rooms) before you head south on SR 127 across the Snake River. Turn west on US 12, then near milepost 361 turn left (east) up the Tucannon River Road to see wild turkeys (Hot Spot D). Head south again on US 12 to Walla Walla.

Food and lodging: Most cities along the way offer all services.

7

February

Walk to Cure the Winter Blues

An urban nature walk is just the thing to perk up your spirits and remind you that spring is on the way. Here's a favorite and reliable event on Yakima's riverside path.

Site: Yakima Greenway, along the Yakima River in Yakima.

Recommended time: The Yakima Greenway Winter Walk is held every year on the third weekend in February.

Minimum time commitment: An afternoon or a day, plus travel time.

What to bring: Warm clothing, good walking shoes, binoculars, even the family dog (on a leash, please).

Directions: Take I–82 exit 33, drive east on Terrace Heights Drive, then turn right (south) on Eighteenth Street to Sarg Hubbard Park.

The background: This event showcases birds, mammals, and flora in a winter setting. There are informal walks to view the riparian area in stark winter mantle. If you don't want to walk, you can take a horse-drawn wagon ride along the greenway, or you can bicycle or in-line skate—dogs are welcome, too. Listen for the sounds of raptors and red-winged blackbirds. See eagles, great blue herons, ducks, and Canada geese. You may also see beavers and muskrats in the ponds.

The fun: The Yakima Greenway, a National Recreation Trail, is a 10-mile walking/biking path system with paved pathway, three parks, playground, two fishing lakes, and four river access landings. All facilities have rest rooms and picnic areas and are open and free year-round from dawn to dusk.

This event is based out of Sarg Hubbard Park and runs from 10:00 A.M.

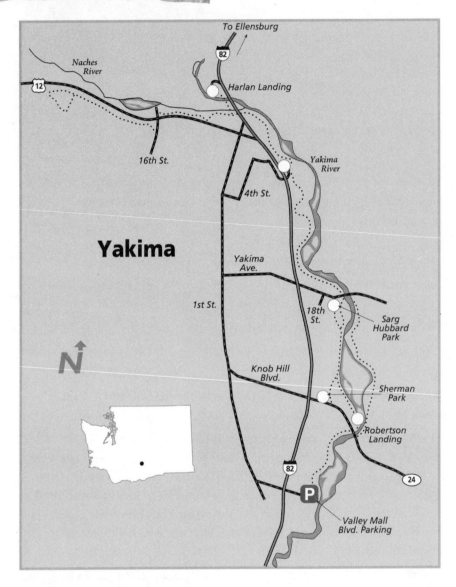

to 2:00 P.M. Audubon members are available for birding walks. The Greenway staff serves hot chocolate and muffins, and T-shirts are on sale to benefit the Greenway Foundation.

Year-round, the Greenway is a pleasant and convenient outdoor recreation area. Sarg Hubbard Park is also the location of the E.A.G.L.E. Earth Day celebration in mid-April, the Gap-to-Gap Relay Weekend in June, and a blues/jazz festival in the amphitheater in August.

The paved pathways are accessible from several parks and landings along the Yakima River; access points (from north to south) are:

■ *Harlan Landing* (take Resthaven Road exit from I–82; turn west over the freeway to parking lot).

■ *Rotary Lake* (drive north on Fourth Street, east on R; follow dirt road under freeway to parking lot—lake is 0.25 mile north on pathway).

Two hardy souls enjoy a winter walk on the riverside path during the Yakima Greenway Winter Walk.

■ *Sarg Hubbard Park and Landing* includes the Sarg Hubbard Natural Area, viewing platform, and amphitheater. The Washington Fruit Place Visitor Center is also located here—a great place to learn about apples.

■ *Sherman Park and Robertson Landing* (enter from Nob Hill Boulevard across from K-Mart). The Yakima Arboretum is also here, with its eleven acres of natural riparian wetland, a lovely Japanese Garden, plants from around the world, and the Jewett Interpretive Center.

■ *Valley Mall Boulevard parking lot*

Next best: Take a side trip to view elk and bighorn sheep west of Yakima (chapter 3). Or drive north on I–82 and look for early-spring activity in the great blue heron rookery on the west side of the freeway (just before milepost 28). Then turn onto SR 821, drive north through Yakima Canyon toward Ellensburg, stop near milepost 19 or 20, and search the butte across the river for bighorn sheep.

Food and lodging: Yakima offers all services.

For more information:

Yakima Greenway Foundation
(509) 453–8280; www.yakimagreenway.org

8

February

Cute, Cuddly, and Floats on Its Back

Journey to Washington's coast for a good chance to see sea otters bobbing on the water like furry corks, often eating from their "tummy tables."

Site: Olympic Coast National Marine Sanctuary, near Neah Bay on Washington's northern Pacific Coast.

Recommended time: February; from December to April sea otters are closer to good viewing locations.

Minimum time commitment: A day to look and observe, plus traveling time.

What to bring: A spotting scope or binoculars; warm, wind-resistant, water-repellant coat; hat, gloves; patience.

Directions: Drive to Sappho (US 101/SR 113 junction) from Forks or from Port Angeles. Follow SR 113 north to Clallam Bay and SR 112 west to the Sekiu/Neah Bay viewing areas.

The background: Commercial hunting for their fur eliminated these animals off our coast by the early 1900s. Sea otters were protected by international treaty in 1911. They were reintroduced to Washington in 1969 and their numbers are increasing.

The thick, luxurious fur, which nearly brought about their demise, is a good insulator and the reason they can survive so well in the cold coastal water. It is also the reason oil spills can be a tragedy for these animals. Even a small spot of oil on their fur can let in so much cold that the animal dies.

Biologists consider sea otters a "keystone predator" because their behavior can have a huge effect on the rest of their ecosystem. Large kelp beds are a sign of a healthy marine environment because so many fish, other sea creatures, and birds depend on them. When sea urchin numbers increase, they consume too much kelp habitat, and the ecosystem is thrown off balance. Sea otters maintain this balance by eating sea urchins in large quantities.

Populations of sea lions, the normal prey of transient orcas, have been decreasing, especially in the Aleutian Islands, so the whales have switched to hunting sea otters (as many as 45,000 otters over the last decade). As a result kelp beds there are disappearing and the ecosystem is collapsing. Fortunately, our resident San Juan Islands orcas prefer salmon, and our kelp beds are healthy.

Sea otters must eat 25 percent of their weight—up to seventy sea urchins—every twenty-four hours. They find their prey mostly by feel on the ocean floor. They bring the food to the surface, flip over on their backs, and use their stomachs as tables, often using rocks as tools to open shells. The males weigh 65–85 pounds; females, 35–60 pounds. They can get bigger—the largest male sea otter tagged in Washington weighed 102 pounds!

Sea otters normally breed twice a year; the heaviest pup populations occur in late March and early November. Only one pup is born in each litter because it is a full-time job feeding just one. Only the mother is on parenting duty, finding enough food for both herself and her baby.

In early December male otters leave their summer feeding areas along Washington's north coast and move around Cape Flattery into the Strait of Juan de Fuca to feed on the red sea urchins. Because sea otters dive to the sea floor for their food, they stay in fairly shallow water. This is fortunate for us nature enthusiasts; they sometimes come close enough for us to see them from the shore.

The fun: Be patient when searching for sea otters. Catching sight of the gregarious animals is worth the effort. They are often very active—floating on their backs and moving their feet. You can sometimes see them with the naked eye; with a spotting scope, you have an even better chance. A hint on spotting the floating groups or "rafts"—look for sea gulls hovering above in hopes of scavenging food.

There are good viewpoints right on SR 112; a good place to start is Chito Beach Resort, west of Sekiu. Call Pat Ness or stop in and ask where they were last seen; she is a volunteer for the U.S. Geological Survey, collecting data on the sea otters. You can often observe rafts of up to forty otters

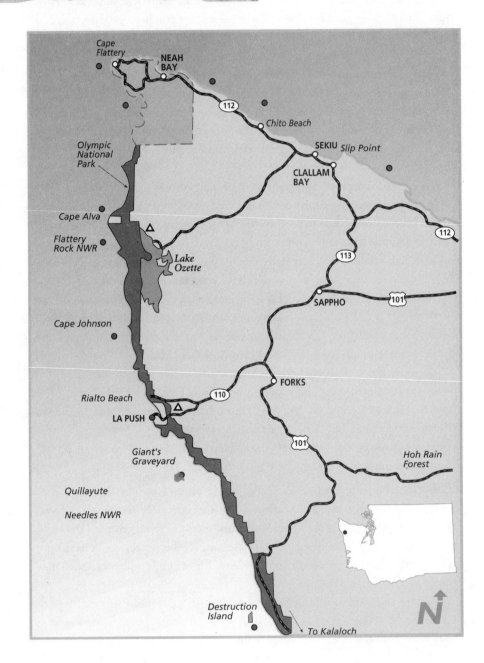

Cape
Flattery

NEAH
BAY

112

Chito Beach

SEKIU Slip Point

CLALLAM
BAY

Olympic
National
Park

112

Cape Alva

113

Flattery
Rock NWR

Lake
Ozette

101

SAPPHO

Cape Johnson

FORKS

Rialto Beach

110

LA PUSH

101

Giant's
Graveyard

Hoh Rain
Forest

Quillayute

Needles NWR

Destruction
Island

→ To Kalaloch

N

From the Cape Flattery viewing platforms, you can look south at the rugged cliffs along the coast. At times, hundreds of birds roost here.

from the bluff east of Bullman Beach. The best viewpoint is at a small pullout just west of milepost 2; a larger pullout is 0.5 mile farther east.

You can also see sea otters in the surf off Cape Alava, a 3.3-mile hike from Lake Ozette. Sea otters have been seen near Waadah Island in the Strait of Juan de Fuca (also east of Clallam Bay by helicopter); from Cape Flattery and in Mukkaw Bay on the ocean; and, recently, north of Kalaloch. Backpackers and kayakers can view otters between Sand Point and Oil City.

Next best: See chapter 13 for more nature activities and larger Neah Bay area map.

Food and lodging: The highway from Clallam Bay to Neah Bay has all amenities.

For more information:

Chito Beach Resort
(360) 963–2581; www.chitobeach.com
Ozette Ranger Station
(360) 963–2725
North Olympic Peninsula
www.northolympic.com

River Otters and Sea Otters

Both river and sea otters are members of the family *Mustelidae*. They are some-times confused, but distinguishing between them is not that difficult if you just keep a couple things in mind—habitat and behavior.

In Washington the northern river otter lives in and around both fresh and salt water and is frequently seen on shore and on docks. The sea otter stays in salt water, rarely and reluctantly coming on shore. I guess you could say their feet determine their behavior—at least that's anoth-er way to remember the differences.

River otters are versatile; they have webbed feet for strong swimming but also can run with ease on shore. Sea otters' flipperlike hind feet make them very efficient in water also but very awkward on land.

The two kinds of otters even look a lot different, once you start noticing. River otters are very dark brown and a lot smaller than sea otters—a weight range of eleven to thirty pounds for river otters but thirty-five to eighty-five pounds for sea otters. Sea otters have round, fuzzy, light-colored heads. River otters have longer, more streamlined,

Sea otters eat mussels, clams, and a favorite, the kelp-eating sea urchin—a valuable contribution to the kelp forests on which fish depend.

but powerful, tails. Sea otter tails are stocky and short; they don't extend much beyond their hind feet when they're lying on their backs. Sea otters are the ones who are always depicted on postcards and designed as stuffed animal toys—cute, cuddly, floating on their backs.

If you see an otter running and playing along the beach, it is not a sea otter. These marine mammals are always in the water, except when a storm is too severe. Then they will wait, looking vaguely uncomfortable, on the beach. As soon as possible, back they go into the waves. Sea otters live their lives in the water—they sleep in the water (securely tethered by wrapping strands of kelp around their bodies), eat in the water, play in the water, mate and give birth in the water. They are self-contained, using their chests for food preparation, eating, feeding, and holding their young. Sea urchins, crabs, mussels, abalone, and fish are their primary foods.

The river otter can be found in freshwater rivers and also along the shores of Greater Puget Sound and in the San Juan Islands—often around boat docks and marinas.

Except when seriously hunting for fish, river otters are like frolicking children. In and out of the water, sliding down banks, running down the beach, bodysurfing in swift streams, playing, wriggling. They're very gregarious; you almost never see just one. They can dive up to 55 feet deep, swim underwater for up to a 0.25 mile, then come up to the surface, tread water, and raise their heads high to look around. River otters can hold and carry fish in their forepaws, often dining on land. They also eat small mammals, diving birds, and nesting birds and their young. River otters live in dens but do not enjoy construction, preferring to move into natural cavities or abandoned dens of other animals, including beavers.

The sea otter, on the other hand, is found along the coast in ocean water, in and among kelp beds within about a mile of shore. It is occasionally found in Greater Puget Sound, especially in areas that are close to the outer coasts.

Despite their habits, river otters are not considered a "marine mammal" and do not enjoy the legal protection of the Marine Mammal Protection Act as do sea otters.

9

March

Glass Balls and Other Treasures

Are you getting cabin fever? Does the beach beckon? Check out the Beachcombers' Fun Fair at Ocean Shores. Or bundle up and go beachcombing. You may find glass Japanese floats, bottles, or other treasures—and a fresh appreciation for the Pacific Coast.

Site: Beachcombers' Fun Fair at the Ocean Shores Convention Center, Ocean Shores, 70 miles west of Olympia on Washington's coast.

Recommended time: The annual Beachcombers' Fun Fair is the first full weekend in March. The entire month of March, especially right after or during a storm, is recommended for the best beach treasure hunting up and down Washington's Pacific coast.

Minimum time commitment: A few hours plus driving time for the festival, a day if you want to join a volksmarch, a whole weekend if you want to get out and search for treasures.

What to bring: Warm, wind-resistant outerwear; layers of warm clothing including a wool sweater; hat and gloves; rain gear; waterproof boots; extra dry clothes; plastic bags and boxes to carry your salty discoveries back home.

Directions: From I–5 in Olympia, take exit 104 and drive 48 miles west on SR 8 and US 12 to Aberdeen. Take US 101 west to Hoquiam, then follow the signs to Ocean Shores via SR 109 and then south on SR 115.

The background: Because many people visit the beach only on a warm summer day, enjoying the coast at this time of year adds considerably to your wealth of year-round outdoor experiences. Although Japanese fishing floats made of green glass seem to be the most sought-after prizes, there are many

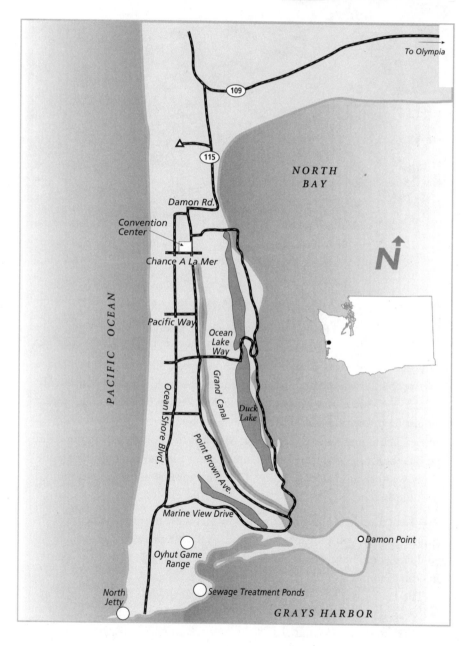

To Olympia

109

115

NORTH BAY

Damon Rd.

Convention Center

Chance A La Mer

PACIFIC OCEAN

Pacific Way

Ocean Lake Way

Grand Canal

Duck Lake

Ocean Shore Blvd.

Point Brown Ave.

Marine View Drive

Damon Point

Oyhut Game Range

North Jetty

Sewage Treatment Ponds

GRAYS HARBOR

N

"Bottles From Around the World" is one of the many displays judged at the Beachcomber's Fun Fair.

others to seek. Plastic floats, bottles, fishing gear, wooden objects (signs, crates, lumber), plastic items with Asian or other foreign labels, driftwood, shells, fish and whale bones, rocks of many colors and shapes, and colorful agates and jasper pebbles. Even the popular glass floats come in all kinds of shapes, colors, and sizes. Some of what you find may be valuable to a collector; most will just be interesting and fun to add to your home or yard.

Beachcombing experts advise that March is the best month in the entire year. The best time is during or just after a storm. If you can't go during stormy weather, at least choose high tide, with some wind blowing toward or across the beach.

The fun: Beachcombing is a treasure hunt, pure and simple. Like most treasure hunters, you probably won't find a valuable prize every time, but you'll find something worth looking at and won't be able to resist bringing something home.

The Beachcombers' Fun Fair, a small but worthwhile festival, is held in the Ocean Shores Convention Center. There are displays of beachcombed items such as driftwood and glass floats, artwork about or created from beachcombed treasures, with judging in forty-four categories. A Science-Go-Round is held on Saturday of that weekend where kids can talk to experts from the Audubon Society, the National Oceanic and Atmospheric Administration (NOAA), the University of Washington, and the Washington Department of Natural Resources about coastal creatures and plants, ocean currents, and wildlife rescue. There are also adult and family presentations on both days on such topics as coastal erosion, ocean currents, surf and water safety, razor clams, wildlife rescue, whales, and birds.

Next best: The Volkssport Association holds its Annual Seabreeze Weekend on the first weekend in March, with 6.2-mile (10-km) walks along the bay (go early to see the deer) and along the ocean. All walks are self-paced and clearly marked.

The annual Beachcombers Driftwood Show is held two weeks after the Beachcombers' Fun Fair in Grayland, about 25 miles southwest of Aberdeen on the coast. Good beachcombing areas can be found at Ocean Shores, Copalis Beach, Iron Springs, Pacific Beach, and Moclips. Be a courteous visitor; please respect private property and stay off posted Indian reservation areas.

While beachcombing is generally safe, do watch out for sneaker waves—those unpredictable giants that sometimes carry large and deadly logs crashing onto the beach, smashing everything in their path. The best way to beachcomb is to "keep one eye on the beach and the other on the waves." Respect the ocean's power and stay alert. Otherwise just watch the tides so that you don't get trapped on a rocky point, walk carefully on soft sand and slippery rocks, and think before you pick up a sea creature. Some jellyfish, for example, can sting.

Food and lodging: Ocean Shores offers all services; Ocean City Campground is just north of town on SR 115.

For more information:

Ocean Shores Chamber of Commerce
(800) 762–3224; www.oceanshores.com/events/index.shtml
Evergreen State Volkssport Association
(253) 840–1776; www.esva.org/

10

March

Nature's Mating Game

Hundreds of long-legged great blue herons gather in their "heron-ries," or communal nesting areas, to perform their courtship rituals. Flocks of sandhill cranes, Canada geese, and tundra swans add to the spectacle.

Site: Shillapoo Wildlife Area and Ridgefield National Wildlife Refuge, just west and northwest of Vancouver.

Recommended time: March.

Minimum time commitment: Half a day; a weekend to see all the sites.

What to bring: Binoculars or spotting scope, camera with telephoto lens, field guide to birds, WDFW Access Stewardship Decal.

Directions: From I–5, take exit 1D, Fourth Plain Boulevard, and drive 1.3 miles west to Fruit Valley Road and the start of your tour. A large great blue heron colony (357 nests) is 5.5 miles farther, north of Frenchman's Bar Riverfront Park in Shillapoo Wildlife Area.

The background: According to Robert W. Butler, research scientist with the Canadian Wildlife Service, our Northwest Coast great blue heron sub-species (slightly darker plumage) is found only west of the Cascades, from southern Oregon north through coastal British Columbia. It is non-migratory and remains isolated from other great blue heron species. Look for heron colonies in clusters of tall cottonwoods along waterways or wetlands. Huge nests of sticks are used year after year, with additions made each season. One courtship study found that fourteen physical behaviors, including the

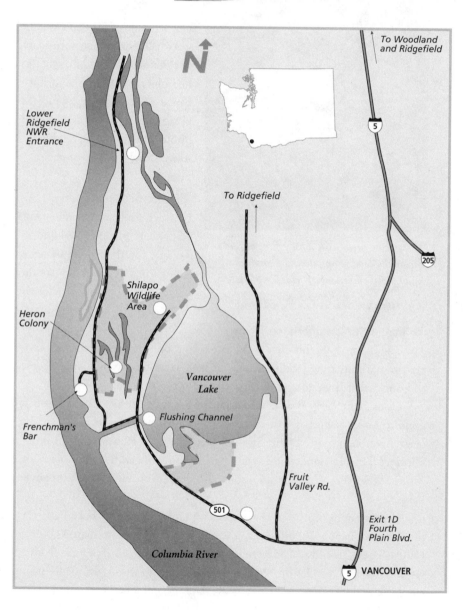

To Woodland and Ridgefield

5

Lower Ridgefield NWR Entrance

To Ridgefield

205

Shilapo Wildlife Area

Heron Colony

Vancouver Lake

Frenchman's Bar

Flushing Channel

Fruit Valley Rd.

Exit 1D Fourth Plain Blvd.

501

Columbia River

5 VANCOUVER

exchange of nest sticks, are connected with pair bonding—rituals well worth watching. Herons are extremely skittish during mating season. The Washington Department of Fish and Wildlife warns, "Despite their formidable size, herons are shy birds that can be vulnerable to human disturbance . . . keep your distance by using binoculars, scopes, and telephoto camera lenses, be quiet, move slowly, and leave pets at home."

Great blue herons eat mostly fish, but occasionally food scraps, nestlings, and small mammals. Their longest recorded lifespan is more than 23 years.

The fun: Herons move between Shillapoo Wildlife Area, Ridgefield National Wildlife Refuge, and the Sauvie Island Refuge in Oregon. They are most active for two hours after sunrise and two hours before sunset; visit the heronry in late afternoon for best light.

The drive to the heronry is full of birding opportunities. You may spot raptors and migrating sandhill cranes, as well as tundra swans, Canada geese, and ducks that have not yet headed north for the summer.

From Fruit Valley Road, head west for 0.8 mile on SR 501 and stop at a pond to look for birds. Great egrets, American white pelicans, and Canada geese have been spotted here. SR 501 then curves northward for 2.5 miles to Flushing Channel, where you'll find parking, toilets, and beautiful views of Mount St. Helens. Cormorants, loons, and grebes inhabit nearby Vancouver Lake.

Head straight (north) at the intersection, past Vancouver Lake Park. On the left is Shillapoo Wildlife Area, a wintering area for more than 30,000 Canada geese. In early March see lesser sandhill cranes all along the fields and wetlands from 1.4 miles on. At 2 miles walk out on the access road—staying clear of the flocks—to see cranes, geese, raptors, and a few egrets and swans.

Return to the intersection, turn right (west) on Lower River Road and drive 1.8 miles to Frenchman's Bar Riverfront Park on the Columbia River, a

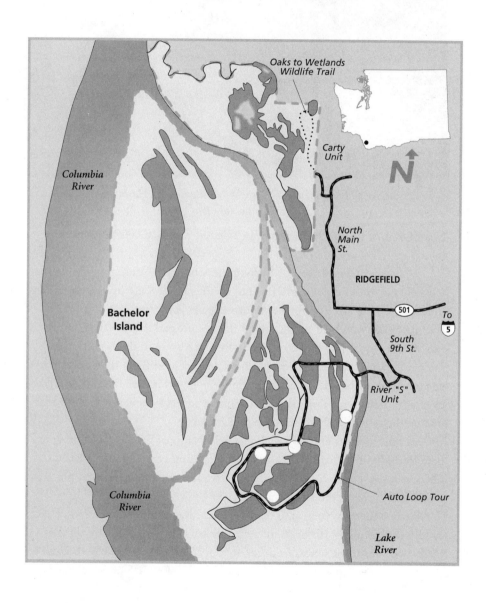

Oaks to Wetlands
Wildlife Trail

Carty
Unit

Columbia
River

North
Main
St.

RIDGEFIELD

**Bachelor
Island**

501

To
5

South
9th St.

River "S"
Unit

Auto Loop Tour

Columbia
River

Lake
River

N

Tundra swans, which remain at Ridgefield NWR through March, are easy to view from the auto-only tour loop.

beautiful place for lunch. Facilities include rest rooms, picnic tables, and a hiking trail.

When you leave, drive north along the Columbia. You'll pass the heronry 0.4 mile north of Frenchman's Bar, but there is no parking on the east side of the road, so save this stop for the return trip. As you drive listen for cranes bugling. When you hear them, stop at the nearest parking access and walk quietly out along the paths to catch a glimpse. Also look up to see small flocks of cranes and large flocks of ducks and geese in flight. Two miles north of Frenchman's Bar, the fields across from the gravel pit are filled with left-over small potatoes, a favorite food of tundra swans, which are plentiful in winter. You're less likely to spot them in March.

In 2 more miles enter lower Ridgefield National Wildlife Refuge. From here to the Post Office Lake parking lot is a string of ponds and wetlands filled with geese and ducks, as well as a few late swans. What a great place to take a walk, look at the river, and enjoy the birds!

Return the way you came, stopping this time at the heron colony. Park at an access to the north or south and walk back, or pull part way off the road's wide west lane across from the heronry. There are great blue herons everywhere—on their nests, in the air, and in the slough. Stay awhile and watch them perform their mating rituals.

Next best: Visit Ridgefield National Wildlife Refuge, 13 miles north on

I–5, to see mating, migrating, or still-wintering birds from your car (entrance fee, Annual Refuge Pass, or Golden Eagle Pass).

Directions: From I–5 take exit 14, SR 501, and drive 2.5 miles west to Ridgefield. Turn left on South Ninth Street, then right in 0.6 mile into the River "S" unit, down the hill and across the railroad tracks.

In early March wintering waterfowl still forage and rest in refuge wetlands and fields, and bald eagles roost in the trees. In February you can see as many as 2,000 tundra swans, 20,000 dabbling ducks, and thousands of the dusky subspecies of Canada goose. They are everywhere in the River "S" unit, which is diked and planted with crops to provide optimal browse for waterfowl.

A 4.2-mile auto-only tour loop opened in 1999; it circles the diked ponds and wetlands—with canals around the perimeter. Highlights on one drive were:

- Hundreds of shorebirds at 1.1 miles
- Four nutria (non-native mammals that destroy wetlands by randomly chewing starchy roots) basking in the sun near the observation blind at 1.3 miles (parking area, trail)
- Several hundred tundra swans in the ponds at 2.3 miles
- Fields covered with Canada geese at 4 miles
- Raptors, ducks, and songbirds everywhere

Ridgefield's Bachelor Island heronry (inaccessible from the public area) hosts about 400 nests. In March great blue herons in full mating plumage may be seen in shallow marshes on the River "S" unit. Three-foot-tall sandhill cranes (red caps on their foreheads) arrive by early March to feed in grain fields at the refuge and surrounding countryside. Black-tailed deer, coyotes, foxes, raccoons, skunks, beavers, and otters are sometimes seen in the early morning.

Food and lodging: Vancouver and Woodland offer all services; camping at Battleground Lake State Park (showers).

For more information:

Shillapoo and Vancouver Lake wildlife areas
(360) 906–6725
Ridgefield National Wildlife Refuge
(360) 887–4106; www.rl.fws.gov/ridgefield/

11

March

Journey of the Giants

The Pacific Ocean along the Washington coast is a highway for migrating gray whales. Luckily these majestic mammals often travel close to shore as they head north from their calving grounds each spring.

Site: Pacific Ocean, near Westport. This area has some of the best whale-watching boat excursions, with captains who have been finding whales for tourists for many years.

Recommended time: March and April are the best months to see gray whales from Washington shores, although they continue to migrate northward from February to July.

Minimum time commitment: Most tours last two to four hours, plus travel time.

What to bring: Warm clothes, rain gear, binoculars, camera and plastic bag to protect equipment from saltwater, sunglasses, hat and gloves.

Directions: From I–5 in Olympia, take exit 104 and drive 48 miles west on SR 8 and US 12 to Aberdeen. Turn left (south) on US 101 over the bridge, then right (west) on SR 105. Follow the signs 23 miles to Westport, on the southern "hook" of Grays Harbor.

The background: Gray whales are just like human "snow birds." They spend fall and winter in warm Baja California waters, where they mate and give birth. In spring they head north to Alaska and beyond to the Bering, Beaufort, and Chukchi seas—a trip of close to 7,000 miles. Males migrate north earlier than the mothers with their young, who follow about a month

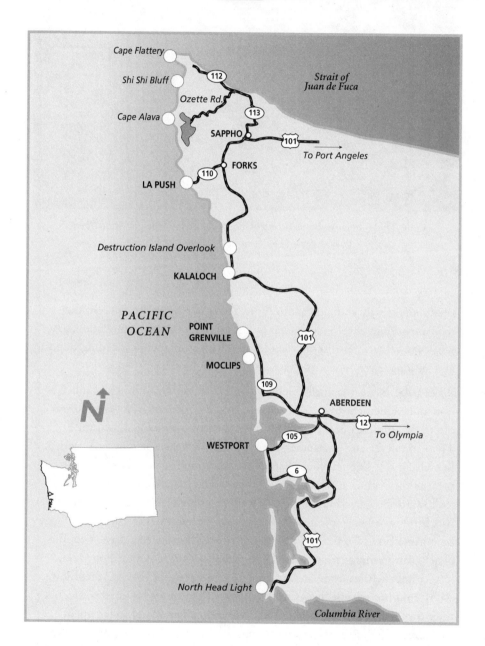

Cape Flattery

Shi Shi Bluff

Ozette Rd.

Cape Alava

SAPPHO

112

113

Strait of
Juan de Fuca

101

To Port Angeles

FORKS

110

LA PUSH

Destruction Island Overlook

KALALOCH

PACIFIC
OCEAN

POINT
GRENVILLE

MOCLIPS

101

109

ABERDEEN

12

To Olympia

WESTPORT

105

6

N

101

North Head Light

Columbia River

Gray whales often swim very closely alongside slowly cruising charter boats. Observers can often even "pet" a curious whale.

later, more slowly and closer into shore. Youngsters grow up fast. On the return trip they travel independently. During the southward migration, gray whales travel farther offshore than in the spring. Gray whales are huge, up to 46 feet long. Even newborns average 16 feet in length.

The fun: Next to actually seeing the whales, the most fun is the anticipation and excitement of looking. Add to that the pleasure of looking for sea otters, dolphins, sea lions, seals, and birds and you will have a great time. There are never any guarantees, but on a good whale-watching boat with a knowledgeable skipper, your chances are very good. On one trip we saw two orcas in the harbor and wondered if they would engage in aggressive behavior toward the grays, but the orcas left them alone. The most unpredictable part is the weather—spring on the coast can be sunny, or it can be too foggy or stormy to see. Be flexible. Just in case the trip is canceled, have a contingency plan in mind (see chapter 17 for other nature activities in the area).

To spot whales from land or from a boat, watch for "blows," those low, wispy columns of mist that whales spew from their blowholes. Also watch for their dark, curved backs rhythmically swimming, under, up, under, up, or sometimes their giant tails pointing high in the air as they search the bottoms of shallow bays for food. Gray whales have no dorsal fins and their bodies look mottled and rough. Closer inspection shows that they are covered with barnacles and whale lice. Don't worry, humans can't "catch" the lice; interestingly, the barnacles are a species unique to this particular whale.

On whale boats or in your own vessel, insist upon the legally required 100-yard limit. Some migrating gray whales have learned to approach boats because of their experiences with friendly Baja whale watchers in inflatable boats. Down there the whales love to have their backs scratched and have shed their natural fear of people. Some of these "tame" whales approach boats all along their route, trusting that humans mean them no harm. This can be exciting to whale watchers but hazardous to the whales, which put themselves in danger of being scraped by a boat engine or harpooned by someone with less-friendly intentions.

If the boat you are on has obeyed the 100-yard limit with idle engines and is approached by a "friendly" whale, it is okay to stay where you are, enjoy the sight, and even "pet" the whale if you're close enough. To avoid injuring the whale keep the engine in neutral until the whale swims away.

Next best: Trying to catch a glimpse from land is more difficult, but it is free and there's no chance of getting seasick—see map for locations.
- Neah Bay: Mukkaw Bay; Cape Flattery (0.75-mile trail—gray whales, sea otters, seabirds); Shi Shi Bluff (trail south of Neah Bay).
- Cape Alava: three-mile boardwalk to the beach—gray whales, harbor seals, sea lions, sea otters, bald eagles, osprey, marine birds.
- Kalaloch: from the lodge or the Destruction Island Overlook nearby.
- Westport: observation tower; also Grayland State Park beaches.
- North Head: walk to lighthouse—seals, sea lions, gray whales.

Food and lodging: Westport offers all services; camping at Twin Harbors State Park, a few miles south of Westport.

For more information:
Westport-Grayland Chamber of Commerce (list of charters)
(800) 345–6223; westportwa.com/chamber/index.html
Gray Whale Watching Charters
westportwa.com/business/charter.html
The Seattle Aquarium (trips and adventures)
(206) 386–4300 or (206) 386–4353;
www.seattleaquarium.org/education/default.asp

12

March

Red Crowns, Gray Cloaks

Sandhill cranes migrate northward through central Washington every spring, inspiring a festival in Othello in the Columbia Basin, where they stop to fatten up on grain and corn in the fields.

Site: Othello, about 20 miles south of Moses Lake.

Recommended time: The annual Sandhill Crane Festival is the last full weekend in March. For a whole month—from mid-March to mid-April—as many as 10,000 cranes fly into the fields from their roosts each morning and afternoon, feed in the fertile fields of the Columbia Basin, and return to their roosts around noon and at dusk.

Minimum time commitment: This festival is worth taking an entire weekend; if you have only one day, go on Saturday.

What to bring: Binoculars, spotting scope, camera.

Directions: From the junction of SR 26 and 17, drive west on SR 26, turn north into Othello, and head for festival headquarters at Othello High School, 370 South Seventh Avenue.

The background: This wildlife celebration is centered on the northward spring migration of lesser sandhill cranes from their wintering areas in California's Central Valley to their Canadian and Alaskan breeding grounds.

The best view of the cranes is from the many roads in the Othello area, but wildlife areas from Crab Creek to the Columbia National Wildlife Refuge and south to Scooteney Reservoir are also good.

The Othello area is agricultural and close to wildlife areas—the major reasons the cranes stop here. Sandhill cranes prefer grain and field corn to all other crops, and they feast on the spillage from the previous harvest. Farmers

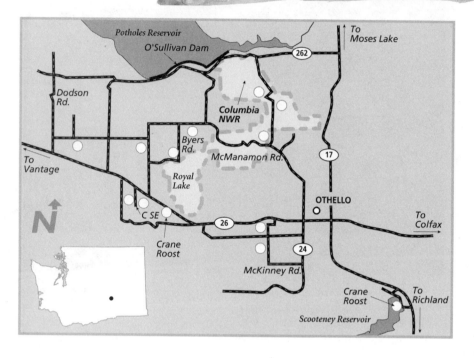

harvest about five tons of corn per acre, with approximately 5 percent loss or spillage; on average there's about 500 pounds of corn left on every acre for the cranes. Cranes also eat rodents, bugs, and worms in alfalfa fields and wet meadows.

When you are out searching for sandhill cranes, stop and listen. You may hear their shrill, rolling, cackling "bugle" before you see them. These gray to rust-colored birds are easy to spot. They are 4 feet tall and have a distinctive bald red crown. In flight you can tell them by their outstretched necks and legs and 7-foot wingspan. Seeing hundreds of cranes flying overhead and hearing the wonderful sound they make is a thrilling combination you won't soon forget.

The fun: If you want to take full advantage of the wonderful opportunities the Sandhill Crane Festival has to offer, arrive in Othello on Friday afternoon for a birding tour of the Columbia National Wildlife Refuge and Potholes Wildlife Area ($10). Then proceed to Othello High School early Saturday

Sandhill crane courtship displays include loud rattling calls and elaborate dances—bobbing heads, bowing and leaping, and running with wings extended.

morning to catch a bus for one of the first ninety-minute or three-hour viewing tours. Crane tours also run late Saturday afternoon and Sunday morning. General festival admission is $5.00; the workshops and talks are free, and the shorter tours are $5.00.

Two guides accompany each tour—an experienced birding guide and a local guide knowledgeable about Columbia Basin agriculture. It makes for well-rounded and extremely interesting presentations. Maps are available at headquarters so that you can explore the back roads on your own.

Channeled scablands geology tours are held midday on Saturday and a series of workshops and informative talks are presented at Othello High School from 10:00 A.M. to 4:00 P.M. Past topics have included crane conservation; Ice Age floods; birds of the Arid Lands Ecological Reserve; local geology; local history; landscaping for wildlife; shrub-steppe flora and fauna; crane folklore, literature and art; birds of the Columbia National Wildlife Refuge and Potholes; and a live falcon demonstration.

On Sunday there are longer tours (five to eight hours; $10 to $30) with limited participation. Destinations have included a sage grouse lek, Wahluke Slope for shrub-steppe birding, Arid Lands Ecological Reserve, Columbia NWR/Potholes WA (Fish and Wildlife staff led), and Cariboo/White Bluffs Trail for an interpretive history walk. All tours are very popular; register by phone or e-mail before mid-March to ensure a space.

The festival is a family affair, with special children's activities running from 9:00 A.M. to 3:00 P.M. on Saturday. These include making bird feeders, origami, mask making, print animals, and wildlife art instruction. Vendors and organizations have wildlife and other Columbia Basin–related displays set up in the high school. A banquet is held each year on Saturday evening, featuring a noted guest speaker.

Next best: You can always take your own crane tour. Large flocks of cranes feed in the fields during the morning and late afternoon; at midday and dusk they take refuge in shallow open water.

We had the most success during the day along SR 26 west of Othello. In the afternoon we saw several large flocks flying in and out of the fields near C SE south of SR 26 and about 12 miles west of Othello. Just before noon we saw hundreds of cranes and large numbers of Canada geese standing in the wetlands at one of the roosts along SR 26, 1.5 miles east of D SE. Cranes can often be seen feeding just southwest of Othello in the fields between SR 26 and Hampton on the south and along Miller or McKinley Road.

Many cranes roost on islands in Scooteney Reservoir at night. They begin to gather a half hour before sunset; by semidark we counted about 600 cranes. They circled and flew into the wind to land. In the morning, they leave at first light; only 40 were left a half hour after dawn. There are lots of Canada geese and ducks flying overhead in the morning, too.

To get to Scooteney Reservoir drive 1 mile east of Othello on SR 26, then 9.5 miles south on SR 17 to the north end of the reservoir. Turn right (west) on Coyan Road, then south into a parking area just past the bridge. Walk down the canal path or out on the road across the earth dam to see cranes roosting on the islands to the south of the dam.

You can also see cranes in the Columbia National Wildlife Refuge and Seep Lakes Wildlife Area (WDFW Access Stewardship Decal required). Get a refuge map at the entrance; the roads are confusing. Paddle the canoe trail on Hutchinson and Shiner lakes south of McManamon Road, which is northwest of Othello. Hike the many trails to see a scenic mixture of rugged cliffs, canyons, lakes, and arid sagebrush grasslands.

The Central Basin Audubon Society Report on Columbia NWR

includes an excellent outline tour of the refuge; check it out at
www.cbas.org/ special/cnwr/index.htm. The site also offers information
about the channeled scablands and the awesome lava flows, ice dams, and
floods that shaped this landscape.

Food and lodging: Othello offers all services. Camping in the Columbia
National Wildlife Refuge and at Potholes State Park (showers) north of
Othello as well as at Scooteney Reservoir south of Othello.

For more information:
Sandhill Crane Festival
www.othello-wa.com/sandhillcrane.htm
Othello Chamber of Commerce
(800) 684–2556 or (509) 488–2683
International Crane Foundation
(608) 356–9462; www.savingcranes.org/

13

April

Slide Across the Strait

When the winds blow from the east, conditions are perfect for raptors to soar high in the sky and glide across the 13 miles of open water from Washington to Vancouver Island.

Site: Cape Flattery, at the northwest tip of the Olympic Peninsula. This is all private land belonging to the Makah Nation; be sure to read the sign at the entrance to the Village of Neah Bay for regulations.

Recommended time: Early April is often the best, but any time from mid-March through April can be good, depending on the weather.

Minimum time commitment: Plan on a weekend because of travel time from nearly everywhere.

What to bring: Binoculars, raptor field guide.

Directions: Take SR 112 to Neah Bay (see chapter 8). The routes to Waatch Valley, Cape Flattery, and the ocean beaches all start by driving west through Neah Bay to the end of the waterfront road, curving left past the Indian Health Service Building, and turning right 1 block to a "T" intersection.

The background: This flyway hosts an average of more than 5,000 migrating raptors each spring, with 2,000 to 8,800 hawks converging in the Neah Bay area in late March and April as they migrate north to nesting grounds. They stop here to rest, feed, and stage before they cross the Strait of Juan de Fuca to Vancouver Island.

The warmth of the land mass (steep bluffs of Cape Flattery and Bahokus and Archawat peaks) colliding with the cold marine air, plus the succession of

weather systems coming through, can create an unusual air flow or "slide" that the raptors use to cross the strait. They rise high on the warm thermals, catch the top of the slide, and glide across to Canada. Falcons, harriers, and sandhill cranes can power across, but soaring raptors are dependent on these special lift and wind conditions to carry them across. Some don't make it, but Canadian rescuers sometimes pick up raptors from the water.

From 1983 to 1987 Bud Anderson's Falcon Research Group focused on falcon studies on Tatoosh Island and Cape Flattery, observing for a four- to six-week period each year. Anderson turned the studies over in 1989 to D. Byrne, founder of

Red-tailed hawks and other buteos make up almost 80 percent of the raptors that concentrate at Cape Flattery before attempting the long, over-water flight.

the NW Raptor Center in Clallam Bay. She, along with others, including members of the Makah tribe and "Ad Hawk volunteers," studied the hawk migration until 1998, the last six years under an arrangement with Hawkwatch International. See results in Welden and Virginia Clark's Cape Flattery raptor migration report at www.olympus.net/opas/birdcf.htm.

The fun: Begin watching the first of April for light east winds and clear weather with rising temperatures. For several weeks in the spring, large numbers of raptors (mostly red-tailed and sharp-shinned hawks with medium numbers of American kestrels, northern harriers, and turkey vultures and a few Cooper's hawks, northern goshawks, merlins, peregrine falcons, golden eagles, and osprey) arrive at Neah Bay along with sandhill cranes from their wintering sites in the south. Bald eagles also fly over, but many of them are residents.

In 1999 one birder observed 1,000 to 1,500 sandhill cranes in four hours. They had been hunkering down in the fields until the east winds and warm, clear weather came, and then they all took off. When conditions are

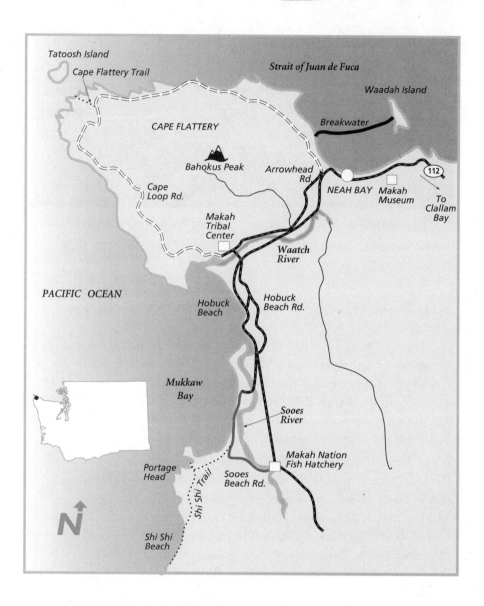

Tatoosh Island

Cape Flattery Trail

Strait of Juan de Fuca

Waadah Island

CAPE FLATTERY

Breakwater

Bahokus Peak

Arrowhead Rd.

Cape Loop Rd.

NEAH BAY

Makah Museum

112

To Clallam Bay

Makah Tribal Center

Waatch River

PACIFIC OCEAN

Hobuck Beach

Hobuck Beach Rd.

Mukkaw Bay

Sooes River

Makah Nation Fish Hatchery

Portage Head

Shi Shi Trail

Sooes Beach Rd.

N

Shi Shi Beach

Take a 4-mile hike to Point of Arches on Shi Shi Beach to enjoy the spectacular tidepools and arches at low tide.

right thousands of birds are observed from Bahokus Peak over just a few weeks.

The road to Bahokus Peak is officially closed to the public, but you can see raptors feeding and resting in Waatch Valley, a tidal-river plain between Neah Bay on the strait and Mukkaw Bay on the ocean. Drive the roads on either side of the Waatch River and look for raptors in the fields, in the trees, and soaring in the air. Enjoy the ducks on the Waatch River, the resident bald eagles, and the bright yellow skunk cabbage everywhere.

Next best: If marginal weather keeps you from seeing the raptors, go to the Makah museum, walk the short trail to Cape Flattery observation points, hike to Shi Shi Beach, or look for gray whales.

The Makah Cultural and Research Center, at the east end of Neah Bay, is open Wednesday through Sunday. The museum features full-scale replicas of cedar long houses, along with whaling, sealing, and fishing canoes and artifacts recovered from an ancient whaling village at Ozette.

To reach the Cape Flattery Trail, go to the "T" intersection (directions above); turn left and follow the road 2.5 miles to the Makah Tribal Center. The road then becomes gravel after 0.25 mile; drive another 4 miles around the south side of the cape and turn left at the CAPE TRAIL sign to the parking area. The new 0.75-mile trail winds through splendid rain forest habitat. Four viewing platforms—each with beautifully illustrated interpretive signs—give you superb views of Tatoosh Island and the rocks below. Bring binoculars or a scope to look for sea otters in the kelp and marine birds (black oystercatchers, cormorants, common murres, and the spectacular tufted puffins) on the rocks and in the waters of the Olympic Coast National Marine Sanctuary. Check out the Cape Flattery online tour at www.northolympic.com/capeflatterytrail/.

Explore the nearby ocean beaches by crossing the Waatch River from the Makah Tribal Center and driving south along Mukkaw Bay. Hobuck Beach is closest; we saw lots of sand dollars the last time we were there (no beach-combing—this is private land). Or hike the new Shi Shi Trail that winds across BLM and Makah Tribal lands, through old-growth forest and logged areas with new interpretive signs and glimpses of wildlife. It ends at the Olympic National Park entrance to Shi Shi Beach; walk 2 miles south on the beach to Point of Arches to explore the magnificent tidepools and arches at low tide.

Visit the Makah Marina in Neah Bay to see California sea lions up close. Puffin Adventures offers whale-watching boat trips out of Neah Bay starting in April. Gray whales are migrating north then (see chapter 11) and often wander into the strait. See porpoises, sea lions, and harbor seals—maybe even a sea otter with a baby on her tummy. Contact Puffin Adventures at (888) 305–2437 or (360) 963–2744; www.olypen.com/puffinadventures.

Check Neah Bay and Ozette day trips at www.forks-web.com/fg/hohrainforest.htm, or see chapter 8 for more places to look for sea otters and other wildlife.

Food and lodging: The highway from Clallam Bay to Neah Bay offers all services.

For more information:
Makah Tribal Council
(360) 645-2201; www.makah.com/

14

April

Creepy, Crawly Critters

*Visit Crab Creek, the longest creek in the nation, and search for
snakes, frogs, lizards, and more as they go a courtin'.*

Site: Crab Creek Coulee, 7 miles southeast of Vantage, across the Columbia
River.

Recommended time: Mid-April through mid-May.

Minimum time commitment: A few hours to a weekend, plus traveling time.

What to bring: Flashlight or headlamp, field guide, high boots to protect
against snakes, WDFW Access Stewardship Decal.

Directions: From Vantage cross the Columbia River on I–90, turn south
on SR 243, drive about 7 miles (through Beverly), and turn left on the paved
road just north of Crab Creek.

The background: Frogs and salamanders are amphibians; snakes and turtles are reptiles. The study of reptiles and amphibians is called "herpetology,"
from the Greek *herpeton,* which means "creeping thing." The informal, short-
hand word sometimes used to refer to all reptiles and amphibians is "herps."

Gary Lentz, area manager of the Lewis and Clark Trail State Park and
Camp Wooten, has studied reptiles and amphibians for many years and says
they are sometimes hard to find. "These animals don't appear on demand like
many birds do," he says. "With herps you take care to find the right habitat,
the right weather, the right time of year, and the rest is 95 percent luck."
Follow his advice below to have the best chance of success. You may be
rewarded with sightings of Great Basin gopher snakes, side-blotched lizards,

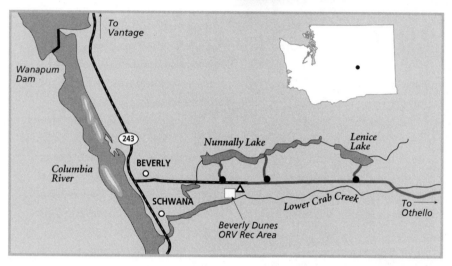

Pacific chorus frogs, spadefoot toads, blue racer snakes, or western rattlesnakes.

Crab Creek Coulee, most of which is owned by the Washington Department of Fish and Wildlife, is worth visiting whether you see any herps or not. It is, according to the WDFW, "a long, magnificent valley carved out of rock by glaciers and prehistoric floods; the stream is officially designated the longest creek in the United States."

The fun: Follow Crab Creek upstream from the Columbia River, stopping at these points of interest:

- Nunnally Lake and fishing access, 2 miles from SR 243.
- Beverly Dunes ORV Recreation Area at 2.2 miles. There is an outhouse here, and you may see painted turtles in Crab Creek as it winds through the dunes.
- Path across the dunes to Nunnally Lake at 3.1 miles.
- Lenice Lake fishing access, 5.1 miles (outhouse).
- Bridge over Crab Creek at 6.1 miles. Walk along the north side of the creek to look for herps.

Most of the snakes at Crab Creek Coulee are from 2.5 to 4 feet long, are most active midday, and are most easily observed in the morning when basking in the sun. The four most common to this area are the western yellow-bellied racer (blue racer) with smooth, olive skin and large eyes; the Great Basin gopher snake (bull snake), which has dark blotches down the back; the wandering garter snake, which has a yellow stripe down its back; and the western rattlesnake, which is readily identified by the "rattles" at the tip of the tail. Sometimes, if you are lucky, you might find a two-lined whip snake, a desert night snake, or a common garter snake with red splotches on its sides.

Lizards also sun themselves on rocks. The side-blotched lizard, with its tiny, rounded back scales, is the most abundant. Look for the short-horned lizard (flat, round, gray, and spiky) in sandy soils—especially near anthills. Also watch for the slim, gray, striped sagebrush lizard and the western skink—long and skinny with smooth shiny scales and a bright blue tail.

There are four breeding species of frogs, toads, and salamanders found in wetlands at Crab Creek. Frogs and toads start calling out at sunset and keep going all night. They're especially vocal when the moon is full. The call of the tiny, slender Pacific chorus frog sounds like "ribbet"; the large, "warty" boreal toad (a subspecies of the western toad) makes frequent birdlike twittering calls; and the small, relatively smooth-skinned Great Basin spadefoot toad repeats a grating "cronk" call—audible for more than 300 feet—over and over again.

The long-toed salamander, dark gray with a stripe down the back, is the smallest and most widespread of all salamanders; large numbers of salamanders may sometimes be seen at night in ponds. A field guide is an absolute necessity

In the Crab Creek area, large numbers of western rattlesnakes overwinter together at a common den site and emerge in the spring.

when trying to identify reptiles and amphibians. Descriptions of eastern Washington reptiles and amphibians also may be found at the Washington Department of Fish and Wildlife Web site: www.wa.gov:80/wdfw/wlm/region1/herps.htm.

Park ranger Gary Lentz asks that sightings of unusual specimens, such as the two-lined whipsnake, be reported to the WDFW. "These animals are not well understood in Washington, and sightings with accurate data are always welcomed."

It is against the law to collect reptiles and amphibians in Washington without a permit from the WDFW. However, if you just want a quick, closer look, here are some guidelines from that agency and others.

- Never collect specimens if another method of identifying is available, such as photographing or on-site identification. Observation is safest for you and the animals.
- Please do not chase or otherwise harass the animals.
- Handle specimens as little as possible. Many herps are quite fragile and injure easily. If capturing a specimen means disturbing sensitive habitat or could result in injury to the animal, don't do it. Wear rubber gloves while handling amphibians—for your protection and theirs. Always wash your hands as soon as possible after handling specimens. Some—most amphibians, for example—secrete toxins through their skin.
- Remember that your specimens need the proper temperatures to survive. Never leave them in direct sunlight or expose them to freezing. Amphibians need temperatures between 35 and 60 degrees Fahrenheit. Reptiles usually do best in 60 to 80 degree temperatures.
- Do not try to feed your specimens. Look at them; then release them in the same place you took them from.
- Never attempt to capture poisonous reptiles without professional training. Keep your distance. Watch where you're walking or putting your hands, especially in spring. Juvenile rattlesnakes are abundant around dens and are even more venomous than adults are.

Lentz says that the 4-mile stretch from Nunally Lake to the Crab Creek bridge is the best place to start looking. "Remember when and where you are looking," says Lentz. "To a reptile, temperature is everything; to an amphibian, water is everything."

During the day, walk into the shrub steppe from the road. From mid-April to mid-May you can see herps all day, but not in the evening—it is too cool. These animals are mating in April, so they are more active and aggressive and therefore, notes Lentz, "out and about more often." You may even see lizards courting and bobbing. If you see a lizard or mouse impaled on the thorns of Russian olive and locust trees here, it is the work of the loggerhead shrike, a bird with a unique method of storing food. A word of caution: When looking for herps, lift flat rocks towards you with a hoe or rake; put them carefully back in place.

In May and June also look at night, Lentz advises. Drive slowly with your lights on and watch the road and ditches closely. Be careful not to run over herps; when you spot movement, pull off and take a look on foot.

"You can also turn off your lights and just listen," says Lentz. "If you hear a 'swooping' noise, it might be a nighthawk diving on bugs." You will hear coyotes at night, too, and occasionally the cry of a bobcat or cougar.

Next best: If you stay overnight in Othello, drive through the Columbia National Wildlife Refuge to see shorebirds, waterfowl, and raptors starting in mid-April. Stop at the wetlands on McManamon Road northwest of Othello, then drive a mile into the refuge to Morgan Lake to see yellow-headed blackbirds, red-winged blackbirds, and prairie falcons. Three miles farther north is a parking area and wetlands walk on the east; you may see American avocets, black-necked stilts, and more. Stop at the right-angle turn in another mile and walk up the gated road to see egrets, shorebirds, and more. Watch for raptors. (See chapter 12 map.)

Food and lodging: Othello, Mattawa, and Vantage have motels and restaurants. Wanapum State Park (showers) is near Vantage; primitive camping is allowed along Crab Creek and the Columbia River.

For more information:
Crab Creek Wildlife Area
(509) 765–6641
Pacific Northwest Herpetological Society, Lakebay
(206) 628–4740; www.pnhs.net

15

Honor Our Precious Earth

*Earth Day, when our attention turns to the state of our environ-
ment, inspires many events across the state. One of the best is held
in the Tri-Cities in a green and sprawling park along the wide
Columbia River.*

Site: Howard Amon Park in Richland, which, along with Kennewick and
Pasco, is one of the Tri-Cities of south-central Washington.

Recommended time: The weekend closest to April 22, which is officially Earth Day.

Minimum time commitment: An afternoon.

What to bring: Sunglasses, lawn chairs or a blanket.

Directions: From I–82, take the Richland exit onto I–182 and then the
exit to George Washington Way, the main street in this small city. The river
will be on your right. At the third light turn right into Howard Amon Park.

The background: The first Earth Day was held on April 22, 1970. It was
the idea of former U.S. Senator Gaylord Nelson of Wisconsin. The idea "took
off like gangbusters," according to Nelson. About twenty million Americans
participated in various events that day.

"Earth Day achieved what I had hoped for," he wrote. "The objective
was to get a nationwide demonstration of concern for the environment so
large that it would shake the political establishment out of its lethargy and,
finally, force this issue permanently onto the national political agenda. It was a
gamble, but it worked. . . . It was truly an astonishing grassroots explosion."
Organizers point to successes that followed that first observance such as the

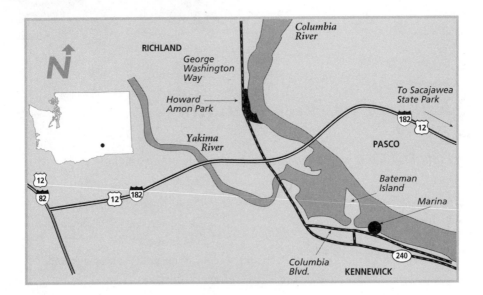

creation of the Environmental Protection Agency and passage of the Clean Air Act of 1970, which eventually led to the elimination of lead in gasoline.

Interest dwindled somewhat for the next twenty years, but in 1990 a worldwide commemoration took place to revive the idea. It also was enormously successful—200 million people in 140 countries took part. Every year since then, Earth Day has been observed with all kinds of events and conservation projects designed to remind us of our connection with and responsibility to our environment.

The fun: Although there are a large number of events from which to choose around the state, the Earth Day Celebration in the Tri-Cities is special for several reasons. There is an excellent variety of activities, something for everyone, and the weather is usually quite pleasant this time of year. The event is held in a beautiful riverside park with grassy areas for picnics or lounging, paved paths along the river, playgrounds, picnic tables, and towering shade trees. There's ample parking, little traffic, and lots of services. And they have very nice T-shirts for sale and food booths for lunch.

A recent Tri-Cities event included more than seventy display booths with environmental information and fun activities for adults and children. The event also offered music and entertainment at a unique stage called "the Fingernail," a fashion show featuring recycled clothing, a kayaking demonstration, a display of Earth Day quilts, and a silent auction to benefit Earth Day. Participants could also choose to help paint an Earth Day mural, listen to Native American storytelling in a tepee, make a fish print or eco-art project, or participate in a communitywide cleanup project. When you are done, be sure to visit the nearby Columbia River Exhibition of History, Science and Technology, which tells the dynamic story of the Columbia Basin.

Next best: If you spend the weekend in the Tri-Cities, enjoy some of the other nature activities in the area.

Take a four-and-a-half-hour Columbia River Journeys jet boat tour of the scenic and historic Hanford Reach, the last free-flowing section of the mighty Columbia River. American white pelicans, osprey, great blue herons, and mule deer still inhabit this unspoiled natural sanctuary. In April the black-crowned night heron colony is filled with courtship and nest-building activities. Contact Columbia River Journeys at (509) 943–0231; www.columbiariverjourneys.com/.

Columbia Park, between SR 240 and the Columbia River in Kennewick, is a great place to enjoy a nature walk on Bateman Island (trail starts a few blocks west of the Columbia Park Marina) or on the Audubon Nature Trail. The bike trail also runs along the river. Or enjoy some early-morning bird-watching at the Sacajawea State Park wetlands (in Pasco, south of US 12 and just west of the Snake River bridge) or the McNary National Wildlife Refuge (4 miles southeast of Pasco); visit McNary NWR at www.rl.fws.gov/mcnwr/McNarypage.htm.

Food and lodging: Richland, Kennewick, and Pasco offer all services.

For more information:
Tri-Cities Earth Day Celebration
www.pnl.gov/EarthDay/
Tri-Cities Visitor and Convention Bureau
(509) 735–8486 or (800) 254–5824; www.visittri-cities.com/

More Earth Day Events

Earth Day events are held all across the state and may include fairs, art events, parades, trail construction, habitat restoration, or cleanup projects. These events are usually held on Earth Day or a weekend near Earth Day. Watch for announcements in area newspapers.

- *Fort Lewis:* Army Earth Day for Kids "Conserving Wildlife." Take a wildflower walk, tour the marsh nature trail, or create a Prairie Oak Preserve. Call (253) 966–2100, ext. 8; www. lewis.army.mil/envcaretakers.
- *Leavenworth:* Hazel Wolf Environmental Film Festival, including presentations by environmental filmmakers and activists, and environmental media workshops. Call (206) 443–7239; www.equinoxfilm.org/.
- *Olympia:* Procession of the Species Parade, held annually on the weekend before Earth Day in conjunction with the Olympia Spring Arts Walk. Contact Earthbound Productions at (360) 705–1087; www.procession.org. Another Procession of the Species Parade, started in 2000, is held in Spokane on the weekend after Earth Day.
- *Puget Sound area:* Earth Work Northwest, the largest hands-on environmental restoration event in the history of the Northwest. More than 5,000 volunteers dedicate a morning of work to more than 300 projects—removing invasive plants, fixing trails, planting trees, and cleaning up streams. There are family-safe projects for parents and children. In the afternoon Earthworkers enjoy a celebration at Seattle Center with music, awards, and activities. Contact the Student Conservation Association at (206) 324–4649; www.sca-inc.org.
- *Seattle:* Earth Day Puget Sound Coalition sponsors a large event, rally, and concert at Seattle Center. Call (206) 264–0114 or e-mail llockard@earthday.net.

Also in Seattle, the Northwest Exhibition of Environmental Photography, held in April, features a two-month photographic exhibit celebrating nature's wildlife, places, and endangered cultures. A multimedia slide presentation is shown on the first Saturday in April. For more information visit www.edie.org.

A father and daughter pose for the camera at Olympia's fun-filled Procession of the Species Parade.

The King County Park System celebrates Earth Day by involving more than 500 volunteers in tours, programs, and other projects at county parks. For a project list visit www.metrokc.gov/ earthlegacy/.

■ *Vancouver:* Earth Action Day, a community celebration of environmental stewardship. Up to 500 citizens participate in hands-on projects to help beautify, renew, and enhance local sites.

For more information:

Find Earth Day events across Washington and the nation at:
Earth Day Network
www.earthday.net/
EnviroLink
(619) 496–6666;
www.envirolink.org/earthday/

16

Let the Blooming Begin

It's the beginning of the wildflower season, Mother Nature's annual garden party. Pack a picnic and take a driving tour of Beezley Hills to look for rare hedgehog cacti and other early wildflowers.

Site: Beezley Hills, 6 miles north of Quincy in the Columbia Basin.

Recommended time: Mid-April through May.

Minimum time commitment: Half a day; more if you decide to explore other BLM wildflower locations.

What to bring: Wildflower field guide, small magnifying lens, camera, binoculars.

Directions: From I–90, take exit 149 and drive 10 miles north to Quincy. Then drive 6 miles north on Q Street NW, curving up the hill on Overen Road to Baird Springs Road and the start of the 17-mile Beezley Hills driving and walking tour.

The background: In the Columbia Basin, where the main habitat is shrub-steppe covered by sagebrush and bunchgrass, spring wildflowers include yellow balsamroot, purple lupine, white phlox, pink mariposa lily, yellow bells, and bluebells. In the lusher riparian habitats, you'll find red geraniums, yellow currant and blanket flowers, white western spring beauty, mock orange, and pink roses.

The fun: This lovely mid-April wildflower drive (with easy walks) takes us through lands managed by the BLM, Washington Department of Natural Resources, and The Nature Conservancy (TNC). From the tour starting point (see directions) drive east on Baird Springs Road and follow the map.

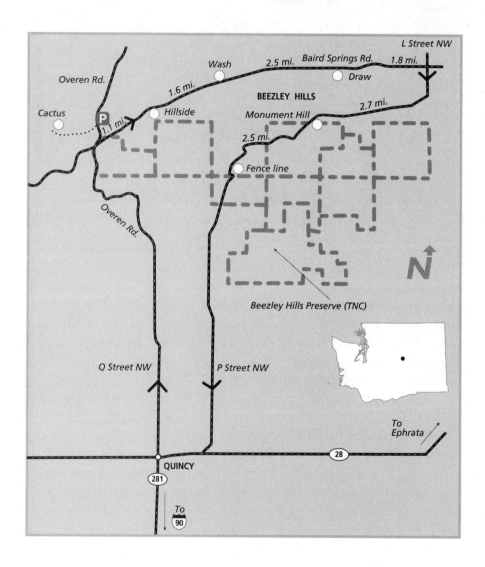

L Street NW

Overen Rd.

Wash   2.5 mi.   Baird Springs Rd.   1.8 mi.

Draw

BEEZLEY HILLS

Cactus   1.6 mi.

1.1 mi.   Hillside   Monument Hill   2.7 mi.

2.5 mi.

Fence line

Overen Rd.

N

Beezley Hills Preserve (TNC)

Q Street NW   P Street NW

To
Ephrata

QUINCY

28

281

To
90

In April, fields of balsamroot cover the hills at The Nature Conservancy's Beezley Hills Preserve.

The first areas are on protected DNR or BLM land; the last on TNC's Beezley Hills Preserve. Stop and walk around at marked locations on the map to explore hillsides covered with shooting stars, bluebells, and phlox; a wash with large numbers of brodiaea and bitterroot; and a wet draw with an impressive display of lupine and balsamroot.

The Beezley Hills Preserve encompasses 4,300 acres of shrub-steppe habitat in the Beezley Hills area, making it the largest Conservancy preserve in Washington state. Purchased in 1998 and 2000, it is home to rare species of birds and flowers. One access to the preserve is at 9.7 miles on Monument Hill across from the repeater/transmitter station. In mid-April Audubon trip participants followed the gravel road to the edge of the hill, feasted their eyes on an incredible hillside of balsamroot, and looked out over the coulees of deep sage—a nesting area for sage thrashers. At 16.8 miles arrive back at Quincy.

For a special treat sign up for a naturalist-guided trip offered by the Central Basin Audubon Society or the Washington Native Plant Society (Wenatchee chapter). These walks start with a side trip onto private land (permission required, 800–359–1417). The big attraction here from mid- to late April is the hedgehog cactus, unusual in the sagebrush habitat and one of

A Gift of Water

In the Lower Columbia Basin, the hottest and driest land in the state, all flowering is an extravagance, a gift of water. In the rain shadow of the Cascades, blooming begins in April as soil slowly warms. Flowers appear first in lowland areas on the sagebrush plains, shifting to higher elevations as temperatures increase and soil loses its moisture. Around the Tri-Cities, in a good water year you can see miles of the long spikelets of lupine scattered across the face of Rattlesnake Mountain; without moisture only a few of these purple-blue passions may bloom.

For a brief time in spring, you can find lupine and the bright sunflowerlike flowers of Carey's balsamroot—two of the most common wildflowers of the shrub-steppe ecosystem—dotting the sunny slopes of Badger, Red, and Candy mountains, long narrow ridges formed by upward folds in the Earth's crust. Between native sagebrush and bunchgrasses, you'll see low-growing mounds of pink or white—one of two species of phlox. The widespread longleaf phlox, often a bright pink, likes sandy areas of the shrub-steppe. Often you will find its stems clambering up gnarled limbs of sagebrush, while Hood's phlox, a cushionlike variety, grows only on rocky ridge tops.

High wind, poor soil, and no escape from sun prevent many plants from establishing on basalt ridges of the Lower Columbia Basin. But if you hike across the crest of the Horse Heaven Hills you likely will see small patches of rosy balsamroot, with yellow flowers that turn to rose as they age. Rosy balsamroot and daggerpod, named for its daggerlike pods projecting out from reddish-purple stems, grow only in the thin rock soil called "lithosol."

Although many people see the shrub-steppe as harsh and unforgiving, the region supports many fragile species of plants. If you look closely you may see single stems of the dark blue cluster lily *(Douglas' brodiaea),* the most widespread lily in the shrub-steppe, or maybe you'll find a mariposa lily, its elegant lavender petals nestled among bunchgrass.

—*Georgeanne O'Connor*

the best displays in the state. The beautiful red flowers open wide on a sunny day.

Next best: If you are spending the whole weekend, enjoy the courting rituals of American avocets, black-necked stilts, and other shorebirds in the Quincy Wildlife Area southwest of Quincy (American white pelicans visit here in spring) or the premier birding locations south of I–90 (see chapter 36).

For spring wildflower and bird locations on BLM lands, order *Washington Watchable Wildflowers, A Columbia Basin Guide* from a BLM office, or access it on the Web. It contains habitat, wildflower, and wildlife descriptions plus driving directions for each BLM location. Good mid-April locations are:

- Douglas Creek (south of Douglas on US 2—riparian corridor, columnar basalt, wildflowers, canyon wrens, cliff swallows, and meadowlarks).
- Wilson Creek Canyon (west of Wilbur on US 2—wildflowers, raptors, songbirds).

Farther east near Sprague (I–90 exit 254) are two April-May hikes:

- Fishtrap Lake (1.5 miles to lake—wildflowers, red-winged and yellow-headed blackbirds).
- Hog Lake (1.7 miles to lake—wildflowers plus waterfall and turtles at the lake).

Food and lodging: Quincy and Ephrata offer all services. Crescent Bar Resort, RV Park and Campground is southwest of Quincy on the Columbia River. Quincy Wildlife Area has primitive lakeside campsites (WDFW Access Stewardship Decal required).

For more information:

The Nature Conservancy, Seattle
(206) 343–4344; www.tnc-washington.org/
BLM Watchable Wildflowers, Washington Sites
www.or.blm.gov/watchable/wflower/sites/maps/maps.html
Quincy Wildlife Area
(509) 765–6641
Guided Trips:

Central Basin Audubon Society, Moses Lake
(509) 246–0641; www.cbas.org
Washington Native Plant Society, Wenatchee
(509) 665–2100; www.geocities.com/RainForest/2745/

17

April

Ballet in White and Black

Don't miss the spectacular shorebird "ballet" at the annual Grays Harbor Shorebird Festival. Up to a million birds gather here to feed before migrating farther north.

Site: Bowerman Basin, 54 miles west of Olympia, in the Grays Harbor National Wildlife Refuge near Hoquiam.

Recommended time: Late April or early May. For many years the peak three-day period occurred around April 25, but in recent years the birds have been returning later.

Minimum time commitment: Half a day plus more for the extra festivities and tours.

What to bring: Binoculars, spotting scope, bird book, camera, tide book, rain gear. Pets are not allowed on the refuge.

Directions: From I–5 in Olympia, take exit 104 and drive 48 miles west on SR 8 and US 12 to Aberdeen, and then another 5 miles west on US 101 to Hoquiam. Pass Hoquiam High School and follow the signs to the airport turnoff at Paulson Road. Drive south and then west to marked parking areas at the airport, where there are portable toilets and a boardwalk, all barrier-free. During the festival a shuttle bus runs continuously between the high school and the refuge.

The background: Birders discovered the Bowerman Basin area many years ago, slogging with dedication through deep mud and wet grass. Later, the Washington Department of Fish and Wildlife realized that the area was in danger of being trampled and sent staff to guide birders to good locations,

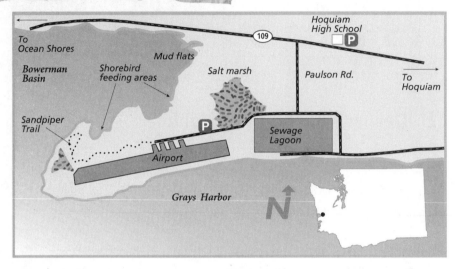

helping to interpret what they saw. In 1988, to further protect this important shorebird habitat, Congress established the Grays Harbor National Wildlife Refuge, managed by the U.S. Fish and Wildlife Service. It has been designated a "Western Hemisphere Shorebird Reserve Network Site of Hemispheric Significance."

The refuge encompasses 1,500 acres of intertidal mudflats, salt marsh, and adjacent uplands, sandwiched between the bluffs of the original shoreline and the Hoquiam Airport, which doesn't seem to bother the birds at all. The mudflats are the first areas in Grays Harbor to be exposed at low tide and the last to be flooded. This gives the shorebirds extra time to feed. It also crowds the feeding birds near the shoreline, allowing birders a close-range view of shorebirds in truly spectacular numbers!

A 0.25-mile walk on the boardwalk (no more boots) takes you to the Sandpiper Trail loop, which winds through riparian habitat and woods and past several shorebird-viewing areas on the rich mudflats of Bowerman Basin. USFWS plans to build an interpretive center when funds permit.

The refuge is open year-round for good birding. Many shorebirds return to the estuary June through October on their way south, and tens of thousands stay for the winter. The Sandpiper Trail is a great place to see wrens and other riparian birds plus hundreds of hummingbirds nesting in the shrubs along the trail.

Watch the varied shorebird feeding habits—dowitchers rapidly probe the mud while greater yellowlegs swing their heads back and forth to catch small fishes.

The fun: The numbers of shorebirds you will see here this time of year is mind-boggling. Thousands swoop and turn together, pirouetting in the air, a shorebird ballet in glistening white and black. They land to probe the mud-flats ceaselessly and intently for tasty invertebrates. These birds are engaged in the serious occupation of feeding, storing fat, and resting up for their nonstop flight to northern breeding grounds.

All the movement and the dense, wheeling flocks are part of the little birds' defensive strategy against peregrine falcons and merlins. Even these skilled predators don't want to crash through a wheeling flock and risk being injured in a midair collision. The shorebirds' very numbers hold the raptors at bay. To add to the scene, northern harriers cruise very close to the ground, occasionally picking up injured or disabled birds. Red-tailed hawks soar high-er, primarily looking for rodents.

For the best spectacle, plan your trip around the tides. Viewing is excel-lent from two hours before high tide to one hour after. For extraordinary viewing find a 10-foot high tide within a week of the festival weekend.

During the festival, there are bird experts to help with species identifica-tion, wildlife arts and crafts vendors, and workshops on shorebird identifica-tion and migration. There are also guided tours to the nearby Quinault Rain Forest, Westport, Ocean Shores, and Point Grenville.

Next best: You can spend a long weekend and just begin to cover all the excellent birding spots in the Grays Harbor area.

On the north side of Grays Harbor, Ocean Shores hosts some of the best birding on the West Coast. More than 290 species of birds have been seen in the diverse habitats of this peninsula—as many as 100 species in one day. Some of the best spots include the Point Brown (North) Jetty, sewage ponds, Damon Point, and Oyhut Game Range. Stop and purchase *A Birder's Guide to Ocean Shores, Washington* by Bob Morse for excellent local birding information. (Also see Ocean Shores detail map in chapter 9.)

On the south side of Grays Harbor, drive west on SR 105, stop at the John's River Wildlife Area (east of milepost 37) and walk the 0.6-mile wheelchair-accessible paved dike trail. Shorebirds, great blue herons, Canada geese, and elk are often seen along here.

Bottle Beach State Park, 0.2 mile west of milepost 35, is a wide, shallow mudflat area—excellent for shorebirds. Park across from Ocosta Third Street and walk past the fence to the beach. Arrive at the beach an hour before high tide and watch the incoming tides push the shorebirds closer to shore. If you stand still they will come within 10 feet of you as they probe for food.

Head west again on SR 105 to Westport, which has excellent birding at the marina and miles of open, sandy, coastal beaches. The long jetty extending from Westhaven State Park is a good place to look for rock sandpipers, western tattler, and seabirds, including shearwaters, but watch your step. The footing is treacherous and the waves unpredictable. Large colonies of Caspian terns nest on islands in the bay. Gray whale watching is still excellent in April (see chapter 11) and you may see California sea lions and harbor seals headed into the harbor toward their rookeries on Sand and Goose islands.

Food and lodging: Hoquiam, Aberdeen, and Ocean Shores offer all services. Pacific Beach and Ocean City state parks both have seaside campgrounds.

For more information:

Grays Harbor Shorebird Festival/Audubon Society
(360) 495-3101; www.ghas.org/bowerm.html
Grays Harbor National Wildlife Refuge
(360) 753-9467; www.graysharbor.fws.gov/
Grays Harbor Chamber of Commerce
(800) 321-1924 or (360) 532-1924; www.graysharbor.com/

18

May

Flyways of the World

Celebrate International Migratory Bird Day by taking part in one or more birding events in northeastern Washington. As a bonus, you may even see a moose!

Site: Little Pend Oreille National Wildlife Refuge, southeast of Colville.

Recommended time: The Saturday closest to International Migratory Bird Day, which is officially May 9.

Minimum time commitment: A half day plus travel time.

What to bring: Binoculars, spotting scope, walking shoes.

Directions: From Colville drive 6 miles east on SR 20 to the Artman-Gibson Road (0.3 mile after milepost 360). Turn right (south) and travel 1.7 miles to an intersection. Turn left onto Kitt-Narcisse Road and go 2.2 miles until the road becomes gravel and forks. Angle right onto Bear Creek Road and drive 3.3 miles to the refuge office.

The background: This event is one of many held across the state to commemorate International Migratory Bird Day, celebrated throughout the Americas. IMBD was created not only to spotlight the habits, importance, and sheer beauty of all migratory birds, but also to shine the environmental warning light in their direction. Millions of birds (350 out of the 660 bird species that breed in North America) make the long journey to wintering grounds in South and Central America, Mexico, the Caribbean, and the southern United States. In spring they travel back north along the major flyways, stopping periodically to rest and eat. In late spring and early summer, many continue on their journey to northern breeding areas. These birds are called "neotropical

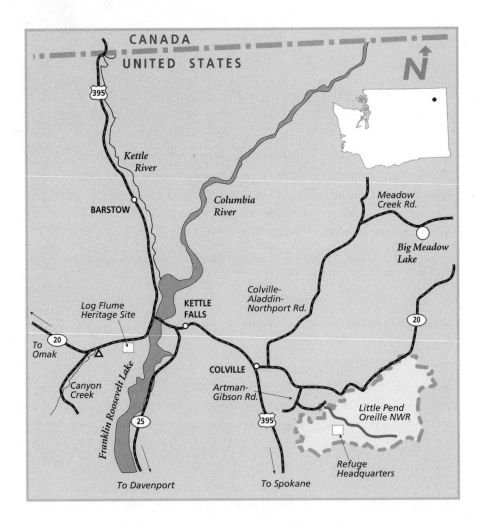

CANADA
UNITED STATES

N

395

Kettle
River

Columbia
River

Meadow
Creek Rd.

BARSTOW

Big Meadow
Lake

Colville-
Aladdin-
Northport Rd.

Log Flume
Heritage Site

KETTLE
FALLS

20

To
Omak

20

Canyon
Creek

COLVILLE

Artman-
Gibson Rd.

Little Pend
Oreille NWR

Franklin Roosevelt Lake

25

395

Refuge
Headquarters

To Davenport

To Spokane

migratory birds," and they include raptors, waterfowl, shorebirds, and songbirds such as orioles, tanagers, warblers, and hummingbirds.

IMBD also points out one more reason to conscientiously conserve habitat worldwide. Although many species of migratory birds are thriving, some are declining due to environmental pollutants, uncontrolled predation, and habitat destruction all along their routes and at their breeding grounds. Various international monitoring programs collect valuable information on population size and trends, distribution, breeding success, and condition of habitats. The importance of this information and of international cooperation is why IMBD is often referred to as "Earth Day for birds."

The fun: The Little Pend Oreille National Wildlife Refuge hosts an annual 2.5-mile bird walk along the ridge overlooking McDowell Lake, with an optional 2-mile walk to some beaver ponds. In early May you'll see and hear migratory birds such as yellow warblers, common yellowthroats, vireos, chipping sparrows, all five swallow species, red-necked grebes, and red-winged blackbirds. You'll also spot resident birds such as woodpeckers, chickadees, juncos, and nuthatches. Later in May even more migratory birds arrive. When we took this walk we also saw delicate forest wildflowers, Canada geese and goslings, several duck species, osprey and eagles (both carrying fish), painted turtles, six species of butterflies, white-tailed deer, moose tracks, and beaver signs. To register call the wildlife refuge at (509) 684–8384.

Little Pend Oreille National Wildlife Refuge extends over 40,200 acres, making it the largest wildlife refuge in Washington. It claims to encompass "six distinct forest vegetation zones." According to refuge staff, 186 bird species and 58 species of mammals (including black bears) have been observed here.

Next best: If you spend the weekend, enjoy more nature activities.

West of Kettle Falls is the Log Flume Heritage Site (milepost 335 on SR 20), a 0.5-mile interpretive trail, and the end of the Canyon Creek bird walk.

Another 0.7 mile west is Bangs Mountain Road, a scenic drive through Donaldson Draw to a vista overlooking the Columbia River (grouse, turkeys).

The Canyon Creek Trailhead (barrier-free, mostly level) is accessible from this road, just across the first bridge. Take a self-guided bird walk along Sherman Creek, across a footbridge, and through the forest to the heritage site or sign up for a guided 2-mile walk sponsored by Colville National Forest. You can also reach the trailhead from Canyon Creek Campground (toilets) just up the same road.

More Ways to Celebrate
International Migratory Bird Day

Some local Audubon chapters offer guided bird walks or "bir-dathons," where a field team is sent out to count as many species as it can in a twenty-four-hour period. Members and supporters pledge money to help support Audubon education and conservation activities. These are fun trips, and beginners are welcome. Contact National Audubon Society, State Office at (360) 786–8020; wa.audubon.org/.

Several national wildlife refuges celebrate IMBD, some with the help of the local Audubon chapter. Look for presentations, bird mounts, open houses, guided bird walks, or mist-netting demonstrations at these refuges: Dungeness (near Sequim), Nisqually (near Olympia), Ridgefield (near Vancouver), Toppenish (near Yakima), and Turnbull (near Cheney).

Gifford Pinchot National Forest sponsors IMBD events at Trout Lake Marsh and White Salmon (Columbia Gorge).

■ *Kirkland:* Visit Juanita Bay Park, where the East Lake Washington Audubon Society holds its annual osprey celebration on the Saturday closest to IMBD. It starts at 10:00 A.M. with a "nest warming" party for the osprey nesting platform in Juanita Bay. This is followed by workshops, storytelling, nature walks, and children's activities until 3:00 P.M. Environmental organizations have booths with information, flyers, samples, and buttons. Visit the Juanita Bay Park Osprey Celebration Web site at www.elwas.org/osprey/.

■ *Seattle:* Go to the Woodland Park Zoo and take a walk with an expert to see wild birds—warblers, wrens, song sparrows, hermit thrush, spotted towhees, swallows, and the brilliant western tanager. In addition to their traditional values of education and species protection, zoos provide valuable habitat for migrating and resident wild birds and animals, usually in the middle of an urban area. For information call (206) 615–0076 (events line) or zookeeper Dawn Garcia at (206) 684–4822.

■ *Spokane:* Assist the BLM with its annual bird survey at nearby Fishtrap Lake. Guides, transportation, and lunch are provided. Vans leave the Spokane District Office, 1103 North Fancher, at 5:00 A.M. Birds are abundant and there are experts to help with identification. People of all physical abilities are accommodated; some even look for birds from inside the vehicles. For reservations call biologist Joyce Whitney at (509) 536–1244, or e-mail: joyce_whitney@or.blm.gov.

The refuge manager and IMBD trip participants look for recently arrived neotropical migratory birds at Little Pend Oreille National Wildlife Refuge.

The national forest offers another biologist-led bird walk at Big Meadow Lake (campground, toilets, viewing tower) northeast of Colville. The 3-mile trail passes through upland forest habitat with views of the lake and wetlands. You may spot moose here, especially at dawn or dusk. To register for either national forest walk, contact the forest headquarters at (509) 684–7000 or visit www.fs.fed.us/r6/colville/.

Food and lodging: Colville and Kettle Falls offer all services. There are five campgrounds (no water) within the Pend Oreille NWR; Cottonwood and Potter's Pond are best for birders.

For more information:

International Migratory Bird Day
americanbirding.org/imbd/
U.S. Fish and Wildlife Service (events by state)
birds.fws.gov/imbd.html

19

May

Butterflies and Blossoms

*Butterflies and wildflowers—look for one, you'll find the other. On
the Prairie Appreciation Day's guided nature walks, look for the
nearly twenty species of butterflies that prefer prairie plants. You'll
also learn about a unique area of Washington, the Mima Mounds.*

Site: Mima Mounds, 15 miles southwest of Olympia, and other natural areas
nearby.

Recommended time: Prairie Appreciation Day, sponsored by the
Friends of Puget Prairies, is held the second or third weekend in May,
depending on weather. Additional guided walks at Thurston County's prairies
are held in June and July.

Minimum time commitment: Each guided walk lasts between one
and two hours; activities end around 4:00 P.M.

What to bring: Butterfly, bird, and wildflower field guides; camera with
close-up lens; binoculars; picnic lunch. All walks are free.

Directions: From I–5 south of Olympia, take exit 95 (SR 121) and drive 3
miles west to Littlerock Elementary School. Mima Mounds is another 0.8
mile west on SR 121 and 0.8 mile north on Waddell Creek Road. Glacial
Heritage Preserve is also on Waddell Creek Road, 2.6 miles south of SR 121.
The north entrance to Scatter Creek Wildlife Area is 4 miles south of SR
121, just west of I–5.

The background: The 445-acre Mima Mounds was designated as a
National Natural Landmark in 1968 by the National Park Service because of

Tiger swallowtail butterflies enjoy a mud seep on a dusty road.

its unique topography and was dedicated as a Natural Area Preserve by the Washington Department of Natural Resources in 1975. No one has been able to explain the origin of the mysterious, regularly spaced, 6- to 8-foot-tall mounds. The site supports a native grassland ecosystem called "Puget prairie" and is the home of the white-top aster, a rare plant on the state's "sensitive" list, which occurs only within grasslands of the Puget Trough.

The Scatter Creek Wildlife Area supports an Idaho fescue/balsamroot short-grass prairie, while Oregon white oak and Douglas-fir dominate the forested portion of the area. Active beaver dams on the creek contribute to habitat quality in the riparian and wetland zones. *Note:* Glacial Heritage Preserve is normally closed to the public, but is open for tours during Prairie Appreciation Day.

The fun: Prairie Appreciation Day kicks off at Littlerock Elementary School at 8:00 A.M. with arts and crafts activities and booth displays by other conservation groups. The first guided nature walks leave for the three different sites soon after. Join docents for a walk to see butterflies, birds, and early May wildflowers such as shooting stars (red-purple), buttercup (yellow-gold), and death camas (white). Fields of common camas (deep blue-violet) blanket the area in early May. Eight other species of wildflowers bloom from mid-May to late July.

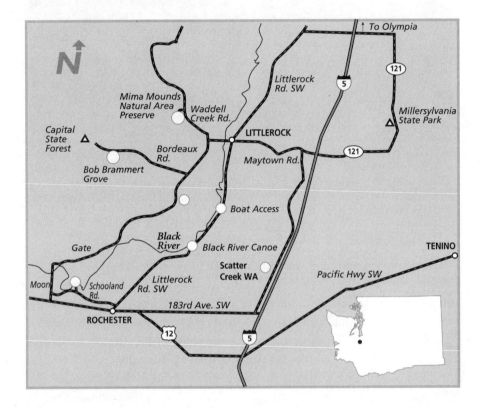

These natural prairie remnants are home to some eighteen species of butterflies including the Mardon skipper. When it is sunny the air is full of these colorful, fluttering wonders—each with its own distinctive pattern. To get close walk slowly and quietly. Butterflies of this habitat include the iridescent silvery blue, the lilac spring azure, the brown Sonora skipper (listed as a state-monitored species), the scalloped, gray-brown hoary elfin, the intricately patterned Mylitta crescentspot, the bright orange western meadow fritillary, the Sara orangetip or Pacific orangetip (cream with bright orange wing patches), the yellow and black tiger-striped western tiger swallowtail, and the mourning cloak (purplish brown with a yellow, lacy border on its wings). You might even see the rare red-orange, black, and cream Whulge checkerspot, a candidate for state listing.

Mima Mounds guided wildflower and butterfly tours are so popular,
visitors even turn out in the rain.

Visitor facilities at Mima Mounds include a 0.5-mile accessible, paved trail, interpretive displays, 2-mile loop trail, and toilet. Farther south, Glacial Heritage features butterflies and oak habitat.

During the spring and summer wildflower blooming season at Scatter Creek Wildlife Area, you can see a variety of butterflies. Walk along the creek from the south entrance to also see birds and oak trees. Walk west from the north entrance to see fields of camas (and hunters training their dogs nearby). Both entrances have portable toilets.

Next best: If you spend the weekend, enjoy other nature activities in the area.

Hike through beautiful second-growth forest on the Bob Brammert Grove Trail in Capitol State Forest. Other trails in this DNR-managed forest are open to hikers, mountain bikes, and horses, but the grove is for hikers only. From SR 121, drive 1.3 miles south on Waddell Creek Road and 2.5 miles west on Bordeaux.

The best time to explore the backwaters of the Black River is May, when the waters are high. According to The Nature Conservancy, "the Black River is one of the best riverine wetland areas left in Western Washington."

Expect to see goslings, herons, ducks, and the largest osprey nest in the state. Watch for the elusive deer, elk, and bear.

You can rent a canoe from Black River Canoe and Kayaking Trips, 3.3 miles south of Littlerock on the Littlerock Road. After a peaceful three- to four-hour meandering trip through riparian habitat (mostly wild lands with lush vegetation), they will meet you and drive you back. Contact Barry Dahl at (360) 754–6190; www.ool.com/blackriver/.

If you take your own boat, you can also paddle through the primitive 283-acre Nature Conservancy Black River Preserve, home to diverse wetland habitats and accessible only by canoe or kayak. It is open year-round during daylight hours for quiet backwater paddling to see migratory birds and native mammals, including black bear, green heron, and beaver. No facilities.

Two WDFW boat launches are available (Access Stewardship Decal required). From Rochester drive 4 miles west on US Highway 12 to the river; the boat launch is on Schooland Road—paddle upstream. Or head north from Rochester on SR 121; look for the PUBLIC FISHING sign on the left at about 5 miles (north of Black River Canoe)—float downstream.

Seattle: two indoor exhibits let you get up close and personal with butterflies. In the permanent Tropical Butterfly House at Pacific Science Center, nearly 1,000 exotic butterflies flutter through the tropical flora and around you. Call (206) 443–2001 or visit www.pacsci.org/public/exhibits/.

Woodland Park Zoological Garden's Butterflies and Blooms enclosure (opens each year in mid-May) includes thirty-nine native butterfly and five moth species, with more surprises in the outdoor conservation garden. Call (206) 684–4800 or visit www.zoo.org/events/butterflies/menu.htm.

Food and lodging: Centralia and Rochester offer all services; there is one restaurant east of Littlerock near I–5. Camping in the Capitol State Forest west of Littlerock. Millersylvania State Park, 5 miles east of Littlerock, has campsites, showers, and hiking trails.

For more information:
Thurston County Parks and Recreation
(360) 786–5595
The Nature Conservancy Events
(206) 343–4344; www.tnc-washington.org/events/
Black River Preserve
www.tnc-washington.org/preserves/black_river.html

20

The Big Bang

Treat yourself to a weekend at Mount St. Helens National Volcanic Monument on the anniversary of its most recent eruption, May 18, 1980.

Site: Mount St. Helens is located northeast of the Kelso/Longview area, on the west slope of the Southern Cascade Range.

Recommended time: The west side visitor centers are open by May 1. Information stations and the Windy Ridge Viewpoint open in mid-May, and most viewpoints can be reached by Memorial Day. The mountain is at its prettiest when covered with snow, and you will have more solitude if you go before Memorial Day. (Call ahead for opening dates.)

Minimum time commitment: A half day, plus driving time, for the west side; a long weekend if you tour the whole mountain.

What to bring: Binoculars, warm clothing, hiking shoes (entrance fee, Golden Eagle Passport, or Northwest Forest Pass).

Directions: You can approach the monument from three directions. From the west take I–5 exit 49, Castle Rock, and drive 5 miles east to the Silver Lake Visitor Center. (See pages 96–97 for directions from the east and south.)

The background: Mount St. Helens erupted in 1980 after 123 years of inactivity. For two of the previous months, scientists watched the steam clouds with intense interest and installed various kinds of monitoring equipment. On May 18, 8:32 A.M., when the entire north side of the mountain exploded, two geologists were watching overhead from a small plane. They actually managed to escape. The enormous explosions resulted in clouds of ash, ash flows, mudflows, acres of blown-down timber, and other general

From the parking lot at Windy Ridge, you can get a close-up view into the Mount St. Helens crater.

devastation. Thousands of animals and fifty-seven people perished. Seeing the timber down, lying all in one direction as if a giant child had arranged toothpicks, is a sight you will not forget. Just as interesting as the eruption, however, is the subsequent recovery of the ecosystem, the amazing resilience of nature. Today flowers are blooming, trees are growing, and wildlife is thriving.

The fun: Stop at the visitor center (normally open May through November, and now operated by the Washington State Parks and Recreation Commission) to see exhibits, magnificent views of Mount St. Helens, and the Silver Lake wetlands. A year-round nature trail also begins here. The 48-mile drive to the end of the road has many viewpoints where you can enjoy Mount St. Helens, the Toutle River mudflow, forests, and wildlife.

The Coldwater Ridge Visitor Center, open all winter (except holidays), is located at milepost 43 and features a video-wall program and interactive exhibits. From the deck see splendid views of the volcano, newly formed Coldwater Lake, and the debris-filled Toutle River Valley.

Johnston Ridge Observatory, 53 miles from I–5 at the end of SR 504 and within 5 miles of Mount St. Helens, opens May 1. State-of-the-art interpretive displays show the sequence of geologic events leading to the eruption—you can actually monitor the active volcano. The wide-screen theater presentation is impressive and, at the end the curtains open up to a magnificent vista of Mount St. Helens! From the patio or the overlook, you have spectacular views of the lava dome, crater, pumice plain, and landslide deposit. Mount St. Helens is radiant in the evening just before sunset.

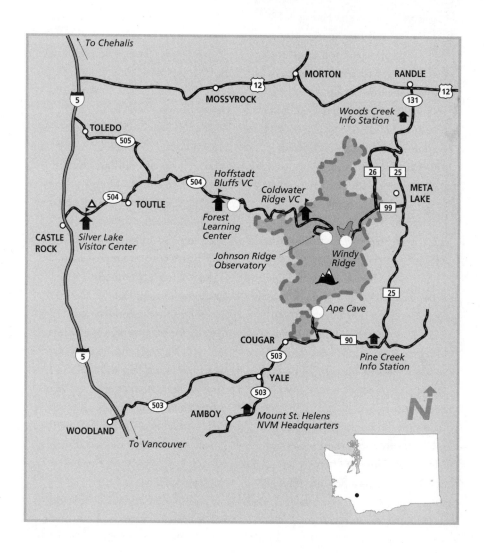

To Chehalis

MORTON

RANDLE

12

MOSSYROCK

5

Woods Creek
Info Station

TOLEDO

505

131

12

Hoffstadt
Bluffs VC

504

Coldwater
Ridge VC

26   25

META
LAKE

504   TOULE

Forest
Learning
Center

99

CASTLE
ROCK

Silver Lake
Visitor Center

Johnson Ridge
Observatory

Windy
Ridge

Ape Cave

25

COUGAR

90

5

503

Pine Creek
Info Station

YALE

503

N

AMBOY

WOODLAND

To Vancouver

Mount St. Helens
NVM Headquarters

If you visit over the extended Memorial Day weekend instead of on the eruption anniversary, you will have time to enter the monument from other directions.

East Slope: For Spirit Lake and Mount St. Helens' east slope, drive to Randle on US 12, then 6 miles south on FR 25 to the Woods Creek Information Station. Turn right (west) on FR 99, then stop at Meta Lake at the FR 26 junction; a forest interpreter leads walks to this emerald lake.

Harmony Falls Viewpoint and Trail is the next stop. "Discover the story of the eruption, its effect on Spirit Lake, and the remarkable return of life. Take a mile-long, downhill hike to the shores of the lake." The lake, literally covered with bare logs, bark peeled off by the blast, is awesome.

Windy Ridge, at the end of the road, affords a spectacular view of Mount St. Helens. At dawn Mount St. Helens turns a delicate pink; at sunset the lake below turns crimson in the sun's afterglow. Ranger talks are held once an hour. At the Windy Ridge outdoor amphitheater, you can relive the unbelievable power unleashed by the volcanic eruption.

Food and lodging: Randle offers all services. USFS campgrounds are located on FRs 25 and 23.

South Side: To see the lava flows and Mount St. Helens's south side, take I–5 exit 22 at Woodland and drive 23 miles east on SR 503. Detour to Mount St. Helens NVM Headquarters (6.5 miles south of this intersection) or continue straight on the SR 503 spur to Cougar, then another 6.7 miles (the spur becomes FR 90 along this stretch) to FR 83. Turn left and follow this 11.2-mile road north into the monument.

At 3 miles is the road to Ape Cave, the longest known lava tube in the continental United States (12,810 feet). A forest interpreter accompanies you through the 1,900-year-old lava tube to explain the life and features of this fascinating cave. Wear warm clothes and sturdy shoes. Less than a mile away is the Trail of Two Forests picnic area and a 0.25-mile, barrier-free boardwalk through a lava tree cast area.

Continue another 7.5 miles to Lahar Viewpoint to see how life is returning to this mudflow-scoured landscape. Lava Canyon Recreation Area is at road end; explore a canyon (accessible trail), see a waterfall plunging over an older lava flow, or hike the Lava Canyon trail.

Back on FR 90, drive 12 miles east to the Pine Creek Information Station. If you have time, continue east on FR 90; the next 15 miles has a splendid variety of 4★ (rating for excellent form and height) and smaller waterfalls along the Lewis River (Northwest Forest Pass required).

Food and lodging: Cougar has limited food, lodging, gas, and helicopter rides. Woodland offers all services. Camp at Pacific Power or USFS campgrounds along Yale Lake and Lewis River.

If you want to visit more volcanic cones, lava beds, palisades, lava tubes, caves, and craters shaped by this area's violent past, read *Washington's South Cascades Volcanic Landscapes* by Marge and Ted Mueller. It describes more than ninety places where you can see these remarkable geological features.

Spirit Lake is still covered by thousands of logs blown down when the volcano erupted.

Two nonmonument visitor centers deserve mentioning:

The Cowlitz County–operated Hoffstadt Bluffs Visitor Center (milepost 27) also opens May 1. From here you can take a helicopter ride over the Toutle River mudflow and up higher to see "spectacular views of the lava dome, crater walls thousands of feet high, steam vents, waterfalls, blown-down timber, and remarkable signs of resurgent life . . . including herds of elk."

The Weyerhaeuser Forest Learning Center, just past milepost 33, opens May 17. It's an excellent place to see both the mountain and elk on the Toutle River mudflow.

Next best: Many people enjoy the elk and deer almost as much as the volcano. You may see black-tailed deer anywhere, especially early in the morning, but the Roosevelt elk herds tend to stay near certain locations. Look down in the North Fork Toutle River Valley from the Forest Learning Center or Elk Rock Viewpoint (milepost 37); look up Maratta Creek (milepost 41); or hike Hummocks Trail #229 (milepost 45), walking clockwise 1 mile past ponds to an overlook of the badlands. In summer elk are often above the east end of Coldwater Lake (look down from the Johnson Ridge Observatory or up from mileposts 48 and 50). Elk give birth to their calves in late May or early June.

Food and lodging: The visitor centers all have food. Castle Rock offers all services. Camp at Seaquest State Park, directly across from the Silver Lake Visitor Center on SR 504.

For more information:

Mount St. Helens National Volcanic Monument
(360) 247–3900; www.fs.fed.us/gpnf/mshnvm/
Individual Visitor Centers
(see Appendices)
USGS/Cascades Volcano Observatory (Washington State volcanoes)
vulcan.wr.usgs.gov/Volcanoes/Washington/framework.html

21

May

Melting Snow, Roaring Water

Dripping, gurgling, rushing, tumbling water—there is nothing more dramatic to remind you of the renewal and abundance of Mother Nature. Pick a waterfall and enjoy.

Site: Locations on the North Cascades' west slope that are easily accessible in late spring.

Recommended time: Late May; in late spring the snow in the mountains is melting and there's sunshine to enhance the sight.

Minimum time commitment: An afternoon or a day.

What to bring: Binoculars, camera, hiking boots.

Directions: See list.

The background: There are hundreds of waterfalls in Washington; some require a wait until summer or early fall, especially in years with heavy snow. Here is a sample of the ninety waterfalls mapped in the North Cascades— ones big enough to impress everyone and easy to get to. Consult *A Waterfall Lover's Guide to the Pacific Northwest* by Gregory A. Plumb for others.

The fun: The sounds of streams and waterfalls in spring push you into peaceful mode quickly. Look at them, listen to them—they will work their magic for you.

On the Nooksack River: Nooksack Falls (5★ rating—exceptional) positively roars. The amount of water that pours through there is impressive, and the falls are easy to find—no hiking needed. Stop at the Glacier Public Service Center at milepost 34 and pick up maps. Remember to check on road conditions, especially in years with heavy, late snowfall.

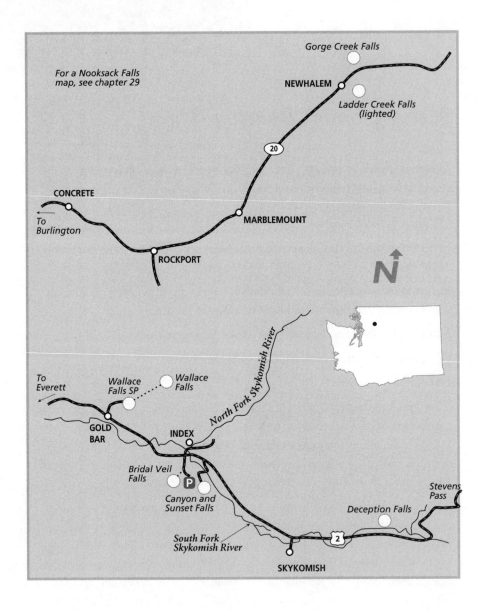

Gorge Creek Falls

For a Nooksack Falls
map, see chapter 29

NEWHALEM

Ladder Creek Falls
(lighted)

20

CONCRETE

To
Burlington

MARBLEMOUNT

ROCKPORT

N

North Fork Skykomish River

To
Everett

Wallace
Falls SP

Wallace
Falls

GOLD
BAR

INDEX

Bridal Veil
Falls

P

Canyon and
Sunset Falls

South Fork
Skykomish River

Deception Falls

Stevens
Pass

2

SKYKOMISH

Drive 34 miles east of Bellingham along SR 542 to Glacier, then 7 miles east to Wells Creek Road #33. Turn right and drive 0.5 mile. Park on the left, just before the bridge, listen for the roar, and walk across the road to see the falls. The area is fenced—please don't let anyone climb around on the other side. The rocks are slippery and there have been accidents.

In the Ross Lake National Recreation Area: Gorge Creek Falls is another falls you can see from the road. It is a very high falls—a wide ribbon of water tumbling many hundreds of feet over rocks and moss. From I–5 take Burlington exit 230, drive east on SR 20 (North Cascades Highway)

See Gorge Creek Falls, east of Newhalem, from the road or a protected walkway.

past milepost 123, and park on the right before the Gorge Creek bridge. Walk across the bridge on the protected pedestrian walkway to view the falls and the creek below. A short, paved, accessible loop trail takes you from the parking lot (toilets) to overlooks of the creek, lake, and dam.

Stop at the National Park Service's North Cascades Visitor Center at Newhalem on the way up (milepost 120). Both adults and kids will enjoy the exhibits and nature trails here. If you go earlier in May, you can join a guided bird walk to celebrate IMBD (chapter 18).

Next best: Drive east from Everett on US 2 to visit five waterfalls with easy to moderate hikes. Rugged snow-capped peaks start at 30 miles.

At Gold Bar follow the signs 1.7 miles northeast to Wallace Falls State Park (campground, picnic area, rest rooms, trails). Wallace Falls (5★) is a popular attraction on a moderately steep trail—2.5 miles one way to view the falls, up to 3.5 miles for more views. There's a safety fence at the viewpoint; hold on to children anyway. Dropping 250 feet, Wallace Falls is one of the tallest in the North Cascades (giant Snoqualmie Falls is 268 feet).

Seven miles east of Gold Bar, Bridal Veil Falls comes off Mount Index in four parts—each a 100- to 200-foot ribbon. From US 2 turn right (south) on Mount Index Road 0.2 mile east of milepost 35, right in 0.2 mile on FR 109, then left into a parking area (toilets). Hike 1.6 miles up the Lake Serene Trail, then 0.5 mile up the spur to the falls.

For Canyon Falls (4★), cross the South Fork Skykomish bridge on US 2, turn south on an unsigned road 0.6 mile east of milepost 36, drive 0.2 mile, and park near the fork. Walk a mile down the gated road to the left for close-up views. It's small, but the geology is interesting; the river has "physically eroded and widened a fracture in the granite to form the falls." For views of Sunset Falls (60- to 100-foot slide) walk 0.5 mile down the red-gated road to the right (kayak put-in, picnic tables).

Continue east on US 2 through Skykomish to Deception Falls; parking and toilets are on the left (north) 0.7 mile east of milepost 56. Hike the easy 0.25-mile loop nature trail (interpretive signs) down through the forest, across the creek (footbridge), and up along the tumbling Tye River with its right-angle waterfall. Or walk the 0.2-mile paved, accessible trail to the big falls where water roars and tumbles under the see-through metal footbridge.

Food and lodging: Services all along the way.

For more information:
Mount Baker–Snoqualmie National Forest
Glacier Public Service Center (seasonal)
(360) 599–2714
North Cascades National Park
North Cascades Visitor Center
(206) 386–4495

22

May

Subtle Blooms and Bold Terrain

For deep canyons and wildflowers more typical of the Rocky Mountains, travel to the eastern slopes of the Blue Mountains.

Site: Blue Mountains, 28 miles south of Clarkston.

Recommended time: Mid-May to mid-June.

Minimum time commitment: A day; a weekend for leisurely exploring; a long Memorial Day weekend for Palouse side trips.

What to bring: Wildflower field guide, binoculars.

Directions: From US 12 in Clarkston, drive 5 miles south on SR 129 along the Snake River to Asotin to begin your tour.

The background: The Blue Mountains were formed by enormous basaltic lava flows, then scoured by glaciers and floods. The cooling of these lakelike flows sometimes forms six-sided basaltic structures called "columnar joining"—see these in cliffs or palisades high above the Snake River. As you drive up the long, looping switchbacks south of Asotin, look around at the deep canyons (Snake River Canyon is the most spectacular) and the huge folds of land that seem to envelop you. Farther south, as you descend the steep winding grade to the Grande Ronde River, stop at the turnouts to absorb the grandeur. The habitat in these mountains is more like the Rocky Mountains than the Cascades. In fact, our local wildflower expert, Priscilla Dauble, uses a Rocky Mountain wildflower field guide.

The fun: From Asotin drive 23 miles south on SR 129 along the eastern edge of the Blue Mountains. This is agricultural land, where yellow canola

From Puffer Butte, you can look across the wild canyons of the Grande Ronde River gorge to Oregon's Wallowa Mountains.

fields peak in mid-June and ancient barns are picturesque year-round. Or get out your *Washington Atlas and Gazetteer* and drive the back roads west of SR 129 for more scenery and wildflowers (avoid slippery clay roads in wet weather). Just south of milepost 16, turn left (east) into Fields Spring State Park.

The park is built on Puffer Butte overlooking the Grand Ronde River. Hike up to the top of the butte for a sweeping three-state view of mountains and canyons (incredible at dawn). You'll see wildflowers of the wetter habitats (calypso orchids, monkeyflowers, etc.) at the start of the trail and the more common sage and shrub-steppe wildflowers at the top. Listen for coyotes, songbirds, and drumming grouse; watch for white-tailed deer and raptors. Trailheads are located near the campground (1.5 miles, 550-foot gain) and south of the Puffer Butte Learning Center (1 mile, 500-foot gain).

Then drive south from Fields Spring State Park on SR 129, down Railroad Grade to the Grande Ronde River. The dry canyon is lush green in spring, with steep, winding roads, lots of pullouts, great views, and more wild-flowers and birds. South of milepost 5 but before the bridge, turn right on the Grande Ronde Road and drive up the winding river canyon. Watch and listen for spring migrant birds and enjoy the wildflowers of this warm canyon (peak color is mid- to late May). Bighorn sheep make their home among the

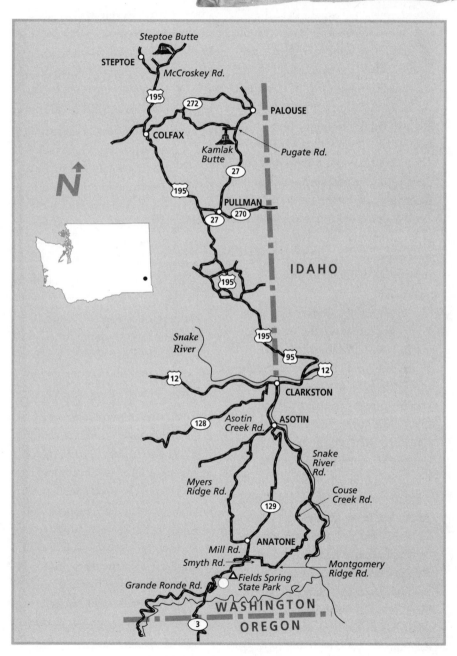

If your trip extends over the whole Memorial Day weekend, you may want to visit the spectacular buttes and rolling hills of the Palouse, 30 miles north of Clarkston. An early-morning trip to either Kamiak Butte or Steptoe Butte north of Pullman will reward you with a panorama of rolling hills covered with sensuous green-and-brown patterns made by the cultivated fields—all bathed in the sun's golden light. Lovely stands of balsamroot, lupine, paintbrush, and other wildflowers are dramatic in this early warm light.

Kamiak Butte County Park is good at all times of day for wildflowers and birds, but for a real treat arrive early enough to reach the top of the butte's east-facing slope before sunrise (fifteen- to twenty-minute hike). Park at the trailhead by the toilets and hike up the half-mile, moderately steep trail. Sit on the bench at the overlook to the southwest and enjoy the incredible vista. After sunrise walk along the ridge and enjoy open slopes with patches of wildflowers, white-tailed deer, chipmunks, and birds (spotted towhees, sparrows, bluebirds, wrens). Take the trail south through the conifers and listen or watch for dark-eyed juncos, western wood peewees, western tanagers, and red crossbills. As the day warms up, check for hawks soaring over the fields.

Directions: From Pullman drive 12 miles north on SR 27 and turn left on Fugate Road (KAMIAK BUTTE sign). Picnic area and campground.

Steptoe Butte State Park is spectacular at both sunrise and sunset. From the bottom you wind around and around up the butte, with the view changing at every loop. The vistas are extraordinary; farm buildings make colorful accents on the rich, green cultivated fields. Go in mid-May for balsamroot, later for fields of purple lupine. Groups of white-tailed deer may be found anywhere on the butte. Be the first person up the road in the morning to see them before they drift away.

Directions: From Colfax drive 6 miles north on US 195 and turn right on McCroskey Road (STEPTOE BUTTE sign). The road becomes Hume Road; the park entrance is on the left (toilets, picnic area).

Drive through the Palouse countryside to enjoy more of the famed rolling hills with their beautiful green crop patterns. You will see intermittent fields of bright yellow canola—a brilliant contrast against the green.

and Wildflowers

The wandering route heads south on US 195 through Colfax, past Pullman, and through Uniontown. Some favorite roads are listed below.

East of Colfax and northwest of Kamiak Butte, drive along SR 272, Glenwood Road, and Clear Creek Road to see barns and rolling hills.

Just west of Kamiak Butte, Abbott and Parvin roads are your best bets.

South of Kamiak Butte, on Four Mile Road, is Rose Creek Preserve, a mile west of Old Albion Road.

South of Pullman, starting at milepost 19, there are many scenic roads near US 195. West of the highway, Druffel, Union Flat, Little, Wawawai, and Meyer roads take you to barns, patterned hills, canola fields, and a windmill.

East of US 195, Johnson, Colton and Bald Butte roads take you through more rolling hills. Explore on your own—it's a fun adventure.

In late May and early June, a short hike over the top of Kamiak Butte will reward you with gorgeous wildflower displays.

rugged cliffs along the near side of the river. They are not always visible, but on one trip at the end of May, we saw nine adults and three tiny lambs in a draw 7.8 miles from SR 129. Watch for mule deer on the lower slopes; black bear have also been seen. You can either complete the loop (through Oregon) or retrace your route to SR 129. If you dip down into Oregon, don't miss the wildflowers between Troy and Flora.

For the return trip to Clarkston, stay on SR 129 to Asotin or drop down to the Snake River and follow it north. For the river route, turn right (east) just north of milepost 15 on Smyth Road, turn right again on Montgomery Ridge Road, and cross the high, flat plateau country. This may be the prettiest wildflower location on the trip. You'll see three or four types of balsamroot, lupine, sheets of onions, and more. At 12 miles turn left (SNAKE RIVER sign) on Sherry Grade Road and head down steep switchbacks through dramatic volcanic ridges, rocky cliffs, and mock orange bushes. The road becomes Couse Creek Road and follows a riparian area (lots of birds) along the creek.

At 20 miles turn left (north) on the Snake River Road to Asotin (30 miles). The lower reaches of Hells Canyon, with its magnificent cliffs and river scenes, are adorned with flowering shrubs—mostly white-flowered varieties. You will also see boats of all types floating the river. If you like jet boats, Beamers Hells Canyon Tours & Excursions runs Snake River trips from Clarkston. You will run the rapids and see lots of beautiful river scenes, bighorn sheep, mule deer, and historical landmarks. Contact Beamers at (800) 522–6966; hellscanyontours.com/.

Food and lodging: Clarkston and Asotin offer all services. Fields Spring State Park has a twenty-site campground (showers). Primitive camping is allowed at fishing accesses on the Grand Ronde River (WDFW Access Stewardship Decal required). Watch for rattlesnakes.

For more information:

Fields Spring State Park
www.parks.wa.gov/alphase.asp

Guided Trips:

Washington Native Plant Society, Columbia Basin Chapter
(509) 372–1526
Blue Mountain Audubon Society
(509) 529–8628

23

Walk, Run, Ride, and Work

Celebrate National Trails Day this weekend at one of the best events in the state, the Spokane River Centennial Trail Festival.

Site: Downtown Spokane's Riverfront Park and the Centennial Trail.

Recommended time: First Saturday in June.

Minimum time commitment: Half a day; a weekend if you want to enjoy other nature activities in the area.

What to bring: Sunscreen, water, walking or running shoes, bicycle or horse.

Directions: From I–90, take exit 281 (US 395) north, then turn left (west) on Spokane Falls Boulevard to Riverfront Park (south side of the Spokane River).

The background: National Trails Day is an annual event sponsored by the American Hiking Society and the State Trails programs in each state. Since 1993 it has grown to more than 3,000 events across the country with more than a million total participants. In Washington there are events all across the state designed to "promote new strategies for community trail planning, increase public awareness of trails, promote trail conservation, and celebrate the values and benefits our treasured pathways provide."

The fun: The Spokane River Centennial Trail Festival is one of the best of the fun events. And as a great side benefit, May and June are Spokane's most beautiful months. The temperatures are mild, the foliage is lush and green, and the flowers are in full bloom.

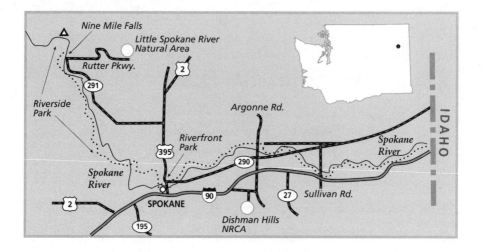

The Friends of the Centennial Trail host the annual Spokane River Centennial Trail Festival from 8:00 A.M. to 1:00 P.M. on the first Saturday in June. The main staging area is at Riverfront Park in downtown Spokane—with music, vendor and user group displays, food, T-shirts, prizes, and awards. Events suitable for families and individuals of all ages are held all along the 37-mile trail. They include a 22-mile bike ride, a 12-mile equestrian ride, a 4-mile hike, and a 4-mile run.

The trail runs from the Idaho state line to Nine Mile Falls and is accessible to wheelchairs. Get a detailed pocket map of the trail for $2.00 from the Friends of the Centennial Trail office. The eastern segment of the trail is mostly flat; the section from Sullivan Road to Argonne Road is quite scenic; and you often see deer, osprey, and herons along the river.

The west segment of trail stays in Riverside State Park most of the way. It is more hilly than the eastern section, as the route moves between the riverbank and the hills. It offers spectacular views of the river (including the Bowl and Pitcher area), Nine Mile Dam, the Spokane Valley, and Seven Mile area vistas.

Next best: Try a rafting trip on the Spokane River. The river is beautiful, with frequent fun rapids and lots of places to just drift. Spokane Parks and Recreation runs river trips in late May and early June. Call (509) 477–4730 or (509) 625–6200.

Visit Dishman Hills Natural Resource Conservation Area (509–456–4730), just 2 miles east of downtown, for peaceful walking through 450 acres of nearly pristine wildlands. Take I–90 exit 285, drive east on Sprague, and turn south on Sargent Road to the parking area. Enjoy lush trails, ponderosa pine, ponds, cliffs, ravines, and numerous wildflowers (no mountain bikes, horses, or in-line skates). Deer, raccoons, coyotes, fifty species of butterflies, and one hundred species of birds inhabit this area.

In Riverside State Park you can hike or bike on miles of trails, horseback ride, canoe, or raft. Drive west on Francis, angling northwest when it changes to Nine Mile Road (SR 291). Access to Riverside State Park is at Rifle Club Road.

For a sense of solitude, turn right off SR 291 onto Rutter Parkway to the pristine Little Spokane River Natural Area, which encompasses 7.3 river miles. Hike the trails or paddle a canoe or kayak down the river. In addition to songbirds, woodpeckers, raptors, and waterfowl, you will see a great blue heron colony in the tall cottonwoods by the river. Please travel quietly because these birds are sensitive to disturbance. The critical nesting season ends in mid-May, so the river will be open and young herons will be active. Also look for beavers, muskrats, porcupines, raccoons, coyotes, marmots, and white-tailed deer. Contact Friends of Riverside State Park or for map visit www.riversidestatepark.org/little_spokane.htm.

Food and lodging: Spokane offers all services; camping is at Riverside State Park.

For more information:
National Trails Day events
www.americanhiking.org/
Spokane River Centennial Trail Festival
(509) 624–7188; www.spokanecentennialtrail.org
Friends of Riverside State Park
www.riversidestatepark.org/

Trails Day events are usually a mix of fun and work. The work often includes some light trail maintenance, and the fun usually includes a nature walk or other out-door activities. We spent one day at a weeklong Washington Trails Association work party in the Icicle Creek area to shore up a trail and build a new bridge. It was active work, but the pace was leisurely, and the cooking, campfire, and cama-raderie were great. Try one; we think you'll like it. See the American Hiking Association Web site for a complete list of National Trails Day events. Or call one of the regular sponsors below to see what event they are sponsoring this year.

- *Bellevue:* King County Parks and Recreation
  (206) 296–4171
- *Everett:* Snohomish County Parks and Recreation
  (425) 388–6600
- *Mount Vernon:* Skagit County Parks and Recreation
  (360) 336–9414
- *North Bend:* Snoqualmie Valley Trails Club
  (425) 885–5148
- *Puget Sound:* The Mountaineers
  www.mountaineers.org/
  conservation/trailm.org

- *Seattle:* City of Seattle, Trails Program
  (206) 684–4122
- *Vancouver:* Chinook Trail Association
  (360) 906–6769;
  www.chinooktrail.org/

Year-round work parties:
Washington Trails Association
(206) 625–1367;
www.halcyon.com/wta/
Pacific Northwest Trail Association
(877) 854–9415;
www.pnt.org/worktmo.shtml

As part of National Trails Day, a Washington Trails Association work party builds a rock wall to shore up a trail near Icicle Creek.

24

June

Feathered Babies

Mid-June is a great time to visit the Pend Oreille River in north-eastern Washington to see osprey, double-crested cormorant, and bald eagle chicks both in their nests and as they learn to fly.

Site: Pend Oreille River, in the northeast corner of Washington. There is an impressive concentration of nesting birds all the way from Usk north to the Canadian border.

Recommended time: June.

Minimum time commitment: Take the whole weekend.

What to bring: Binoculars, spotting scope, camera, bird field guide.

Directions: From Spokane drive 34 miles north on US 2. Turn left (north) on SR 211 and drive 15 miles to SR 20. Cross the intersection into Usk.

The background: This area comes as close as you can get to guaranteed sightings of osprey nests with young birds in them. According to a Sullivan Ranger Station survey, there were seventy-three osprey nests in 1999 on or near the river from Usk to Riverbend, 13 miles north.

Cormorant numbers increased greatly on this stretch of the river starting in 1995. Many locals feared that they were replacing the osprey, but the osprey nest count puts that fear to rest. A fish hatchery was constructed around that time, and the change in fish species may account for the increased cormorant numbers.

The fun: Many osprey nests are back in the trees or on the transmission line poles. If you see owls on top of some of these poles, look again. They're plastic, put there to prevent young ospreys from being electrocuted.

On the Pend Oreille River, ospreys build huge nests on large river pilings. The female osprey and chicks are waiting for her mate to share his fish.

Osprey nests built on pilings in the Pend Oreille River are more accessible since they are right at eye level. You can see into at least ten nests from LeClerc and River roads just north and south of the Lake Road bridge in Usk. In June you will see ospreys in the nests, feeding their young, sitting on pilings, or fishing. Please keep your distance—use binoculars or spotting scopes.

On one trip in mid-June, two little gray heads barely poked up from a nest just north of Usk on River Road—newborn osprey! The proud mama—piercing yellow eyes darting from side to side—made little cries at her mate who was sitting on a piling. When he finally brought his fish to the nest, the parents took turns tearing off the flesh and feeding it to the outstretched mouths. If you go in late June, the young osprey will be bigger, livelier, and easier to see.

More than one hundred cormorant nests sit atop pilings north of the bridge, and in mid-June, about half these nests are full of large, active young with parents feeding them or flying away to catch fish in the river. The chicks are born in late May or early June; if you want to see them fledge, try late June.

Early June is also a good time to see the large diversity of nesting songbirds in the Pend Oreille Valley. You can even see bobolinks at Cusick Flats on SR 20, north of milepost 420.

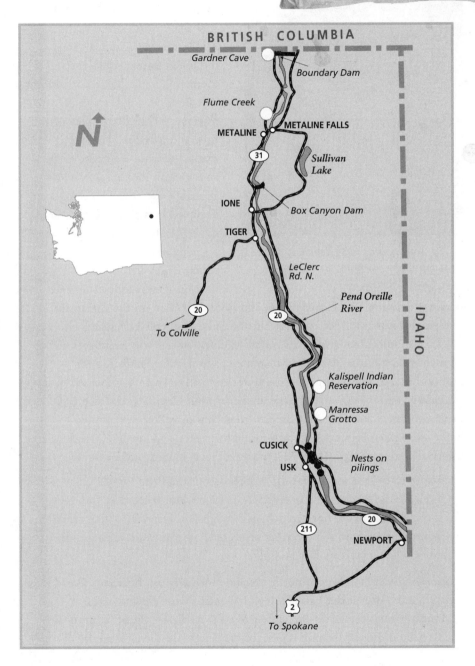

BRITISH COLUMBIA

Gardner Cave

Boundary Dam

Flume Creek

METALINE FALLS

METALINE

31

Sullivan
Lake

IONE

Box Canyon Dam

TIGER

LeClerc
Rd. N.

N

20

20

Pend Oreille
River

To Colville

IDAHO

Kalispell Indian
Reservation

Manressa
Grotto

CUSICK

Nests on
pilings

USK

211

20

NEWPORT

2

To Spokane

The water spilling from Boundary Dam is spectacular when backlit by the early morning sun.

Next best: Drive 31 miles north on SR 20 to Tiger, then continue north on SR 31 toward the Canadian border. At least three pairs of bald eagles nest in the Metaline Falls area; more nest farther south along the Pend Oreille River corridor. The best viewing is south of milepost 10 on SR 31, between Ione and Metaline. There is a marked turnout along the river, and you can look directly across at a large nest that has been occupied by a pair of eagles for more than ten years.

The best way to see the young eagles is from Box Canyon Resort's three-hour jet boat trip between Box Canyon Dam and Boundary Dam on the Canadian border. Also watch for osprey, great blue herons, white-tailed deer, and, rarely, a bear or moose. The driver stops for all wildlife. On one trip passengers saw a pair of young eagles make their first attempt to fly. One landed on the ground, but the other flopped in the water and had to swim to shore. At Boundary Dam we saw a bald eagle attack an adult Canada goose. The eagle made two passes and then flew off; the goose was okay. You will also see impressive Pewee Falls, rock formations, historic sites, and rapids. Contact Box Canyon Resort at (509) 442–3728; www.pal-biz.com/boxcanyonresort/.

Driving tours: If you spend the weekend, tour the Pend Oreille Valley to see mountain goats, deer, elk, or bison. Watch for white-tailed deer throughout the valley; fawns are born mid-May through July. Deer and other wildlife are more active early in the morning or evening, so plan your driving tours accordingly and drive carefully at dusk.

■ *Boundary Road Drive:* From north Metaline turn west on Boundary Road. At 2.1 miles stop at the Flume Creek Mountain Goat Viewing Area. Mountain goats forage on the cliffs across the road—or out of sight on the cliffs behind those. Morning is best for viewing, since the cliffs are in shadow by midafternoon. Kids are usually born in early June; look closely to see if any "nannies" have newborns with them. Binoculars are essential.

The Pend Oreille River is one of the few rivers in the world that flows from south to north throughout its whole course. Boundary Dam is at 11.5 miles; in early summer they open the gates and spill the water. The view from the overlook is spectacular—especially in the morning when the sun shines through the arching stream of water. The road ends at Crawford State Park and fascinating Gardner Cave, where the underground limestone cave temperature remains at 41 degrees Fahrenheit year-round. One-hour guided tours start at 10:00 A.M. Thursday through Monday.

■ *Sullivan Lake Road Loop:* From the Metaline Falls bridge drive 2 miles north on SR 31 and turn right on Sullivan Lake Road to start your tour. At 0.8 miles Rocky Mountain elk can be seen in the evening in the ranch meadows to the north. Calves are born in June, but the cows usually keep them back in the trees. At 3.2 miles is Mill Creek Pond Historic Site and Elk Creek Falls Trail. Take the 2.4-mile round-trip wildflower hike, or walk the paths at Mill Creek Pond. A snowshoe hare with still-partially-white feet surprised us one morning. The Sullivan Lake Ranger Station (5.2 miles) has good wildflower and wildlife information.

Common mergansers frequent the south end of Sullivan Lake near Noisy Creek Campground. See chicks riding on their mother's back in early June. Look for nesting pairs of harlequin ducks along Sullivan Creek in mid- to late June. In early June thousands of butterflies congregate at wet spots on North Sullivan Lake Road and on SR 31 north to the Canadian border. Drive carefully to avoid them.

■ *LeClerc Road:* The Kalispell Indian Reservation (east side of the river south of Ione) is home to a bison herd; calves are born from late April to May.

Food and lodging: Towns along the Pend Oreille River offer all services. Enjoy historic hotels in Metaline Falls and Usk. Campgrounds are plentiful along the Sullivan Lake Road.

For more information:

Sullivan Lake Ranger District
(509) 446–7500
North Pend Oreille Scenic Byway
www.povn.com/cutter/

25

Celebrating Wildflowers

The Mount Baker–Snoqualmie National Forest, the Washington Native Plant Society, and the town of Darrington all work very hard at making this little wildflower festival worthy of your attention.

Site: Darrington is located in the foothills of the Cascades, 35 miles east of Arlington.

Recommended time: The festival is held the third weekend of June.

Minimum time commitment: Plan to spend the day on Saturday, when most of the activities and music are scheduled. The festival continues on Sunday.

What to bring: Prepare for warm or cool weather, rain or sunshine. It can be iffy this time of the year, this close to the mountains. Wear walking shoes or boots. Bring a camera, binoculars, and a wildflower/plant field guide.

Directions: From I–5, take exit 208 to Arlington and continue on SR 530 about 35 miles to Darrington. In Darrington turn right on Sauk Avenue and watch for balloons and signs. The festival is held at the Darrington School District complex.

The background: The Darrington Wildflower Festival is a small, but charming festival set in a spectacular mountain valley. Darrington is close to the highway but feels remote, surrounded by the Mount Baker–Snoqualmie National Forest and mountains, many with snow still on them this time of year. There are three Wild and Scenic Rivers nearby. It's quiet and peaceful and folks are friendly.

Knowledgeable gardeners from the Salal Chapter of the Washington Native Plant Society sell plants and offer advice at the Darrington Wildflower Festival.

The fun: Darrington makes it easy to enjoy yourself, without hassle. There is no entrance fee, and parking is plentiful and free. When you first arrive get a schedule of events and decide which plant walks to join. There are short and long walks, some along Old Sauk Trail, to accommodate nearly everyone's abilities, interest, and time. These walks are led by Native Plant Society experts and often include interesting tidbits about historical plant use and how plants were discovered and named. Sign up and then spend the time in between walks at the numerous presentations. In the past these have included medicinal uses of wildflower essences, photographing wildflowers, identifying the wildflowers of Washington, and organic gardening.

Stroll among the arts and crafts booths, buy a native plant for your own garden, or listen to music. Talk to the USDA Forest Service rangers or call the Darrington Ranger District at (360) 436–1155 for recommendations for additional hikes in the immediate area. Buy a new field guide from the non-profit Northwest Interpretive Association; they offer good "festival discounts" on their books. There are also T-shirts, posters, maps, children's books, and stuffed Smokey Bear toys. Enjoy the quilt show, including Darrington's own

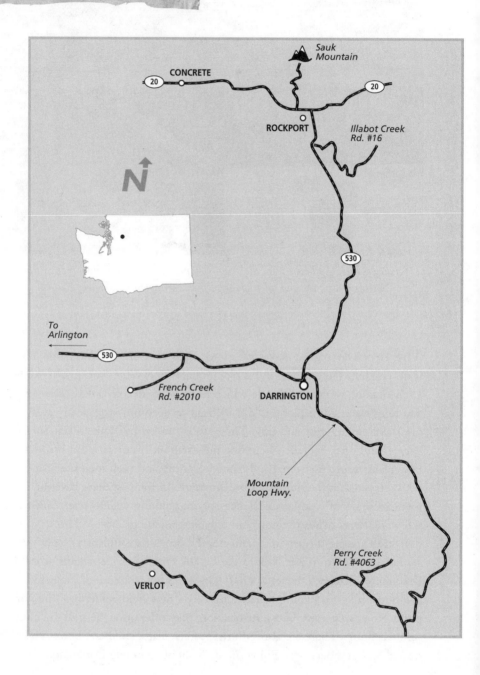

wildflower quilt and the Forest Service Smokey Bear quilt, featuring advertisements from the 1940s to today. The festival includes plenty of activities especially for kids—bubble blowing, walking with llamas, and making hats or other crafts.

The festival continues on Sunday, often beginning with a pancake breakfast and more plant walks and presentations. Take this opportunity to learn about this beautiful area—hikes with wildflowers, ferns, waterfalls, and wild rivers will entice you to come back for more.

Next best: The USDA Forest Service continues its Celebrating Wildflowers events all summer with hikes and activities in the North Cascades. For more information see the National Park Service Celebrating Wildflowers Events Directory at www.nps.gov/plants/cw/states/wa.htm.

If you spend the weekend, enjoy some late June or early July wildflower and waterfall hikes near Darrington (Northwest Forest Pass required). See *Trips and Trails, 1* or *100 Hikes in Washington's Glacier Peak Region* for directions to the hikes listed here, or ask rangers at the festival for their recommendations.

■ *Mountain Loop Highway:* West of Darrington, French Creek Road #2010, Boulder Creek and Falls Trail (easy 1-mile hike).

East of Verlot: Perry Creek Road #4063, Perry Creek Trail. Two-mile hike through forest and wildflowers to the top of Perry Creek Falls. In July hike another steep, switchbacking 2 miles to lush wildflower meadows.

■ *Rockport area:* West on SR 20, Sauk Mountain. Short, steep switchback trail across a wildflower meadow to the top of the ridge and fantastic vistas from the abandoned lookout.

South on SR 503: Illabot Creek Road #16, Slide Lake Trail (forest flowers, easy 1.5-mile hike).

Food and lodging: Food booths and picnic tables on the festival grounds are a great place for meals. Darrington has limited accommodations and restaurants; Arlington, 28 miles west on I–5, offers all services. National Forest campgrounds are located south along the Mountain Loop Highway.

For more information:
Darrington Wildflower Festival
(360) 436–1794
Washington Native Plant Society, Salal Chapter
www.wnps.org/salal/index.html

26

June

In Search of Spock and Spieden

Enjoy a weekend in the San Juan Islands to search for and learn more about orcas, or "killer whales."

Site: Lime Kiln Point State Park on San Juan Island, just 6 miles from Friday Harbor.

Recommended time: In June and July orcas can be seen from Lime Kiln Point almost every day. In general they're in the San Juan Islands and around southern Vancouver Island May through September. If you also want to see the spectacular California poppies south of Lime Kiln Point, go in mid–May.

Minimum time commitment: At least one day, including ferry travel time from Anacortes.

What to bring: Binoculars, spotting scope, camera, sunglasses, sunscreen, lawn chairs or blanket, refreshments, jacket.

Directions: From I–5 take Anacortes exit 230 to SR 20 and travel west, then north at the "Y" into downtown Anacortes. To reach the San Juan ferry terminal, turn left on Twelfth Street and follow the signs.

The background: San Juan Island is one of the best places in the world to watch for orcas. In the San Juan Islands and around southern Vancouver Island, three pods, or family groups, are residents. In these three pods there are about eighty-three individuals, and they have been the subjects of some of the most thorough studies of cetaceans (dolphins, porpoises, and whales) any-where (see sidebar). All summer long you have a really good chance to

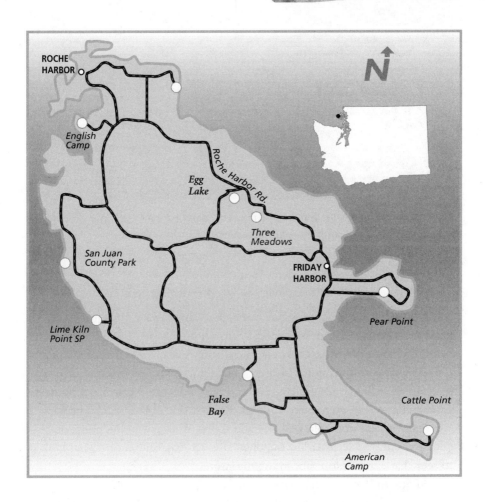

ROCHE
HARBOR

N

English
Camp

Roche Harbor Rd

Egg
Lake

Three
Meadows

San Juan
County Park

FRIDAY
HARBOR

Pear Point

Lime Kiln
Point SP

False
Bay

Cattle Point

American
Camp

Sea kayakers wait quietly near Lime Kiln Point State Park for pods of orcas to travel past them on their circuit around San Juan Island.

observe these animals as they circle the island searching for salmon.

The fun: This is a trip everyone can enjoy. Watching for orcas just takes patience, sitting on the grass, in lawn chairs, or on a boat.

To see orcas from land, take the ferry from Anacortes to Friday Harbor. On the way, start looking for orcas as well as porpoises, seabirds, and harbor seals. When you arrive at Friday Harbor, visit The Whale Museum or bike or drive to Lime Kiln Point State Park on the west side of the island. The park has a new paved, accessible walkway and toilets. Walk out to the point, make yourself comfortable, listen for the orcas' distinct exhalation noises, and look to see what else you can spot in the meantime.

Another place to watch orcas while enjoying the sights on San Juan Island is Cattle Point, located at the southeast tip of the island in American Camp (toilets). It is also a good place to take a walk; see some history; and look for minke whales, marine birds, and deer, as well as the harbor seals that haul out on the rocks just offshore.

To search from the water, make reservations on a whale-watching boat from Friday Harbor or Orcas Island. Or ride the ferry to Friday Harbor another day and take a tour with Island Adventures Whale Watching from Anacortes. You will be accompanied by a naturalist and marine biologist and will have access to an onboard library with whale and wildlife identification charts and books (many of the charters have similar amenities). Contact Island Adventure Whale Watching at (800) 465–4604; www.island-adventures.com.

The Day Trip Adventure from Port Townsend combines both whale watching and a four-hour port of call in Friday Harbor. Contact Puget Sound Express at (360) 385–5288; www.pugetsoundexpress.com/. The Seattle Aquarium has an all-day orca cruise every Saturday all summer. Contact them at (206) 386–4353; www.seattleaquarium.org/.

One of the best ways to get close views of orcas is to take to the water yourself. Sea kayaking has become very popular and many companies offer rentals and tours. If you sit quietly in your kayak, the whales sometimes swim right by you. The great thing is that they know just where you are and will never hit you.

Food and lodging: Friday Harbor, Roche Harbor, Port Townsend, and Anacortes offer all services. San Juan County Park Campground is a wonderful place to camp and even watch the whales, but it fills up early in the season. Reservations for both whale-watching boats and lodging are strongly recommended, especially in the summer.

For more information:

The Whale Museum, Friday Harbor
(360) 378–4710 or (800) 946–7227; www.whale-museum.org/
Whale Watch Operators Association Northwest
www.nwwhalewatchers.org/

What's Next for "Our Orcas"

Orcas are often called "killer whales," but they are actually not whales at all. They are, rather, the largest of the dolphins.

In the San Juan Islands and around southern Vancouver Island, there are three resident pods, the J–pod, the K–pod, and the L–pod. Even during winter it was thought that our resident pods stayed within 200 miles of this area, traveling only as far as nearby Georgia Strait when they needed to find more-abundant salmon. It is still generally true that in April, local salmon runs increase, and "our" pods continue to stay close to "home," in Washington waters for many months. However, during the winter of 1999, K– and L–pods were spotted near Monterey, California and didn't return to Puget Sound until mid-June (with one new calf). Scientists will continue to monitor this behavior.

Most Washingtonians have a special fondness for "our orcas," partly because there is so much information about them. Researchers at Friday Harbor's The Whale Museum and The Center for Whale Research have been studying these beautiful black and white mammals since 1976. Identified by the shape and size of the dorsal fin plus the saddle patch or markings beneath and behind the fin, each animal has been photographed and given an identification number and a common name. Thanks to the more than twenty years of tenacious research, we know interesting and vital details of their personal lives, which make them even more special to us. For example, "Granny," one of the oldest females, baby-sits many of the young calves; "Spock," the oldest of three siblings, helps his mom, "Skagit," take care of the others in the family; and "Spieden" makes a distinctive wheezing sound that enables researchers to hear J–pod passing by, even at night or in fog.

According to The Center for Whale Research, there is also a transient group of orcas, about 170 total, which sometimes venture into Puget Sound. Generally, however, they can be found farther offshore from Mexico to the Bering Sea. Unlike the resident population, which prefer salmon, these orcas eat a diet of marine mammals—harbor seals, sea lions, porpoises, otters, and even whales—plus other sea creatures such as turtles and squid. In 1991 another community, which researchers call "offshores," was discovered. They are most often seen in the Pacific Ocean, 15 to 25 miles out at sea, off Vancouver Island and the Queen Charlottes.

Unfortunately, the number of orcas seems to be declining, and it has been proposed that Washington's resident orca population be added to the state's endangered species list. Whether they will be listed remains both likely due to toxins. This is a serious environmental issue: The pollution in our once-pristine waters may be threatening the existence of our orcas and all other life in and around Puget Sound!

Orcas sometimes leap out of the water close to slowly moving charter boats. This female's baby is hidden in the spray.

to be seen at this writing, but there is no doubt that there are threats to their existence. Fish populations are declining, and the accumulation of toxins in marine mammal tissue in the Puget Sound area has been found to be some of the highest levels recorded anywhere. In March 2000, J18 (Everett) died at the young age of twenty-two, leaving J–pod with only one older breeding male; his mother died a few months later—

We all must be more active in helping these special Northwest mammals to survive. Support efforts to reduce the many different kinds of toxins that eventually find their way into Washington waters. You can also "adopt an orca," through The Whale Museum. You get a certificate and information about the orca you select, and the money goes into education and research. Makes a great gift, too! Call the museum for details.

27

Flourishing Wildflowers, Newborn Wildlife

Visit Hurricane Ridge to see gorgeous meadows of wildflowers, dramatic sunrises and sunsets, scenic mountain views, and close-up looks at black-tailed deer fawns and baby marmots.

Site: Hurricane Ridge in Olympic National Park, 19 miles south of Port Angeles.

Recommended time: Blooming usually begins in late June, peaks in early to mid-July, and continues through August.

Minimum time commitment: A day or a weekend, plus driving time.

What to bring: Wildflower field guide, camera, binoculars (entrance fee, National Parks Pass, or Golden Eagle Passport).

Directions: From US 101 in Port Angeles, take Race Street 1.5 miles south to the Olympic National Park Visitor Center, then 5 miles to the park entrance and 12 more miles to Hurricane Ridge.

The background: Hurricane Ridge offers ample parking, rest rooms, picnic areas, a variety of trails, and ranger-led walks. Wildflowers and mountain views are impressive, black-tailed deer are everywhere, some with fawns, and marmots fill the air with their high-pitched whistles. As if all this weren't enough, sunrises and sunsets are terrific, and it's a short drive back to town.

The fun: If you want to experience it all, drive up to Lookout Rock Vista

*Just after the snow melts, avalanche lilies cover the meadows
on the south side of Obstruction Point Road.*

before sunrise to catch the predawn glow. Then watch the sunrise over the
Strait of Juan de Fuca with the rolling foothills of the Olympics spread out
before you. Scattered clouds create drama; fog is soft, with foothills rising out
of the mist in subtle, delicate patterns. Continue up Hurricane Ridge Road
to the top, stopping to see more views, wildflowers, and deer along the way.
Deer at Hurricane Ridge are not tame, but they are accustomed to humans.

Obstruction Point Road heads sharply left (east) at the top of the road. It
opens in early July (call ahead to see if it is snow-free). At 1 mile from the
start of the road, walk over the ridge to the north-facing slope thick with
wildflowers. From 4.5 to 6 miles there are numerous wildflower locations—
bright orange Columbia lilies by the side of the road, a meadow full of avalanche lilies to the south, red paintbrush around weathered snags, lots of
lupine and other wildflowers.

At 6.2 miles is a pullout on the north side—another good sunrise location with great views in all directions. Explore the north-facing slope to see
marmots and wildflowers, beautiful in morning light. At 7.7 miles the road
ends at a large parking area. Black-tailed deer (mainly bucks with velvet)
seem to hang out on both sides of the road the last 2 miles. Olympic marmots make their home on the rocky talus slopes in the meadows in this area.

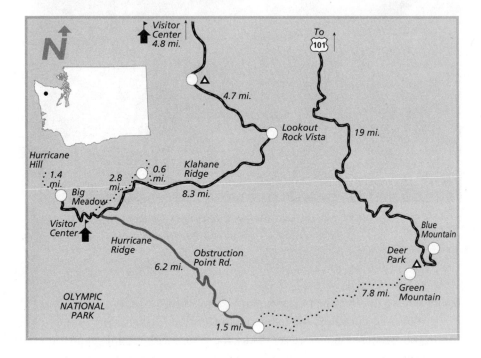

You can see the adults—and a few babies—near the entrance to their burrows, sometimes munching on flowers. For hikers the Badger Valley Trail starts from the parking area and drops steeply to a small tarn with wildflowers. The round trip in and climb out is less than 3 miles.

The Hurricane Ridge Visitor Center provides information and park naturalist guided walks. A picnic area with scenic views and rest rooms is located to the west along Hurricane Hill Road. Just across the road from the visitor center is Big Meadow, with easy trails that take you to scenic vistas, beautiful wildflower meadows, and more deer. Signs at intersections show the way; the paved meadow trails are wheelchair-accessible with assistance. The Mount Angeles Trail from Big Meadow is for more hardy souls. The first leg of the hike is 2.8 miles (400-foot elevation gain) to Switchback Trail. See wildflowers, mountain

A black-tailed doe nurses twin fawns near a Big Meadow trail.

vistas, deer, and sometimes a black bear in the lush valleys below.

In the evening, hike up Hurricane Hill Lookout Trail for a glorious sunset. If you travel all the way to the end (2.8 miles round-trip, 750-foot elevation gain), take a flashlight for the trip back. Grand vistas and wildflowers keep you company along the way—all bathed in warm evening light. Wheelchair accessible first 0.5 mile.

Next best: If your Hurricane Ridge trip extends over a Fourth of July weekend, take time to enjoy other nature-oriented activities around Port Angeles.

Olympic National Park's Deer Park (5,200-foot elevation) offers wildflowers, wildlife, mountain views, gorgeous sunsets, and a campground. Deer Park Road (16 miles, first half paved) begins at milepost 253 on US 101, east of Port Angeles. Enjoy several short but good wildflower hikes here. Take the 2-mile Green Mountain Trail to wildflowers and views, or follow the Slab Camp Trail 1 mile along a ridge to enjoy meadows, flower-decorated rock outcrops, and deer. You can also take a short walk to the top of Blue Mountain, then wander paths to see wildflowers, deer, vistas, and sunsets.

Drive 9 miles west from Port Angeles on US 101 to the Elwha River entrance to Olympic National Park, then up the lovely Elwha River. Check the guidebooks for hikes and backpacks starting from this area, or hike 2.5 miles to Olympic Hot Springs.

Olympic Raft and Kayak, near the Elwha River bridge on US 101, offers leisurely sea kayak trips to view wildlife and scenics on the Strait of Juan de Fuca. On one trip we saw harbor seals, bald eagles, rafts of seabirds, and a large number of cormorants nesting on a cave wall. Watch for sea lions and otters. Two- and three-hour trips on Lake Crescent (amazingly clear water, beautiful mountains) and Lake Aldwell (up-close views of bald eagles, osprey, and waterfowl) are also available. Contact Olympic Raft and Kayak at (888) 452–1443; www.northolympic.com/olympicraft.

Drive another 8 miles west on US 101 to the Storm King Ranger Station parking lot at Lake Crescent and hike to majestic, 90-foot Marymere Falls (1.8-mile round-trip). For another lovely falls, drive 10 miles farther west to Olympic National Park's Sol Duc River entrance. Sol Duc Falls (1.6-mile round-trip hike) and Sol Duc Hot Springs Resort are located 12 miles up the road from the entrance.

Food and lodging: Port Angeles offers all services. Heart of the Hills Campground is just inside the Hurricane Ridge park entrance.

For more information:
Olympic National Park Visitor Center
(360) 565–3130; www.nps.gov/olym/
Port Angeles day trips
www.cityofpa.com/daytrips/index.html

28

July

Ebb Tide Treasures

Visit the Low Tide Fest, learn about all the plants and animals you can see when very low tides occur, then visit some other prime tidepooling locations.

Site: Port Townsend Marine Science Center at Fort Worden State Park.

Recommended time: The annual Low Tide Fest is held in mid-July, usually the second weekend of the month. In general, tidepooling is excellent at minus tides of -1.0, but the very best tidepooling occurs with a minus tide of –2.0 or lower. These usually occur in June or July, sometimes in April and May. If you can find a weekend anytime with a −1.5 tide or lower, go!

Minimum time commitment: Half a day or a day, plus driving time. If you plan to spend the weekend on the Olympic Peninsula, see chapter 27.

What to bring: Nonslip, sturdy shoes or boots and walking stick for exploring slippery rocks and beaches; field guide or waterproof card to identify sea life; binoculars for bird-watching; extra set of dry clothes and shoes; camera with close-up lens.

Directions: Port Townsend is on the northeastern tip of the Olympic Peninsula at the end of SR 20. You can also take the Keystone Ferry from Whidbey Island. Fort Worden State Park is at the west end of town.

The background: The ebb and flood of the tides can bring all kinds of pleasures. One of those is tidepooling at low tide, when salt water recedes from the beach and rocks and leaves in its wake tiny pools of sea life. There are always surprises—sea urchins, anemones, sea stars, hermit crabs, fish, and mussels. If you enjoy visiting coastal areas, keep a tide book on hand at home

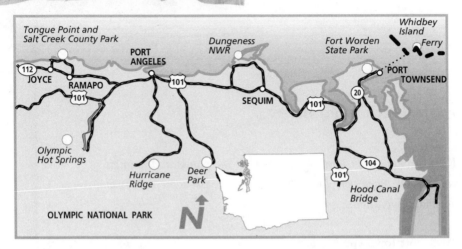

Tongue Point and Salt Creek County Park · PORT ANGELES · 112 · JOYCE · RAMAPO · 101 · 101 · Dungeness NWR · 101 · SEQUIM · Fort Worden State Park · Whidbey Island · Ferry · PORT TOWNSEND · 20 · Olympic Hot Springs · Hurricane Ridge · Deer Park · 101 · 104 · Hood Canal Bridge · OLYMPIC NATIONAL PARK · N

to schedule your trips. Once in a while, look up. You may find sea and shore-birds or marine mammals.

The fun: Very low, or minus, tides occur at different times every year, but Port Townsend's annual Low Tide Fest is scheduled on a mid-July weekend. All-day activities include beach walks, exhibits, presentations, touch tanks, kids' crafts and games, fish printing, seafood, sand creations, music, and more. During the lowest tide, beach naturalists are stationed at Port Townsend beaches to answer questions.

Next best: Other prime tidepooling locations on the Olympic Peninsula include Port Angeles, Clallam Bay, Cape Alava, and Rialto Beach. On Whidbey Island visit Deception Pass State Park and tidepools at Rosario Beach. Seattle offers "urban tidepools" and tanks at the Seattle Aquarium and the Pacific Science Center.

■ *Port Angeles:* The Arthur D. Feiro Marine Laboratory (located on City Pier) has nearly a hundred local marine species in its tanks to see and touch (call 360–452–9277, ext. 26, or 360–417–6254). At July's lowest minus tide, knowledgeable lab naturalists are available at Tongue Point, Salt Creek County Park, west of Port Angeles. The park is on the Strait of Juan de Fuca and features campsites, a picnic area, a marine life preserve, and hiking trails.

- *Clallam Bay:* Slip Point, home of an automated lighthouse and horn, also has excellent tidepools. Access is from the county day-use park right in town, below the lighthouse property.

- *Cape Alava:* To reach the tidepools drive about 2 miles west of Sekiu, turn south on the Hoko-Ozette Road, and drive 21 miles to Lake Ozette. Hike the 3-mile boardwalk trail to Cape Alava, then walk north on the rocky beach. In about 2 miles are "the best" tidepools, but you'll see plenty along the way—often sea otters, too.

Giant green anemones are found in tidepools and surge channels. Their brilliance comes from algae growing in their flesh.

- *Rialto Beach:* Farther south on US 101 (just north of Forks) is the road to Rialto Beach. Drive 13 miles west to the parking area, keeping right at the fork to LaPush. During low tide take the 1.5-mile walk to Hole-in-the-Wall to see tidepools with one of the coast's best variety of sea stars. Watch the tide changes, or you may get wet or stranded.

- *Poulsbo:* The Poulsbo Marine Science Center, on the shore of Liberty Bay, features marine plant and animal exhibits including a gray whale skeleton. Call (360) 779–5549, or visit www.poulsbomsc.org/.

Food and lodging: Port Townsend offers all services; camping is available at Fort Worden State Park (reservations advised).

For more information:
Low Tide Fest
www.olympus.net/edu/ptmsc/events.html#LowTideFest
Port Townsend Marine Science Center
(360) 385–5582; www.olympus.net/edu/ptmsc/

29

Ancient Ice

Glaciers creep, grow, shrink, make streams roar, and carve and move rock. Study glaciers this weekend, appreciate their power and beauty, and enjoy the scenery!

Site: Heather Meadows, Mount Baker–Snoqualmie National Forest.

Recommended time: July, August, and September; mid-July is best for wildflowers.

Minimum time commitment: At least a full day.

What to bring: Binoculars, camera, lunch, water, hiking boots, Northwest Forest Pass.

Directions: From I-5, take SR 542 east to the Glacier Public Service Center at milepost 34. Listed on the National Register of Historic Places, it is jointly operated by the USDA Forest Service and National Park Service and has rest rooms, maps, and information. Buy a pass here and then proceed to Heather Meadows, milepost 53.

The background: Washington is geologically dynamic and geographically diverse, with volcanoes, high mountains, swift streams, snow, ocean beaches, and glaciers—great hunks of ever-changing ice.

The rugged, geologically complex Cascade Range cuts our state in half. South of Mount Rainier, this mountain range is a volcanic tableland, studded with volcanic cones (e.g., Mount Adams and Mount St. Helens) that are minor players in the glacier contest. The North Cascades, however, are a mass of granite that includes the most extensive valley glaciers in the forty-eight

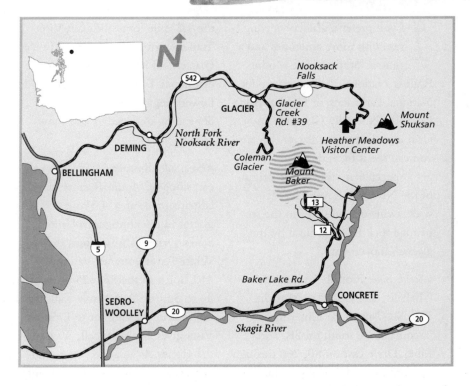

contiguous states. Glacier Peak is a small volcano with over one dozen glaciers; but Mount Baker, the northernmost volcano in the United States Cascade Range, is the king. Due to heavy snowfall Mount Baker is heavily glaciated—its glaciers cover an area of more than 40 square miles, even more than Mount Rainier's 35 square miles.

The fun: Start at the Glacier Public Service Center, and take an immediate side trip to see dramatic, close-up views of glaciers on the northwest slopes of Mount Baker. Turn south 1 mile past the center and drive about 10 miles to the end of Glacier Creek Road #39 to see, among others, Coleman Glacier, the only advancing glacier in the contiguous United States.

Back on SR 542 drive 15 miles farther to the Heather Meadows area at 4,742 feet. See magnificent close-up views of glacier-draped, 9,127-foot

Mount Rainier Glaciers

*I*f you prefer a glacier-viewing site with more amenities and a central location, visit Mount Rainier National Park (entrance fee, National Parks Pass, or Golden Eagle Passport). Nisqually Glacier is an ideal introduction to glaciers because you can see it from the road and also get a spectacular view of the origin of the Nisqually River. Here it is wide, swift, and milky from the suspended rock finely ground by the glacier's movement.

■*South Side:* From I–5 south of Chehalis, take US 12 to Morton, then SR 7 north to Elbe (from Tacoma, drive south on SR 7 to Elbe). Drive east on SR 706 through Ashford to the Nisqually entrance, Longmire, and Paradise. As you make the scenic drive to Paradise, you will cross a large bridge over Kautz Creek to a parking lot with viewpoint and picnic area. Look upstream—that's the Nisqually Glacier up there. You can see evidence of the long-ago Kautz Creek flood—boulder fields and many large, dead, standing trees.

Continue up to the visitor center at Paradise and learn about other mountain phenomena from their many exhibits. Then take a walk on the 1.2-mile loop Nisqually Vista Trail to a great view of the Nisqually Glacier and Mount Rainier's southern slopes. For an added bonus, wildflowers begin popping out in July, depending on weather and snow cover.

■*East Side:* Emmons Glacier, on the east slope of Mount Rainier, has the largest surface area, 4.3 miles, of any glacier in the contiguous United States. Drive 11 miles from the White River entrance station (SR 410, north of the SR 123 junction) up to Sunrise. A 0.2-mile walk from the Sunrise parking lot to Emmons Vista gives you an excellent view of the glacier. As an added treat wildflowers and marmots are abundant on the Berkeley Park Trail in mid-July.

For a closer look follow the Glacier Basin Trail (3-mile round trip) from White River Campground to a viewpoint overlooking Emmons Glacier. Hike 1 mile, then take the 0.5-mile Emmons Moraine Trail to the viewpoint. Look for mountain goats and climbers on the surrounding slopes.

■*North Side:* Carbon Glacier, on the north side of Mount Rainier, is another record holder. It has the greatest measured thickness (700 feet) and the greatest total volume (0.2 cubic mile) of any glacier in the contiguous United States.

Drive south from Buckley on SR 165, turning left on Fairfax Forest Reserve Road before you enter the park. The graveled Carbon River Road is rough; trailers may have difficulty. Call ahead because it is prone to flooding.

The Carbon Glacier Trail (7-mile round-trip, 1,200-foot elevation gain) gives you a close-up look at the glacier. The trailhead is located at Ipsut Creek Campground, 5 miles inside the Carbon River entrance. The first 3 miles of the forested trail parallel the Carbon River. After the Seattle Park Trail junction, cross the river on a suspension bridge below the snout of the Carbon Glacier (beware of falling rocks), right alongside this hunk of ice. This is your destination; however, another 2 miles takes you to Moraine Park, Mount Rainier views, and colorful wildflowers.

For more information:
Mount Rainier National Park (360) 569–2211;
www.nps.gov/mora/Individual Visitor Centers
(see Appendices)

From the Austin Pass parking lot at road end, trails take hikers to excellent views of both Mount Baker and Mount Shuksan glaciers.

Mount Shuksan and 10,778-foot Mount Baker. Even from your vehicle, the scenery is impressive; it's a 360-degree, "up close and personal" view of these spectacular mountains. The roads open later than anywhere else in the mountains most years; check road conditions before you go. There is no food or fuel here, so plan ahead.

You can snap a gorgeous photo of Mount Shuksan right from your car (the best viewpoint is Picture Lake). Or climb to Artist's Point for a view of Mount Baker's northeast side. The extensive trail system in the Heather Meadows area will lead you to more glacier views, wildflowers, marmots, pikas, and mountain goats. Trails into the Chain Lakes, to the top of Table Mountain, along Ptarmigan Ridge, and to Lake Ann are magnificent alpine experiences. There are naturalist programs at the Heather Meadows Visitor Center, open all summer.

Next best: Mount Baker's southern glaciers. If you want to get really close to a glacier, wait until late July for snow-free trails, and hike to Morovitz Meadow (5 miles round-trip, 1300 feet elevation gain) on Mount Baker's south side. The Mount Baker National Recreation Area trailhead is 12 miles north of SR 20 via the Baker Lake Highway (15 miles east of Sedro-Woolley), FR 12 and FR 13. Park Butte Trail #603 climbs through Schriebers Meadow, boulders and gravel, and forested switchbacks to the lower meadow, then through heather fields to Upper Morovitz Meadow—pleasant campsites, wildflower gardens, streams, and marmots. To get close to Easton Glacier, wander up Railroad Grade and look down the wall of gravel and boulders (unstable) to the wasteland below the ice. (See *101 Hikes in the North Cascades* for hike details.)

Food and lodging: Glacier, 19 miles away, has several B&B's and inns; Maple has a few more, as does Concrete on the south side of Mount Baker.

For more information:
Mount Baker–Snoqualmie National Forest
Mount Baker Ranger District
(360) 856–5700
USGS/Cascades Volcano Observatory (glaciers and glaciation)
Mount Baker
vulcon.wr.usgs.gov/volcanoes/Baker/
Mount Rainier
vulcon.wr.usgs.gov/volcanoes/Rainier/

30

July

Starry, Starry Night

If you are looking for a fun and relaxing chance to camp, stargaze, and mix with lots of enthusiastic and knowledgeable amateur astronomers, the Table Mountain Star Party is the place to be.

Site: Table Mountain (elevation 6,357 feet), about 20 miles north of Ellensburg.

Recommended time: This annual event is held between mid-July and mid-August—usually at the first new moon so that moonlight doesn't interfere with telescope viewing.

Minimum time commitment: The Table Mountain Star Party is held on Thursday, Friday, and Saturday nights. Many people come on the weekend; others, as early as Wednesday.

What to bring: Lawn chairs for daytime lounging, food, camping equipment, and all the water you'll need for the weekend—there is none available here. Bring binoculars and red-light flashlights if you have them, but no special equipment is needed. Everything you'll need is there and freely shared.

Registration fee ($25 in 2001) includes camping fee for the whole weekend and admission to all presentations and activities. Saturday-night, chuckwagon dinners are about $10.

Directions: From I-90 at Ellensburg, take exit 106 and follow the signs (directions are in the registration packet and on the Web site).

The background: The Table Mountain Star Party is an annual gathering of people interested in astronomy. Most people attending are amateur

This specialized astrophotography telescope is one of hundreds set up in the meadow for Table Mountain Star Party viewing.

astronomers who enjoy the great viewing, which the mountain provides without interference from city lights. However, anyone with an interest or curiosity is welcome to register and enjoy the experience.

The fun: It is truly fun as well as educational—a family event. Everyone is interested in astronomy and the great outdoors, and the atmosphere is upbeat and friendly. You don't need to be a dedicated astronomer to enjoy yourself and to learn something. On the other hand, if your interest is piqued, this is an ideal event to learn about all the different telescopes and activities from participants and vendors alike. It's also a great time to introduce children to another dimension of the world in which they live.

If you decide to camp—and most people do—you may set up on the perimeter of the main telescope meadow (blackout area) or back in the trees along the road (limited light allowed). Participants camp in everything from huge motor homes to small backpacking tents.

Many of the amateur astronomers set up their telescopes around the big meadow, while others keep them near their vehicles. There are usually more than 600 scopes including many large ones (some more than 40 inches). A

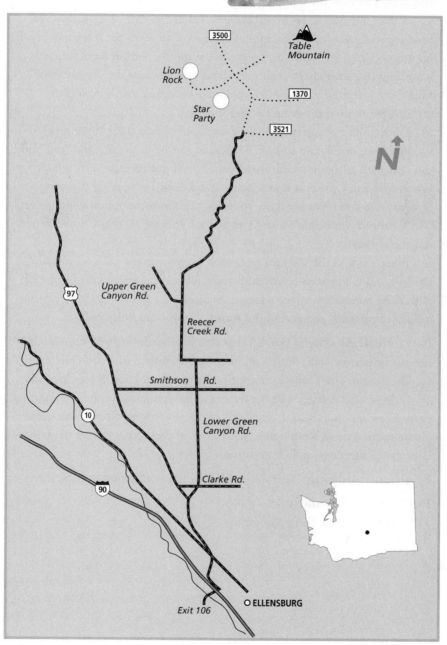

Table Mountain

3500

Lion Rock

Star Party

1370

3521

N

Upper Green Canyon Rd.

97

Reecer Creek Rd.

Smithson Rd.

10

Lower Green Canyon Rd.

Clarke Rd.

90

Exit 106

O ELLENSBURG

special area is provided for astrophotography. Night and day you can roam the area and talk with people about different types of scopes, tracking devices, and photographic equipment. Everyone is willing to answer your questions and show you how the equipment works.

If the Table Mountain Star Party is scheduled in early August, you will have a special treat—the Perseid meteor shower. In 1999 the star party began on August 12, so we were able to watch the meteor shower (and the satellites) from our lawn chairs with our naked eyes. Because the sky north of Ellensburg is relatively dark and unpolluted, we could see thirty to forty meteors per hour at the height of the shower.

During the day participants sleep late (quiet hours until 10:00 A.M.), socialize, hike or bike up to Lion's Rock, or just lie in the sun and read. You can chat with astronomy club members, learn about Project Astro, which brings astronomy projects into schools, watch a mirror-making demonstration, or walk down Vendor Row to check out the astronomical goodies for sale. A Saturday-morning Swap Meet and a Telescope Makers Contest round out the activities.

Participants in the young astronomer program attend talks on meteors, sundials, and falling stars (many adults also feel more comfortable beginning with these more-elementary sessions). Student activities also include a nature walk, face painting, games, and the annual "1,000-yard Solar Walk."

Next Best: Astronomy Day is celebrated in May throughout the state by various astronomy clubs. This is an international public education and entertainment event. The Camp Delaney Star Party at Sun Lakes State Park near Dry Falls is held in August or September as an alternative to the Oregon Star Party. There are more than twenty astronomical societies, observatories, and planetariums around Washington State. Most of these have regular star parties, educational meetings, and other astronomy events.

Food and lodging: Ellensburg offers all services; camping at the site.

For more information:
Table Mountain Star Party Association
www.tmspa.com

31

August

Living on the Seas of the World

Take an offshore boat trip from Westport to see pelagic and coastal seabirds, including alcids, brown pelicans, shorebirds, and marine mammals.

Site: Pacific Ocean, 42 miles offshore from Westport.

Recommended time: August.

Minimum time commitment: Trips last an entire day; add travel time or other activities in the area and make it a weekend.

What to bring: A good pair of binoculars (and plastic bags to protect them from salt water); sack lunch; sun hat; sunscreen; sunglasses; warm clothing, rain gear, and gloves for cold, windy, or wet conditions out on the water.

Directions: From I–5 in Olympia, take exit 104 and drive 48 miles west on SR 8 and US 12 to Aberdeen. Turn left (south) on US 101 over the bridge, then right (west) on SR 105. Follow the signs 23 miles to Westport, on the southern "hook" of Grays Harbor.

The background: Pelagic birds are very different from the many species of land birds we are more accustomed to seeing. They live their entire lives over, around, and on the seas of the world, flying great distances to find food and to nest. It might seem to us to be a hostile environment, with strong seas, high winds, ferocious storms, and few rest stops over thousands of miles of ocean water, but these birds are well built to survive. It is also a very rich environment, with a huge assortment of food—including scraps and garbage from fishing boats and other ships. Some pluck most of their food off the sur-

Charter boats attract a variety of birds that can be only seen offshore.

face; some dive in the water and swim using outstretched wings. Most stop only briefly on land to nest and raise their young, and then off they go again.

Unlike most land birds, many seabirds have a sense of smell, which may help them find food or, returning with food for their young, the correct burrow or nest in the dark. Some tour boat operators will chum with fish oil or scraps, and birds flock to the area like coyotes sensing an overflowing garbage can.

Albatrosses, storm petrels, and petrels are called "tubenoses" because their nostrils are well-protected, hard tubes in the tops of their bills.

Most seabirds nest in colonies on offshore islands, sometimes millions of them in one place. Many nest for life; most have very long life spans. Albatrosses live more than 40 years, for example; even the tiny storm petrels may live twenty years or more.

The fun: Westport Seabirds Offshore Trips offers pelagic trips to Grays Canyon, 42 land-miles out to the edge of the continental shelf, every weekend in August, with fewer trips in September and October. They leave Westport around 6:00 A.M. and return before 4:00 P.M. (2001 cost: $80). These trips are very popular, so reserve early.

Species that are regularly seen in large numbers on these offshore trips

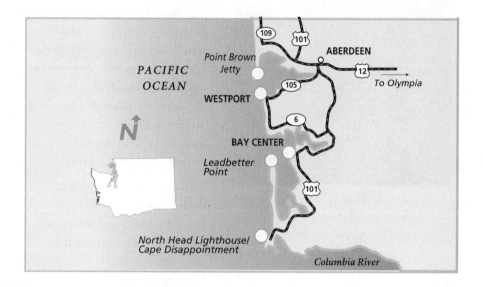

include black-footed albatrosses and fork-tailed storm petrels. According to Westport Seabirds, small numbers of Leach's storm petrel and long-tailed jaeger are highly likely in August. You will see northern fulmar (occasionally thousands) and smaller numbers of pink-footed shearwaters. Watch for albatross and fulmar concentrations at fishing vessels—also sooty shearwaters at foraging opportunities nearer to shore.

Sooty shearwaters are one of the most abundant seabirds on the Pacific Ocean. You may be lucky enough to observe them on their semiannual flights between winter feeding areas in the North Pacific and nesting areas in the Southern Hemisphere. In August and September thousands may be seen in coastal harbors and offshore.

Look for common murre, pigeon guillemot, marbled murrelet, rhinoceros auklet, Cassin's auklet, and the tufted puffin. Hundreds of brown pelicans are seen in the nearshore area and Grays Harbor in summer and fall. In early August Heermann's gulls occur in huge numbers near shore, along with

Albatrosses are normally surface feeders, but have been known to submerge completely in pursuit of a sinking morsel.

glaucous-winged, western, and California gulls. Arctic terns and Sabine's gulls are farther offshore. Rare seabirds are also seen; experts on board are eager to point them out.

Huge schools of gray Grampus (Risso's) dolphins sometimes hang out over Grays Canyon. As many as 75 northern right-whale dolphins, 120 Pacific white-sided dolphins, and 10 gray whales have also been seen, along with northern fur seals and harbor porpoises.

Next best: If you prefer to explore land-based seabird-watching sites along the coast, start with Westport's south jetty observation towers. Other good locations for seabirds (and also shorebirds that migrate down the coast in August and September) are:

■ *Bay Center on Willapa Bay:* Good viewing from the east end of the bay. From late July to mid-August one observer saw "hordes" of immature western sandpipers, several thousand short-billed dowitchers, a flock of 300 whimbrels, almost 200 sanderlings in the bay, and large numbers of black-bellied and semipalmated plovers.

■ *Leadbetter Point at the north end of Long Beach Peninsula:* Leadbetter Point State Park is north of Oysterville on the east side of the peninsula. From the parking lot you can walk 2.5 miles north up Willapa Bay's west side. When the tide is coming in, you may see black-bellied plovers, California and glaucous-winged gulls, quite a few Caspian terns and brown pelicans, and huge flocks of sanderlings, many still in breeding colors. Red knots and golden plovers also stop here during migration.

Farther south on the bay, expect to see semipalmated plovers, a few dowitchers and black-bellied plovers, and the usual huge numbers of western sandpipers in Willapa Bay's west beach salt marshes.

On Leadbetter Point's ocean side, look for big flocks of sooty shearwaters off Long Beach, big flocks of common murres offshore, and sanderlings and big flocks of western sandpipers on Leadbetter Point.

Mike Patterson's *Watching Seabirds from Land* Web site has bird checklists for three more excellent locations: Point Brown Jetty (Ocean Shores), North Head Lighthouse (Ilwaco) and Cape Disappointment, and the North Jetty of the Columbia River (Ilwaco).

Food and lodging: Westport offers all services (reservations advised on weekends). The closest campground is south of Westport at Twin Harbors State Park (reservations, 800–452–5687).

For more information:

Westport Seabirds

(360) 268–5222; hometown.aol.com/trwahl/

Watching Seabirds from Land

home.pacifier.com/~mpatters/seabird/seabird.html

32

Secret in the South Cascades

*Bird Creek Meadows has one of the most splendid displays of
wildflowers in Washington. You will find them everywhere—in
rocky gardens, in boggy wetlands near the streams, and near cascad-
ing waterfalls.*

Site: Bird Creek Meadows, northeast of Trout Lake on the Yakama Indian
Reservation, Mount Adams Recreation Area.

Recommended time: Above 6,000 feet, wildflower blooming peaks in
mid-August (later if there's heavy snow pack); color is good from mid-July
through August.

Minimum time commitment: A half day plus travel time; a weekend
is better.

What to bring: Wildflower field guide, camera, hiking boots, sunscreen,
mosquito repellent, water, food, camping gear, trail fee, map (from the ranger
station or on site).

Directions: From White Salmon on the Columbia Gorge, drive 25 miles
north on SR 141 to an intersection 1.2 miles north of Trout Lake (or start at
Randle on US 12 and drive 56 miles south on FR 23). Angle northeast on
Mount Adams Recreation Area Road and follow the map 13.5 miles to
Mirror Lake. Turn left just past the lake to Bird Lake Campground (nineteen
primitive forested sites). The last 5 miles are rough—high clearance recommended.

A large day-hike parking area is located 1.1 miles straight past Mirror
Lake. The Helispot Overlook is 0.9 mile farther, and Bench Lake (thirty-three

Trekkers can take llamas on several scenic trails in the Bird Creek Meadows area.

campsites) is another 0.7 mile. Campground reservations are not accepted, but campsites are almost always available.

The background: The 1855 treaty describing the Yakama Indian Reservation was lost and not found again until 1930. By this time the boundaries were many miles east of the Cascade Crest. Over the years 100,000 acres of the original claim passed into private ownership. In 1972 the 21,000 remaining acres around Mount Adams, including the summit, were returned to the Yakama Nation by U.S. Presidential Executive Order. The Yakama Nation collects small fees for day hiking and camping.

The fun: Paintbrush, monkeyflower, penstemon, pearly everlasting, yarrow, larkspur, lupine, and a multitude of other blooms cover the meadows with a profusion of color. The wildflower loops (2.5 to 5.75 miles) can be done easily in a day, but camping overnight allows for more leisurely meandering through the meadows.

Bird Creek Meadows can be approached from three trailheads. From Bird Lake Campground, follow the lake to the administrative area to pay your fees and get a map. Hike up forested trail #100 to beautiful Crooked Creek Falls, then meander through flower-strewn meadows and across gentle brooks

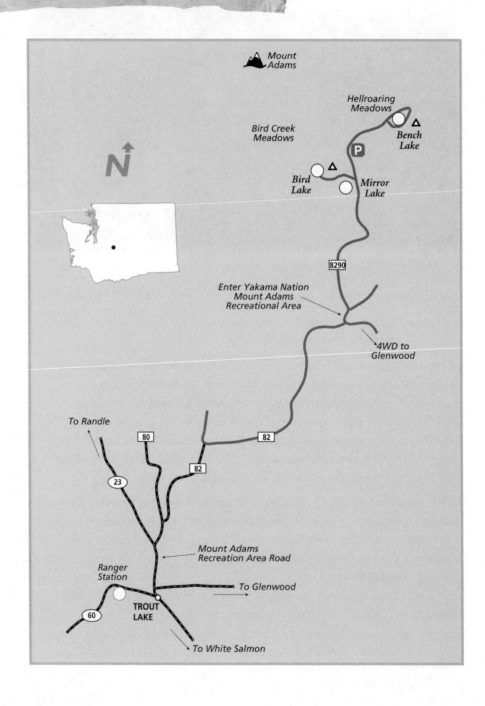

to trail #9 at 1.5 miles. Turn right, walk 0.75 mile to Bird Creek Meadows and wander among the brilliant wildflowers and rock gardens. Trail of Flowers (#106) makes a 1-mile loop around these meadows.

Take trail #67 0.5 mile to the ridge and magnificent views of Mount Adams. It's a peaceful place; the quiet is interrupted only by the occasional rumbling of avalanches and the "thunk" of pinecones as squirrels drop them to the ground. Eat your picnic lunch on Bird Creek Meadows tables or at the viewpoint.

To return via another trailhead, hike down to trail #9 and find Bluff Lake Trail (#105) near the picnic tables. This trail descends 1.5 miles past a small but lovely waterfall and Bluff Lake and ends at the campground near site 17.

For the easiest access to the Trail of Flowers loop, start at the day hike parking area and hike 0.7 mile up trail #9. Llamas and other pack animals are also permitted on this trail and can be kept at Mirror Lake. What a great way to get into the backcountry without shouldering a heavy pack.

Look for marmots, pikas, gray-crowned rosy finches, and humming-birds—they all use wildflowers as a food source. Watch for butterflies on the southeast-facing wildflower slopes—orange and black fritillaries and check-erspots, black with squares of red or yellow.

For an easier hike, drive to the Helispot Overlook and take the 0.8-mile forest trail to Hellroaring Meadows. Cross the creek, wander the meadow, search for little Heart Lake, and enjoy the wildflowers. Beautiful views of Mount Adams from the overlook and the meadow.

Food and lodging: Services in Trout Lake and nearby Glenwood, 14 miles east.

For more information:

Mount Adams Ranger Station, Trout Lake (road and wildflower conditions)
(509) 395–3400
Bureau of Indian Affairs, Toppenish
(509) 865–2255

Mount Rainier

*I*f you prefer an August wildflower site with more amenities
and a central location, visit
Mount Rainier's Paradise area
(entrance fee, National Parks Pass, or
Golden Eagle Passport). Park information describes it perfectly: "The
lush subalpine meadows of Mount
Rainier host a display of flowers
unequaled anywhere. Some flowers
bloom at the edge of the melting
snow pack in late June, while others
wait to bloom in August."

A number of paved trails traverse
the wildflower meadows of Paradise
Park; most start near the Henry M.
Jackson Memorial Visitor Center
(maps available here). You can wander
through the wildflowers and streams
of the lower meadows or hike the
Alta Vista Flower Trails (1- to 3-mile
round trip). The easy 1.2-mile
Nisqually Vista Trail has brilliant displays of flowers plus mountain and
glacier views. Naturalist-led walks are
held every morning; check at the
visitor center for times.

For the path less traveled, drive
0.7 mile east from the end of the
Paradise parking lot to 4th Crossing
Trail. This trail takes you 0.2 mile up
a pretty tumbling creek to intersect
with the Skyline Trail. Turn east

(right); meander across the meadows,
up the long switchback, and over the
ridge for more wildflower meadows.
You can retrace your steps or continue on past Sluiskin Falls and return
via the Golden Gate Trail down
through Edith Basin.

Reflection Lake is several miles
east of Paradise. Mount Rainier's
reflection in the lake is awesome at
sunrise, and the wildflowers around
the lake are lovely.

The Bench and Snow Lakes Trail
is 1.5 miles farther east. Expect to see
a variety of wildflowers and an abundance of bear grass on this 2.5-mile
round-trip hike, along with a silver
forest of trees from a past fire. Good
views of Mount Rainier.

Hoary marmots and ground
squirrels are easy to see in the
Paradise wildflower meadows, and
deer are fairly common along the
roads and in the meadows. We have
also seen red foxes in the evening
along the road to Paradise and black
bears in the early morning near
Reflection Lake.

Directions: From I–5 south of
Chehalis, take US 12 to Morton,
then SR 7 north to Elbe (from
Tacoma drive south on SR 7 to
Elbe). Drive east on SR 706 through

Ashford to the Nisqually entrance, Longmire, and Paradise.

Food and lodging: Inside the park, food and lodging are available at Longmire and Paradise. Camping is at Cougar Rock, Sunshine Point, or Ohanapecosh campgrounds. Outside the park, Ashford offers all services.

For more information:
Mount Rainier National Park
(360) 569–2211;
www.nps.gov/mora/
Individual Visitor Centers (see Appendices)

The majestic scenery at Reflection Lake, along the Stevens Canyon Road in Mount Rainier National Park, makes it a popular lunch stop.

33

August

Fascinating Felines and Other Predators

See the elusive lynx and cougar, plus bobcats, black bears, wolves, coyotes, foxes, and grizzlies, up close and in natural settings.

Site: Northwest Trek Wildlife Park.

Recommended time: Tooth and Talon Weekend is held early to mid-August.

Minimum time commitment: Half a day plus traveling time.

What to bring: Walking shoes, camera, entrance fee.

Directions: From Puyallup drive 3.5 miles south on SR 512, exit at SR 161 (Eatonville), turn left, and drive 17 miles to Northwest Trek (left side). From Tacoma travel east on SR 512, exit at SR 161, and turn right.

The background: Northwest Trek Wildlife Park started with Dr. David and Connie Hellyers' vision and their first purchase of land in 1937. Since the park's opening in 1975, it has developed into an internationally recognized wildlife sanctuary and resource for conservation education. In the free-roaming area the beauty of the terrain and the wildlife that moves freely within its boundaries have been a delight to more than two million visitors. Northwest Trek is now part of Metro Parks Tacoma, but the Hellyers still live in the free-roaming area and are active supporters of the park.

The fun: Lynx, cougars, and bobcats are difficult to see in the wild, but there is a fun solution. The Tooth and Talon Weekend offers an opportunity to see and learn about these reclusive felines and other predators including bears, wolves, and raptors. Take part in demonstrations, lectures, crafts, and videos.

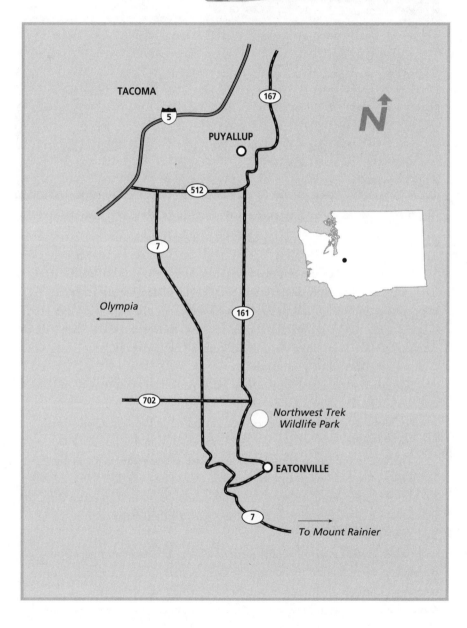

Because bobcats are so difficult to observe in the wild, they are a treat to see at Northwest Trek.

Lynx live only in the remote forested regions of northeast Washington. They are the most aggressive toward people, but since they are extremely rare, elusive, and weigh less than twenty-five pounds, they are not a threat. Their big feet act as snowshoes and carry the cats over the snow with ease to catch snowshoe hares, their main food supply. The lynx population rises and falls with the snowshoe population.

Bobcats are solitary, shy, nocturnal hunters that live in a variety of habitats across the state. They are excellent climbers and spend a lot of their time in trees. Bobcats compete with coyotes for the same prey (small mammals, birds, and reptiles) and act as a check on rodent and rabbit populations.

The larger and more common cougars are solitary cats that inhabit mountains, deserts, forests, and even urban areas. They eat deer, elk, and a variety of small mammals, birds, and reptiles. Cougars can leap more than 20 feet from a stationary position; their long tails aid their balance in leaps and high-speed turns.

Other predators also live at Northwest Trek. The wolf and bear compounds are large, with a variety of habitats giving animals a natural place to roam and humans a natural environment in which to view them. Compounds containing the small forest predators can be viewed through the glass from below or from a bridge above.

To see some of the predators' natural prey, tour the 435-acre fenced free-roaming area at Northwest Trek. Hoofed mammals and birds native to western Washington are free to roam the area and choose which habitat suits them. A free one-hour tram carries passengers through the area every half hour to get close-up views of these beautiful animals. Reminder: Wildlife is livelier early in the morning, late in the afternoon, or on overcast days.

Note: Northwest Trek has year-round events to let adults and kids become better acquainted with wildlife. These include Kids and Critters Naturefest in January, Baby Shower & Birthday Bash in mid-July (baby animals); Elk Bugling Tours starting in mid-September; Hoot 'N Howl in late October, and Free Roaming Area Keeper Tours most weekends.

Next best:

■ *Spokane:* Cat Tails Zoological Park is the home of a training center where students learn the profession of zookeeping. North American bobcats, lynx, and pumas, South American jaguars, Asian leopards, African lions, and Indian tigers are on view. The tour guides care for the animals each day, so the animals interact with them naturally—and they have great stories about each animal. Contact Cat Tails at (509) 238–4126; www.cattales.org.

■ *Issaquah:* Cougar Mountain Zoological Park has two exhibits that focus on endangered cats. Six to twelve cougars live in the World of Mountain Lions exhibit; these are wild orphaned young on exhibit for education only. Four to six cheetahs live in the World of Cheetahs; these endangered animals are bred here. Both worlds are naturalistic, with several habitats, open tops, trees, bushes, rock formations, and caves. Contact Cougar Mountain at (425) 391–5508; www.cougarmountainzoo.org/.

■ *Sequim:* Olympic Game Farm (opened to the public in 1972) is where many animals were humanely trained to be stars of television and movies—many of them with Disney Studios. You can see performing grizzly bears on the driving tour; cubs are born here every year. Contact them at (360) 683–4295 or (800) 778–4295; www.olygamefarm.com/.

Food and lodging: Northwest Trek has a cafe; nearby cities offer all services.

For more information:
Northwest Trek Wildlife Park
(360) 832–6117 or (800) 433–8735; www.nwtrek.org/

34

August

A Delectable Feast

*It's huckleberry-picking time—don't miss it. These delicious berries
are produced in abundance in many locations around the state. One
of the best is near Trout Lake, in southeastern Washington.*

Site: Sawtooth Indian Huckleberry Fields, Gifford Pinchot National Forest,
about 40 miles north of the Columbia River.

Recommended time: Late August, but huckleberries usually begin
ripening in mid-August and continue into September. Always call before you
go! Prime berry-picking time changes slightly from year to year, depending
on weather.

Minimum time commitment: At least half a day plus travel time.

What to bring: Buckets for gathering, containers with lids for transport-
ing, lunch (something that goes well with huckleberries), water, Northwest
Forest Pass.

Directions: From Vancouver travel about 65 miles east along the Columbia
River on SR 14. Turn north on SR 141 before White Salmon, drive 21 miles
to Trout Lake (last gas station), then west on SR 141, which turns into FR
60. There are rest rooms at the intersection of FR 60 and FR 24. Turn north
on FR 24, a good gravel road, and get ready for great views of Mount Adams
starting at 9 miles. The well-marked Sawtooth Berry Fields extend from 10.5
to 13 miles on the west side of the road.

The background: Huckleberries, along with other edible berries, were a
staple in Native American diets. The berries were eaten fresh, of course, and
also cooked and dried in cakes. They were also smoke-dried and cooked with

The black and Cascade huckleberries are the most delectable. The red huckleberry (red, sour) and evergreen huckleberry (very dark fruit) are smaller and not as sweet.

salmon roe. Small wonder that today we still cherish the juicy berries, eat them fresh from the bushes, and take them home to make pies and jams.

Native huckleberries and blueberries are all in the same plant family and all are edible. There are several species of huckleberries, but the black huckleberry is the most abundant and, some claim, the most delectable. The berries are very large—picture the size of the most expensive domestic blueberries at the supermarket. The blue-leaved or Cascade huckleberry is also delicious and is often abundant in subalpine meadows. It looks like a dwarf blueberry, dark blue berries with a "frosty" look. Other huckleberries are smaller and not as sweet.

Huckleberries are a serendipitous blessing from wildfires—turns out the shrubs really thrive in old burn sites that are only sparsely regenerated. Native Americans used controlled burning to encourage huckleberries to grow.

Some of the more remote berry areas may also be favored by black bears. If you see a bear, stay quiet, keep your distance, briefly enjoy the sight, then calmly "yield the berry right-of-way" and find another place to pick. Bears, after all, eat the berries to survive.

The fun: This site is a traditional berry gathering area and is commemorated

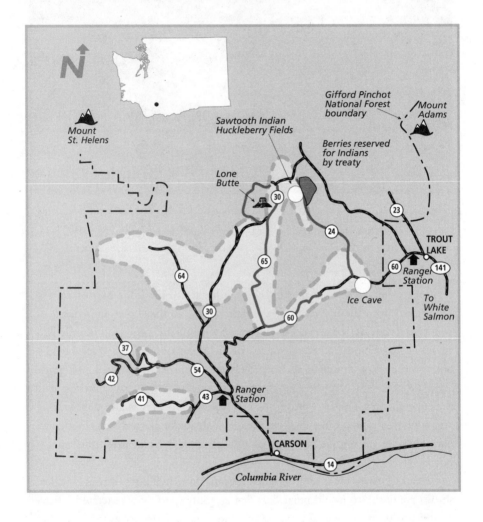

N

Mount
St. Helens

Sawtooth Indian
Huckleberry Fields

Gifford Pinchot
National Forest
boundary

Mount
Adams

Berries reserved
for Indians
by treaty

Lone
Butte

30

23

24

TROUT
LAKE

65

60

Ranger
Station

141

64

30

60

Ice Cave

To
White
Salmon

37

42

54

41

43

Ranger
Station

CARSON

14

Columbia River

with a monument and signs telling of the history of the fields. The areas open for public gathering are on the west side of the road; watch for pullouts and a public rest room.

Native Americans have encampments throughout the traditional berry fields (the east side of the road) and sell five-gallon containers of huckleberries. When the word gets out that "the berries are ready," the public fields can be crowded. This area is easily accessible and everyone always seems to be having a good time picking, eating, and enjoying some of the simple pleasures that Nature gives us. The map shows huckleberry picking locations south to the Columbia River.

Next best: The Ice Caves are 6 miles west of Trout Lake and on your route to the berry fields. This 400-foot-long cave was formed by volcanic action and retains ice formations into summertime (best in spring). There are wooden steps into the caves; the icy floor can be slippery (bring warm clothing, boots, head protection, and a dependable flashlight). The Natural Bridges, a lava tube that has partially collapsed leaving two bridges and a small canyon, is about a mile down the road.

As you exit the north end of the Sawtooth Berry Fields, head south on SR 30. Drive 8 miles, then turn right (west) on Lone Butte Road to Lone Butte Wildlife Emphasis Area—a secluded place to explore by foot, bicycle, or horseback—and again pick huckleberries. The area (a mix of buttes, lush meadows, creeks, forests, and logged areas) is gated, and interior roads are closed to motorized vehicles to reduce stress on the wildlife. Go before hunting season.

In the early morning see elk and deer running across the road and up the hills; at dusk see elk in the meadows (we also saw a black bear). Watch for beavers, coyotes, and many bird species. Mosquitoes are tolerable in late August.

Food and lodging: Closest services are in Trout Lake. Gifford Pinchot National Forest has numerous campgrounds plus picnic areas.

For more information:

Mount Adams Ranger District, Trout Lake
(huckleberries, campground, waterfall maps)
(509) 395–3400
Gifford Pinchot National Forest Huckleberry Report
www.fs.fed.us/gpnf/rec_report/index.html

35

August

Hail the Mighty Waters

Water sustains and entertains, soothes and moves, cools and gives us peace. Washington WaterWeeks reminds us how important clean water is and gives everyone a chance to make a difference and have fun, too.

Site: WaterWeeks activities are held in communities bordering Puget Sound, the Strait of Juan de Fuca, and the Pacific Ocean and along the Columbia Gorge, the upper Columbia River, and its tributaries.

Recommended time: Starts on the last Saturday in August or the first Saturday in September and runs through mid-October.

Minimum time commitment: Half a day to six weeks.

What to bring: See each activity.

Directions: Order a *Washington WaterWeeks Adventure Guide* to find out where individual activities are held (see below).

The background: Washington WaterWeeks is "an annual statewide series of events designed to help residents of all ages understand and take action to protect Washington's waters and habitats . . . 'keeping our waters healthy for people and fish.'" WaterWeeks is sponsored by Washington State Departments of Ecology, Natural Resources, Health, Transportation, Fish & Wildlife, and Community Development; Washington State Parks & Recreation Commission; Washington Sea Grant Program; Seattle Public Utilities; U.S. Environmental Protection Agency; Puget Sound Water Quality Action Team; Clean Sound Cooperative; and Olympia Networking Services. Nearly every nonprofit environmental organization in Washington takes part.

According to Washington WaterWeeks, our state's waters provide a rich variety of habitats "for more than 200 kinds of fish, 14 species of marine mammals, 31 species of waterfowl, 57 species of birds, and thousands of species of shellfish, anemones, sea stars, worms, and other invertebrates. Washington's marine shorelines add up to 2,656 miles in length. The shoreline of Puget Sound alone—1,411 miles of it—is enough to stretch halfway across the country." It's an impressive picture of our state—one worth cherishing.

Get out and enjoy some of the WaterWeeks activities over the next six weeks. Have a fun time learning about our water and our salmon. If you're new to this, go on a nature hike or habitat walk, explore tidepools and forests, take a cruise or canoe trip, go to a festival, or attend some lectures. These are all fun and inspiring things to do.

Tours of facilities from salmon and shellfish hatcheries to water treatment plants are available during WaterWeeks.

When you're ready to be a bit more serious, take a water quality tour, participate in a habitat restoration project, or attend some workshops. Volunteer for a cleanup project. They're work, but they're *fun* work.

The fun: Here is a sampling of fun activities usually held during Washington WaterWeeks. The dates and times vary from year to year, so check your *WaterWeeks Adventure Guide.*

- *Water-related festivals:* Dungeness River Festival in Sequim; Pipers Creek Watershed Festival in Seattle; Water Celebration Day in Keyport; OysterFest in Shelton; Commencement Bay Maritime Fest in Tacoma; National Estuaries Day, Puget Sound Kid's Day near Mount Vernon; Olympia Harbor Days, Project Wet Water Festival in Vancouver; Wooden Boat Festival in Port Townsend; Nisqually Watershed Festival in Olympia.

- *Salmon festivals and events:* Return of the Columbia River Salmon Powwow in Richland; salmon tours, plantings, programs, and workshops galore; the Leavenworth, Seattle, and Issaquah salmon festivals featured in chapter 37.

- *Scuba diving events:* Dive the Canadian Shipwreck HMCS *MacKenzie,* Great Northwest Scuba Festival at Hoodsport.

- *Cruises and boat trips:* Yankee *Clipper* Duwamish ecology tours in Seattle, Bellingham Bay evening cruises, *Lady Washington* boat trips out of Aberdeen, Commencement BayKeeper Tours out of Tacoma.

WaterWeeks offers float trips down the Lower Yakima River and Hanford Reach in addition to the many western Washington activities.

- *Canoe and kayak trips:* Snohomish River Estuary trip out of Everett; canoe the Chehalis River from Oakville, Bellevue's Mercer Slough, seabird trip out of Sequim; salmon estuary out of LaConnor; Chuckanut Bay/Island out of Bellingham; Skagit River Estuary exploration out of Conway; Baker Lake kayak/hike from Concrete.

- *Float trips:* Lower Yakima River trip from Benton City, Hanford Reach trip from Richland.

- *Hikes, walks, and nature watching:* Pipers Creek Watershed walk in Seattle, Mercer Slough walk in Bellevue, Annual Lake to Lake Walk in Bellevue, birding trips in Kent and Bellevue.

- *Tours, cleanups and restorations,* educational talks and readings, and much more.

For more information:

Washington WaterWeeks (and to order the *Adventure Guide*) (360) 943–3642 or (800) RECYCLE; www.waterweeks.org/

36

Pelicans in the Potholes

Do some bird-watching along the Columbia Basin corridor in an extensive wetlands area known as the Potholes. Fall migration brings many interesting shorebirds, wading birds, and white pelicans.

Site: Potholes Wildlife Area southwest of Moses Lake.

Recommended time: Labor Day weekend brings the most variety, but birding is good all August and September.

Minimum time commitment: Set aside the entire weekend if you can. Birding will be especially rewarding for people who are willing to sit and wait for the birds. If you like instant results, you may be disappointed. While migration is an annual occurrence, local movements of birds are unpredictable.

What to bring: Binoculars, spotting scope, field guide to birds, WDFW Access Stewardship Decal.

Directions: From I–90 take exit 169 (Hiawatha Road) west of Moses Lake, drive east 2.5 miles, then turn south on D.5 (unmarked) and follow the map 5 miles to the Job Corps Dike in the Potholes Wildlife Area, staying right at each intersection.

The background: The Potholes area is named for the hundreds of bowl-shaped ponds formed in ancient geologic times by great rivers and floods. These lakes and wetlands are a wonderful legacy of that process for both wildlife and wildlife watchers.

Spring shorebird migration is characterized by huge numbers of birds

The black wing tips of pelicans and other white birds may be a defense against wear; feathers containing more pigment are more resistant to wear than white feathers.

moving up the coast in a short time period (see chapter 17). Fall migration, however, is spread over several months, with smaller numbers of birds seen each weekend. Many birds migrate south through the Columbia Basin corridor. Prime months are August for adults and September for juveniles. Some of the most spectacular birds you will see are great egrets, American white pelicans, great blue herons, black-crowned night herons, and double-crested cormorants, as well as avocets, terns, stilts, yellowlegs, sandpipers, killdeer, and gulls.

The fun: Start your weekend in the Potholes Wildlife Area. Park on the Job Corps Dike at sunrise to see the golden light bathing the shrub-steppe habitat, the potholes, and the birds that are feeding or flying overhead. Then walk north out among the ponds and look for birds, following whatever route looks interesting. Be sure to wear footgear appropriate for mud and stickers.

The birds are plentiful but skittish, and you must move quietly. In spring egrets, cormorants, and both great blue and black-crowned night herons nest here in large rookeries. They are surrounded by an expansive system of water-filled potholes that isolate them from human disturbance at this critical time. In fall these potholes partially dry up, exposing fish for the wading birds and

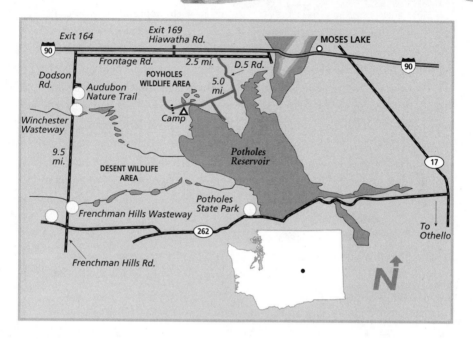

Exit 164 · Exit 169 Hiawatha Rd. · MOSES LAKE · 90 · Dodson Rd. · Frontage Rd. · 2.5 mi. · D.5 Rd. · 90 · Audubon Nature Trail · POYHOLES WILDLIFE AREA · 5.0 mi. · Camp · Winchester Wasteway · 9.5 mi. · Potholes Reservoir · 17 · DESENT WILDLIFE AREA · Potholes State Park · Frenchman Hills Wasteway · 262 · To Othello · Frenchman Hills Rd. · N

mudflats full of goodies for migrating shorebirds. Since the young birds have already fledged, you are not harming them if you walk quietly through the shrub-steppe habitat around the partially-dried-up potholes. In early September we saw hundreds of egrets and cormorants as well as lesser numbers of other shore and wading birds.

The large groups of pelicans you sometimes see flying overhead usually roost in the area know as the West Arm. According to the Potholes Wildlife Area manager, this area is best accessed by kayak or canoe from the Potholes State Park.

The west side of the wildlife area is best in late afternoon. Walk 0.5 mile past the barricade at road end, then head east across the shrub-steppe, through the almost impenetrable willows, into the pond and rookery area. The birds know you're there but will accept you after a while if you are quiet and move slowly. You will see egrets, cormorants, and other birds roosting in the trees and in flight. You are also likely to see mule deer, coyotes, and beavers.

Follow the Migration

If your trip extends over the whole Labor Day weekend, follow the shorebird migration south. The Walla Walla River Delta shorebird-monitoring site is located where the Walla Walla River flows out into the Columbia River. When the water is lowered in the fall, it becomes a huge mudflat and a rich shorebird habitat.

The route to the delta follows SR 17 south through Othello. Large numbers of shorebirds are often seen at the saline ponds 10 miles west on SR 26. In mid-September one year, 5,000 sandhill cranes were seen west of Othello.

Continuing south on SR 17, turn right on Coyan Road at milepost 19, left after the slough, and park at Scooteney Reservoir's earth dam. If you time it right (only a few days in early September), you may see more than 500 yellow-headed blackbirds flying in formation and feeding in the grain fields, preparing for their flight south. Other birds such as barn swallows, red-winged blackbirds, great blue herons, pied-billed grebes, cormorants, waterfowl, and American bitterns are here longer. A campground and a put-in for canoes are located on Scooteney Reservoir's east side.

Continue south on SR 17 and US 395 to Pasco, then east from Pasco on US 12 across the Snake River. Turn left at the MCNARY NATIONAL WILDLIFE REFUGE sign— excellent birding, easy walking.

White pelicans gather in the Potholes Reservoir in early fall before migrating south.

American white pelicans, immature pied-billed grebes, black-crowned night herons, and red-winged blackbirds are here in September. Huge numbers of wintering waterfowl arrive at the end of October. Contact the refuge at (509) 547–4942 or visit www.rl.fws.gov/mcnwr/.

To reach the Walla Walla Delta viewing area, continue south on US 12 to milepost 307, turn west on the gravel road across the railroad tracks and then north to a parking area. Cross the tracks and take the trail that angles down to the Columbia River. The right fork goes up to the bluff; the left fork drops down to the mudflats.

Early morning is the best for shorebirds. Lots of shorebird migration occurs at night, so during early morning hours they rest and feed. In the evening activity starts up again; the shorebirds come in and feed until dark, then take off. Phalaropes, yellowlegs, and avocets fly back and forth between there and the overview pond east of Madame Dorion Park (rest rooms; overnight stays permitted).

For easy morning viewing sit on top of the bluff and look out from shore to see as many as a thousand or more shorebirds. For closer observation walk north on the mudflats, sit on a stool, and let the birds come to you. Western sandpipers and other shorebirds fly in to feed in the mud-flats and eventually drift toward the bluff. You will be walking in about 2 inches of mud, so bring rubber boots or old tennis shoes. If McNary Dam is closed downstream, the water backs up and floods the mudflats; the shorebirds have no place to feed, thus no shorebird viewing. To check call the U.S. Army Corps of Engineers, McNary Lock and Dam Business Office, at (541) 922–3211.

Pullouts are located near US 12 mileposts 299 and 300. Look for pelicans and greater white-fronted geese on sandbars in the Columbia River. More than a thousand greater white-fronted geese arrive in early September and stay about a week, feeding here, in the river, or in the grain fields.

The only known nesting area in Washington for American white pelicans is on islands in the Columbia River just southwest of these pullouts. You can see them just off the spits near these islands, off the delta mudflats, or flying overhead. Use binoculars or a scope.

Food and lodging: Pasco offers all services. Hood Park, Charbonneau, and Fishhook Park campgrounds are on the Snake River (www.nww.usace.army.mil/corpsoutdoors/.

Go to www.reserveusa.com for online campground reservations.

The second day, continue your tour through the Desert Wildlife Area via Dodson Road (I–90 exit 164). The Audubon Nature Trail is accessed from Route 1 SW. Farther south the ponds near Winchester Wasteway fishing access are the most productive for shore and wading birds; large numbers of great egrets have occasionally been seen east of the road. Drive west on Frenchman Hills Road to a parking area on the right (north) for more ponds and shorebirds. Look for burrowing owls farther west (July is best). Drive east and explore fishing accesses along Frenchman Hills Wasteway and the reservoir north of O'Sullivan Dam for terns, parasitic jaegers, and shorebirds.

Food and lodging: Moses Lake offers all services. Potholes State Park campground (showers) is on SR 262, west of the O'Sullivan Dam. Camping at the Potholes Wildlife Area is ideal for good birding access, but there are *no* facilities. If you are self-contained, park in the cleared areas next to the road and enjoy the solitude. Bring mosquito repellent and water.

For more information:
Desert and Potholes wildlife areas
(509) 765–6641

37

September

Return of the Salmon

Honor salmon as they begin making their way from the sea, persistently focused on the journey to spawn at their freshwater birthing place. Three popular festivals make it fun to celebrate this spunky fish.

Site: Leavenworth, 19 miles west of Wenatchee on US 2.

Recommended time: The Wenatchee River Salmon Festival is the third weekend in September; other salmon festivals are two weeks before and after.

Minimum time commitment: A day plus travel time.

What to bring: Camera.

Directions: From downtown Leavenworth drive 2 miles south on Icicle Road to the Leavenworth National Fish Hatchery.

The background: Honoring and celebrating the salmons' return from the sea and their difficult journey upriver to spawn is an ancient rite. Salmon are, after all, one of the basic building blocks in Washington's ecological foundation (see chapter 4). What an amazing life cycle. Details differ somewhat between species of salmon, but generally all these fish are born in freshwater streams from eggs deposited by parents in shallow depressions they make in the gravel, called "redds." The adults die soon after spawning. When the eggs hatch the young fish make their way to salt water and live and grow there, facing all kinds of predators and other obstacles to survival. If they survive, their biological clock directs them back up those same streams—no small feat considering currents, predators, and human-built barriers—to spawn and perpetuate the species. The males of all the different kinds of salmon develop

Kids are fascinated by close-up looks at salmon in the big aquarium at the Wenatchee River Salmon Festival's School Days.

hook-shaped jaws at this time and turn bright colors for the spawning cycle of their lives. Chinook turn a golden brown; sockeye become deep red with green heads; coastal chinook turn black.

At all stages of their life, as well as in death, salmon provide food for all manner of creatures, among them marine mammals, humans, and eagles. Native Americans were the first to observe, protect, and celebrate the position of honor that salmon hold here in the Pacific Northwest. Nearly all salmon-related events include at least some of that tradition and cultural history.

The fun: The Wenatchee River Salmon Festival in Leavenworth features a variety of activities, all held on the grounds of the Leavenworth National Fish Hatchery, just a five-minute drive from downtown Leavenworth. Hundreds of thousands of chinook salmon are raised here and released into the Wenatchee River, where they can be seen making their nests in the gravel. Chinook are the largest of the Pacific salmon; mature chinook are called king salmon.

Activities include music, stories for kids, education displays on salmon (including the Giant Aquarium), fish print classes, Native American dancing, and barbecued salmon to eat. A favorite event on Friday, School Days, is "Kids in the Creek." The kids, walking up the path in their tall orange boots and holding their samples of river water, are so proud that they found microorganisms in the water.

Next best: If you spend the weekend in Leavenworth, guided nature walks and volksmarches on the Icicle Gorge Trail and Icicle Ridge provide pleasant exercise (Northwest Forest Pass required). Cascade peaks tower over this narrow canyon, filled with sparkling Icicle Creek and gorgeous scenery. To explore on your own get an Icicle Gorge Trail brochure from the Leavenworth Ranger Station (509–548–6977).

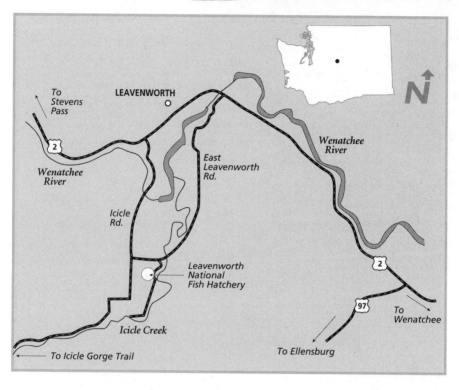

- *Seattle:* The Salmon Homecoming Celebration is held the second weekend in September, on the waterfront at The Seattle Aquarium, Waterfront Park, and Piers 62 and 63. It is sponsored by the Northwest Indian Fisheries Commission and The Seattle Aquarium. The four-day festival features Native American songs, dances, and ceremonial presentations by hundreds of performers; a powwow with intertribal dancing accompanied by traditional drums; a salmon bake; environmental exhibits; a run/walk along the waterfront; and much more. It is a tribute with thousands of years of Pacific Northwest history behind it and is well worth visiting. For more information call (206) 386–4300 or (206) 386–4320, or visit www.seattleaquarium.org/.

- *Issaquah:* The Issaquah Salmon Days Festival is held the first weekend in October. Take I–90 exit 17 and follow the signs. It is a bustling urban street fair with a parade, crafts booths, entertainment, and food. At the fish hatchery,

Sights of huge numbers of salmon returning upstream to spawn once were common; now many species are endangered.

crowds of people enjoy watching salmon try to swim up the Issaquah Creek fish ladder; the observation windows are also a great hit. For more information call (425) 391–9019 or visit www.salmondays.org/.

Food and lodging: Host cities offer all services.

For more information:
Wenatchee River Salmon Festival
www.salmonfest.org/
Leavenworth National Fish Hatchery
(509) 548–7641;
www.leavenworth.fws.gov/
Leavenworth Chamber of Commerce
(509) 548–5807

38

Haul Out at High Tide

Harbor seals in Hood Canal and Puget Sound spend most of each day in the water feeding except during their annual pupping and molting seasons, when they are hauled out and highly visible much of the time.

Site: Hood Canal and Marrowstone Island.

Recommended time: Females give birth to and nurse their pups from July through September (September is less crowded). We cannot emphasize enough that these beautiful, sleek animals deserve privacy during this time; if a harbor seal is looking at you, you are too close.

Minimum time commitment: A day; a weekend for all the sites.

What to bring: Walking shoes or boots, binoculars, tide table.

Directions: Take a ferry across Puget Sound to Bainbridge Island, then cross the Hood Canal bridge. The SR 104 junction with Quilcene-Chimacum Road is 9.5 miles west of the bridge. Check the tides. Fort Flagler State Park is best at low tide; Hood Canal, at high tide. For Fort Flagler, drive 7 miles north through Chimacum and follow the signs to Marrowstone Island. For Hood Canal drive 8 miles south, join US 101 at Quilcene, and continue 12.5 miles to Dosewallips State Park.

The background: Hundreds of harbor seals inhabit shallow estuaries and rivers in Hood Canal and South Puget Sound. They feed on fish when the tide comes in, enjoying salmon when available. Typically they haul out on flat sandbars, beaches, or log booms as the tide goes out, basking and sleeping until the tide rises again. In Hood Canal they also haul out at high tide on

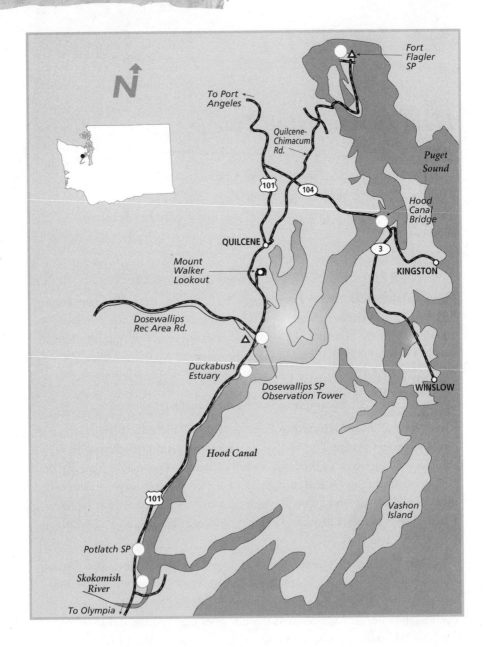

N

To Port Angeles

Quilcene-Chimacum Rd.

Fort Flagler SP

Puget Sound

101

104

Hood Canal Bridge

QUILCENE

3

KINGSTON

Mount Walker Lookout

Dosewallips Rec Area Rd.

Duckabush Estuary

Dosewallips SP Observation Tower

WINSLOW

Hood Canal

101

Vashon Island

Potlatch SP

Skokomish River

To Olympia

Harbor seals spend most of their time in the water, but large numbers haul out on the log boom in Henderson Inlet to nurse their pups.

marsh edges along river-mouth channels.

Seals are 5 feet long, with a streamlined shape for swimming and a thick layer of blubber for insulation. They have a smooth head with no visible ears, big black eyes, and a short, doglike muzzle. Females give birth to one pup on land or in the water—usually from July through September. Newborn pups grow rapidly on their mother's rich milk—quickly learning to swim, dive, catch prey, and haul out. After pups are weaned, harbor seals remain hauled out during molt, gradually replacing all their hair over several months.

The fun: At low tide, seals can be viewed from Marrowstone Island. Drive to Fort Flagler State Park, then west to the boat launch area (rest rooms, picnic tables). Walk south on the spit; on sunny days several hundred harbor seals often haul out on Rat Island (visible only at low tide) west of Indian Island. Scan the waters for grebes, seabirds, and ducks—and occasional rafts of loons. Bald eagles and great blue herons nest here.

Hood Canal seal viewing is generally best at high tide. Harbor seals haul out near Dosewallips State Park, south of Brinnon, year-round—as many as 300 during fall, as few as 30 in winter. To reach the day-use area, turn left off US 101 south of the bridge. Park at the far end, walk west up the river through the primitive camping area, and cross to the river's north side on a footbridge. Turn right and take the path back down the river to the salt marsh and the 15–foot viewing tower. Bring binoculars and scan the sloughs to the south for harbor seals. They swim up the sloughs with the rising tide

Harbor Seals by Kayak

Get close to hundreds of harbor seals by kayak, without over-stressing them, in southern Hood Canal near Hoodsport or in Southern Puget Sound near Olympia.

■ *Skokomish River, Hood Canal:* Kayak access is from Potlatch State Park, 3.4 miles south of Hoodsport. Paddle about 2 miles southeast along the mud and salt grass tideflats of Anna's Bay to the river's wide estuary and then up the west (nearest) channel. As many as 150 to 250 harbor seals swim up the west channel on a rising tide to catch fish, then haul out to bask and rest. The best times to be there are at high tides, with a height of 8 to 10 feet ideal (haul outs are covered at higher tides). The estuary, which is also home to abundant waterfowl, is too shallow to navigate at low tide. Be careful not to get stuck when the tide goes out.

■ *Henderson Inlet, Olympia:* Kayak and foot access is from Woodard Bay Natural Resources Conservation Area (Washington Department of Natural Resources) north of Olympia. From northbound I–5 take exit 108 and drive north 4.5 miles on Sleater-Kinney Road NE. Bear left (west) on Fifty-sixth Avenue N for 0.4 mile, then turn right on Shincke Road. In 0.5 mile curve left onto Woodard Bay Road NE; the entrance to Woodard Bay NRCA is another 0.5 mile on the right. From southbound I–5 take exit 109 and drive 0.6 mile west on Martin Way, then right on Sleater-Kinney Road.

In 1988 the Department of Natural Resources established this conservation area to pro-vide habitat for "shorebirds and songbirds, harbor seals, river otters, bald eagles, a maternity colony of bats, and one of the most significant heron rookeries in the state." The area includes a large parking area, barrier-free toilets, and several lovely trails.

For best harbor seal viewing drive 0.2 mile farther, cross the bridge, and turn right into a small parking area. Kayak access is just inside the gate; be sure to put in on an incoming tide unless you enjoy slogging through mud on your return. Paddle north out of Woodard Bay under-neath the trestle into Henderson Inlet, then turn left (west). The old pilings and structures are a few hun-dred yards along the near shore; hun-dreds of harbor seals haul out on the log booms to rest and give birth.

You can also see these seals on foot by walking about 0.75 mile along the slightly hilly road from the parking area to a grassy area with picnic tables. From here you look out on the log booms used by the seals. Check your tides before you go; midday high tides are best.

Harbor seal numbers have increased dramatically at Woodard Bay since regular monitoring began in 1977. Henderson Inlet is one of the most important pupping areas for harbor seals in Puget Sound. In 1996 Gertrude Island and Woodard Bay peak counts were 714 and 608 animals, respectively, including 280 pups.

This is a wonderful opportunity to see harbor seals up close, but please be cautious. The seals are vulnerable to disturbance by people visiting the site in recreational boats. Actions taken to protect them—signs warning people not to disturb the seals, buoys and lines closing off the entrances to the log boom interior—have been extremely successful, with a dramatic decrease in the rate of disturbances. Let's keep this success story going by being careful to not harass wildlife at these unique locations.

For more information:

Woodard Bay National Resources Conservation Area
(360) 748–2383

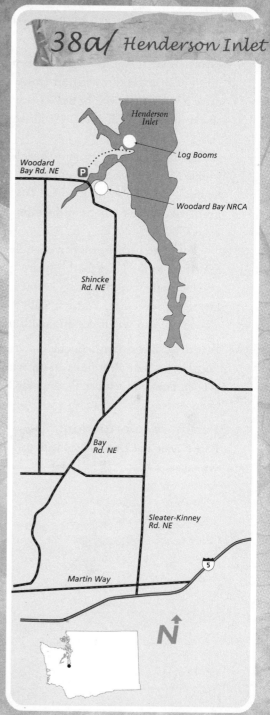

38a/ Henderson Inlet

to catch fish, then haul out on the mudflats to rest and sun themselves. You will see many different bird species—in flight, on the shore, and swimming in the sloughs.

Next best: If you spend the weekend, visit some waterfalls. One mile north of Brinnon turn west on Dosewallips Recreation Area Road (FR 261), drive 3 miles, park west of the Rocky Creek bridge, and walk to the base of an excellent waterfall (rated 4★). Drive 11.2 miles farther to see Dosewallips Falls.

Six miles north of Brinnon, turn east off US 101 and drive up the 4-mile Mount Walker Lookout Road. On a clear day the view of Puget Sound is spectacular. Back on US 101, Falls View Campground is 1.8 miles north; take a short trail from the campground's south side to see another waterfall.

For more harbor seals drive 3 miles south on US 101 from Dosewallips State Park to the Duckabush Estuary (parking area at Duckabush Road). On one high-tide visit the estuary teemed with seals, herons, and waterfowl; at low tide it was empty. Potlatch State Park (24.5 miles south of Dosewallips) is a good place to watch seabirds and launch a kayak (see preceding sidebar).

Food and lodging: Establishments along Hood Canal offer all services. Fort Flagler State Park hosts an American Youth Hostel, and the campground is open through October. Dosewallips State Park campground (showers) is open year-round.

For more information:
Fort Flagler and Dosewallips state parks
www.parks.wa.gov/alphanw.asp

39

September

Follow the Leading Lines

Observe hawks migrating south along the ridges of the eastern Cascades. Sixteen species of North American birds of prey funnel through this corridor.

Site: Chelan Ridge near Cooper Mountain, north of Lake Chelan.

Recommended time: Early September to mid–October; peak numbers often occur at the end of September.

Minimum time commitment: A full day.

What to bring: Field guide, binoculars, spotting scope. Be sure to wear hiking boots; the trail to the ridge is narrow, rocky, and sometimes steep. *Important:* Bring several layers of clothing including a warm coat, rain gear, hat, and gloves. It can snow at this elevation in September.

Directions: From Pateros on US 97, drive northwest on SR 153, turn left between mileposts 6 and 7 onto Black Canyon Road (FR 4010), and follow the map 12.3 miles to the flagged parking area. The ribbon-marked trail to the site is on the south.

The background: The newest and best hawk watch site in Washington requires a drive of 12 miles and a hike of 0.6 mile, but the rewards are great. This is not a suitable area for young children. It's very steep and there are no guardrails. Individuals not wishing to hike can still see a lot from the parking lot—especially if volunteers are banding birds that day.

This new site was discovered in 1996 during an aerial reconnaissance flight. Counting commenced in 1997 and a full-scale hawk watch site was established in 1998—cosponsored by HawkWatch International and the

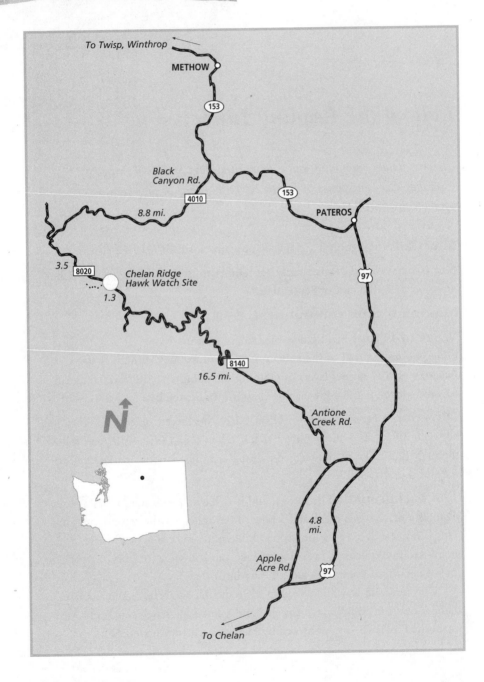

To Twisp, Winthrop

METHOW

153

Black
Canyon Rd.

4010

8.8 mi.

153

PATEROS

97

3.5

8020

Chelan Ridge
Hawk Watch Site

1.3

8140

16.5 mi.

Antione
Creek Rd.

N

4.8
mi.

Apple
Acre Rd.

97

To Chelan

USDA Forest Service. In 1999 banding was added to gain further information about this site and the raptors that use it.

Volunteers count and band hawks from late August to late October or until snow forces them to stop. In 1998 the peak occurred the last week in September; in 1999 the peak number sighted on one day was 151 hawks on October 1. In 1999, 220 hawks were also banded.

The partnership also pursues research to understand raptor populations along migration flyways. The HawkWatch database is becoming an important source of information for understanding the status and trends of western raptors.

There are many large, rocky outcroppings on Chelan Ridge; the hawk watch site is at the top of one of the highest and steepest. The prevailing south winds hit the steep face of the cliff and soar up; this is called a "ridge lift." Hawks use that lift to gain altitude. On sunny days there is often a warm-air "thermal lift," which the hawks also use.

As part of the education program, Falcon Research Group volunteers take a break from Chelan Ridge bird banding and carry a goshawk down for visitors to see.

Sometimes they fly right below the rocky outcropping where the hawk watch site is, using the ridge lift to gain altitude. At least once a day a hawk will fly by one of the two owl decoys at the site and attack it.

The fun: A warm, sunny day with a light to moderate south wind is best for hawk soaring; when it is too windy the numbers go down. Watch for a period of cold rainy weather, then go up to Chelan Ridge on the first sunny day. The raptors tend to back up in bad weather, hunkering down in the shelter of the trees. They continue their journey south when the weather turns. Raptors can also feel the pressure change before a front; they will often fly before the front comes in.

If you observe for a few days, you are likely to see a number of sharp-shinned hawks, red-tailed hawks, Cooper's hawks, northern harriers, and

Studying Hawk Migration

According to Kent Woodruff, wildlife biologist for the Methow Valley Ranger District and project manager for the Chelan Ridge Raptor Migration Project, a number of factors have come together at Chelan Ridge to make hawk migration work. First of all, the topography. The North Cascades get narrower and narrower the farther south you get. East of here the birds that are migrating down get funneled in this direction; north and west of here the same thing happens.

The second factor is that the hawks suddenly hit Lake Chelan and, like a lot of other hawk migration sites, the water becomes a "leading line." As autumn progresses, migration takes place with the young birds first and the parents afterwards. Leading lines are necessary because the birds that have come out of the nest this year don't know where they are headed and have no idea why they're going south. As they are flying they find something on the landscape that helps lead them in one direction. "Those are called leading lines because they really help the birds find their way," says Woodruff.

The spine of the North Cascades is a long, long ridge; the broadwing hawks seen here are probably coming from way up north in British Columbia. "The ridge is one of the things I saw when I was flying over here in 1996," he said. "We decided to take a look and see if this might prove to be a good hawk migration sight—and sure enough it was." There have been observers here since 1997.

The third factor is the way the wind works. When the wind comes from the south, it hits the ridge and pushes air up. "The hawks ride the 'elevator' up," says Woodruff. "They circle around and go up and up." Birds that flap their wings don't need lifts, but it's hard to soar without using air currents to rise.

In 1970 60,000 acres burned in this area. Woodruff speculates that the young, vigorous, diverse vegetation in the burn area provides insects that become food for migrant songbirds as they're going through. Seeds from the variety of plants here are also valuable energy food. As this burn matures, the vegetation will probably not be as diverse. "But now the songbirds are able to get full, top off their fuel tanks and head south in really good condition," he says.

Hawks, in turn, stop and feed on these migrant songbirds. Some days we see a lot of migrating hawks with full crops, so they, too, are fueled up for the migration. The Chelan Ridge

HawkWatch personnel and volunteers can spot as many as ten species of raptors in a day from the top of Chelan Ridge.

Raptor Migration Project is a coalition of partners: USDA Forest Service, HawkWatch International, and Falcon Research Group. "In order to coordinate that effort," Woodruff explains, "I asked everybody to work together and try to cooperate. It wasn't hard at all.

"We had a big campfire where we sat around and discussed the key things that were important to each of us," he recalls. They were all fairly compatible—with a few differences—and the partners agreed to support three goals:

- *Teaching*—providing an educational opportunity

- *Understanding*—learning more about raptor migration
- *Conserving*—working hard on the conservation of raptors

"In my career I've spent a lot of time learning about and studying raptors," he says. "The agency that I work for today is a habitat management agency. We don't do much species manipulation, but we do have the opportunity to work closely with others. This project is a perfect example of what we call collaborative stewardship—it's a nice blend."

golden eagles. Less numerous are American kestrels, northern goshawks, ospreys, rough-legged hawks, and merlins. Just a few turkey vultures, Swainson's hawks, broad-winged hawks, peregrine falcons, prairie falcons, and bald eagles migrate through here. Consider yourself very fortunate to see any of these.

Volunteers from the Falcon Research Group are often at Chelan Ridge banding birds. One Sunday they caught a juvenile sharp-shinned hawk in mist nets. They banded its leg, put a hood on the bird, and brought it down for visitors to look at briefly. Then they took off the hood and released it. Later they brought down a large goshawk and two sharp-shinned hawks—an adult and a juvenile. What an opportunity to see these elusive birds up close!

Food and lodging: Cities and towns in the Methow Valley offer all services. Camping is available at USDA Forest Service and private campgrounds throughout the valley.

For more information:

Okanogan National Forest
Methow Valley Visitor Center, Winthrop
(509) 996–4000
Chelan Ridge Raptor Migration Project
www.fs.fed.us/r6/oka/birds/migration.html
HawkWatch International (migration research sites)
(800) 726–HAWK; www.hawkwatch.org/
The Falcon Research Group
www.frg.org/frg/

40

September

Wooing Wapiti

*Visit the Olympic Peninsula to see and hear Roosevelt elk
"bugling" up close, at their noisiest and most visible, during breeding season.*

Site: Hoh and Quinault rain forests, south of Forks on the coast.

Recommended time: Elk breeding season begins early in September
and lasts until mid-October; activity often peaks at the end of September.

Minimum time commitment: A half day plus travel time; a weekend
is better.

What to bring: Camera, binoculars, rain gear (entrance fee, National
Parks Pass, or Golden Eagle Passport).

Directions: See below.

The background: There are two species of elk in Washington—Rocky
Mountain and Roosevelt. The smaller, lighter colored, and more plentiful of
the two, Rocky Mountain elk are found mainly east of the Cascades—most
of them in wildlife areas and national forests that are managed for hunting.
You may hear bugling elk in the eastern part of the state this time of year, but
it is less likely that you will see any. Elk are smart and try to disappear when
hunting season starts.

On the west side of the mountains, Roosevelt elk live along the coast
and in some parts of the Cascades' western slopes. Here there are several areas
protected from hunting, and the elk have become accustomed to human
presence. They are also very busy and focused this time of year, so it is amazingly easy to see them.

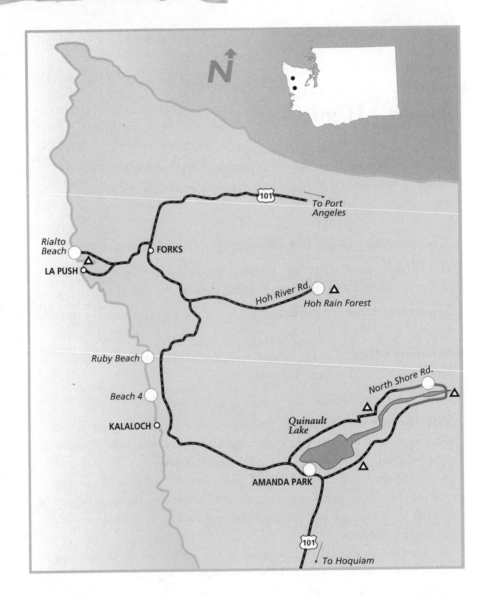

N

To Port
Angeles

101

Rialto
Beach

FORKS

LA PUSH

Hoh River Rd.

Hoh Rain Forest

Ruby Beach

Beach 4

North Shore Rd.

KALALOCH

Quinault
Lake

AMANDA PARK

101

To Hoquiam

Precipitation in the temperate rain forest of the coastal river valleys ranges from 140 to 167 inches—12 to 14 feet—every year.

The fun: Elk exhibit fascinating social behavior during breeding season. At this time they are preoccupied with the task at hand and sometimes allow people to approach fairly close to watch them gather and protect their harems (see sidebar). There are two Olympic Peninsula locations where elk have become acclimated to humans.

■ *Hoh Rain Forest:* Olympic National Park's Hoh Rain Forest Visitor Center is located about 14 miles south of Forks and 18.5 miles up the Hoh River Road.

About 200 Roosevelt elk live in the Hoh River Valley; most of them move up into the park (12.5 miles up the river) during hunting season. The Hoh Campground elk herd is the easiest to see and hear; they will often walk right by you if you stand still. A warning: Do *not* get between the bull and his harem. He will object—sometimes aggressively. Remember that these are still wild animals and that their hormones are raging.

From mid-September through mid-October, the dominant bull elk and his harem of around thirteen cows and calves can often be seen around the campground; the unoccupied C loop is a favorite place to browse. They also move downriver into the occupied A loop and the picnic area, over to the visitor center, upriver (visible from the 1.25-mile Spruce Nature Trail),

Elks in Rut

Breeding season is in progress in earnest this time of year for both Rocky Mountain and Roosevelt elk in Washington. They are genetically programmed to perpetuate the species—and it is very serious business indeed.

During the four- to six-week breeding period, called the "rut," the enormous male elk, or "bull," emits a very loud "bugling" call. This eerily shrill sound declares the bull's masculinity and announces to the rest of the elk world where the boundaries have been drawn. The biggest, "baddest" bull, called the dominant bull, gathers the most females or "cows" for his harem, as many as fifteen to twenty. He must then protect them from all intruders. He shakes his huge antlers or "rack," and attacks trees, other bulls, and anything else that gets in his way.

In late September it is not unusual to see the dominant bull thrashing around in the small trees, moving his antlers back and forth. He will also urinate in the mud and roll in it—all behavior to establish his territory. Some of the younger bulls with smaller racks or spikes stay near the herd and spar with one another—waiting for an opportunity to steal some cows from the dominant bull. The young bulls' bravado is tempered with realism however. Sometimes all it takes is a look from the dominant bull to send them running.

This bugling bull elk is part of the resident Hoh Campground herd whose foraging creates a park-like appearance in the rain forest.

The whole point of this, of course, is that the strongest, most successful males have a chance to impregnate many females and thus perpetuate the strongest genes. It is a demanding task, and the bulls eat very little during this time.

After rutting season the bulls must attend to serious eating; they have only a short time to accumulate enough body fat to survive the winter. Elk society becomes matriarchal once more, and the older cows resume their leadership roles—watching over the rest of the herd, barking alarms, and leading them from summer range to winter range.

or onto islands in the river. Look in all the open parklike areas that are a by-product of their grazing.

Elk are most visible in the evening and early morning. It's an extra treat to actually hear bugling from your campsite here.

Next best: Enjoy short walks through magnificent rain forests and visits to giant trees. Stop in the visitor center for information about Hoh Rain Forest attractions. In early morning watch for river otters, spawning salmon, and harlequin ducks on the Hoh River. If you spend the night in nearby Forks, ask at Tinker's Tales for in-town elk locations. Rialto Beach, 15 miles west of Forks on the ocean, has magnificent sunsets.

Food and lodging: The Hoh Campground is open year-round. There are accommodations and food along the Hoh River Road; Bogachiel Campground is on US 101 (showers). Forks offers all services.

■ *Quinault Rain Forest:* The second protected location for hearing and seeing bugling elk is in the Quinault Rain Forest. Lake Quinault is located about 52 miles south of the Hoh River Road on US 101 at Amanda Park. When you exit the Hoh River Road, head south on US 101, stopping at any of several lovely beaches along the way (see map). Most have tidepools; some have sea stacks.

Look for Roosevelt elk feeding in the meadows on Lake Quinault's North Shore Road about 14 miles from US 101. Evening and early morning are the most reliable. For other attractions on the 28-mile Lake Quinault loop, see chapter 49.

Food and lodging: Lake Quinault Lodge is 2 miles from US 101 on the South Shore Road, along with several smaller resorts and restaurants. Lake Quinault Resort is on North Shore Road; Amanda Park also has services. Several campgrounds are open in September.

For more information:
Olympic National Park, Hoh Rain Forest Visitor Center
(360) 374–6925
Olympic National Forest, Quinault Visitor Information Office
(360) 288–2525

41

October

On the Trail of the Golden Larch

Go in search of the colorful larch—a magnificent deciduous conifer with bundles of long needles that turn a brilliant gold before they drop in the winds of late October.

Site: Harts Pass, 20 miles northwest of Mazama in the North Cascades Mountains.

Recommended time: Early to mid–October.

Minimum time commitment: A day or a weekend.

What to bring: Camera, warm clothing, and boots; Northwest Forest Pass. Four-wheel drive, studded tires and/or chains, and other winter supplies are recommended in case of snow.

Directions: From SR 20 turn north at Mazama (milepost 180). Turn left (west) on Mazama Road and follow it northwest to Harts Pass (about 20 miles of paved and then narrow gravel road). Turn right to the Slate Peak parking lot or left to the campground.

The background: Washington's autumn does not have the magnificent reds and oranges of the northeastern states, but we do have lots of yellows and golds—accented with reds, oranges, and rusts. And Washington is home to large expanses of evergreens, which provide a dark green backdrop for the golden larches, aspen, and cottonwoods in our beautiful mountains.

Larches are the only conifer in Washington that changes color in the fall. They first turn a delicate yellow-green and then a luminous gold, reaching their peak sometime in the first three weeks of October, depending on location. The larches at Harts Pass are the smaller subalpine larches, which grow to over 80 feet tall. In Washington they are found mainly in North Cascades

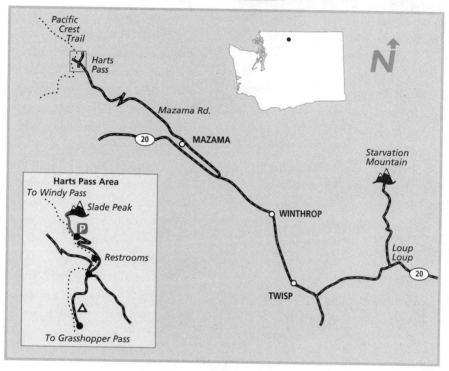

National Park at elevations of 6,000 to 7,800 feet.

The larches found near Curlew (see sidebar) are the larger western larches, which grow in mountain valleys and lower slopes of the Eastern Cascades and Blue Mountains. They grow to over 160 feet tall; the tallest known tree (192 feet; Van Pelt, 2000) is in northeast Oregon.

The fun: Follow the directions above to Harts Pass and the Slate Peak parking lot. At 6,800 feet elevation it is the highest place you can drive to in Washington. A short, steep walk takes you to the top of the 7,440-foot peak, a large flat area with a radar station in the middle. From the top of Slate Peak you can see mountain peaks and ridges for miles in every direction—a splendid place to be at sunrise or sunset (brrrr!—bring your insulated boots for standing in the cold). The larches, which grow in thick patches all over the hillsides, glow in the morning light.

Fall Color Driving Tour

*I*f you prefer a fall color experience with more amenities (no camping or snowy gravel mountain roads), take a driving tour or an excursion train in northeast Washington.

- *Colville National Forest Scenic Byway Drive:* The Colville National Forest sponsors an annual fall foliage event the first weekend in October, the Sherman Pass National Scenic Byway drive (SR 20 between Republic and Kettle Falls). Participants usually meet at US 395/SR 20 junction west of Kettle Falls. Larches may not reach their peak until mid-October; contact the Kettle Falls Ranger District at (509) 738-6111 or (509) 738-7700 for fall color and drive information.
- *Kettle Falls/Curlew Loop Drive:* Your best bet to see magnificent views of western larches during the first three weeks in October is from a self-guided 100-mile auto tour that heads north on US 395, west to Curlew, south on SR 21, and back east across Sherman Pass. Starting at the US 395/SR 20 junction, drive about 17 miles north along the Kettle River and turn west on Boulder Creek/Deer Creek Road towards Curlew.

View larches, cottonwoods, and aspens all along this 23-mile stretch of paved and little-traveled road. From about 8 miles to the 4600-foot summit at 13.5 miles, there are gorgeous stands of western larches both along the road and on the hillsides. There are no official pullouts, just wide places in the road where you can stop.

Two gravel roads exit from the south side of the road for closer views. One is just west of the summit (high clearance required). The other is 2.3 miles further west, just across from the NATIONAL FOREST sign (last good turnaround is 0.4 mile in). At 21 miles look down on lovely fall color views of the Kettle River (west arm) and surrounding valley below.

At Curlew, take an optional 22-mile round trip to the Canadian border to see golden cottonwoods thick along the Kettle River. Then drive 12.5 miles south on SR 21 to Curlew State Park (more fall color) and continue 19 more miles to intersect SR 20 just east of Republic.

The 40-mile trip back to Kettle Falls takes you east over 5,575-foot Sherman Pass (open all winter). In

October, it is resplendent with western larch, aspen, and cottonwood trees—bright yellow to dark gold, with a few fiery orange accents. Stop at the White Mountain burn overlook for rest rooms and splendid views.

- *Ione:* For an old-fashioned fall color steam train ride, travel 50 miles east on SR 20 to the northeastern corner of Washington. The Lions Excursion Train runs between Ione and Metaline Falls on fall weekends, with color usually peaking the first weekend in October. For information, call (509) 442-5466 or visit www.povn.com/byway/train/schedule.html. Take your own fall color driving tour along the Pend Oreille River, around Sullivan Lake, and up Salmo Mountain. Contact the Sullivan Lake Ranger District at (509) 446-7500 for more information.

Food and lodging: Curlew, Republic, Kettle Falls, Ione, and Metaline Falls offer all services.

Special Fall Color Note: Brilliant fall color starts with enough moisture during the summer; sunny, but cool days in September and early October; and chilly-but-not-freezing nights. These conditions boost the formation of anthocyanin that adds more intense colors. During an optimum season, many aspen will turn orange instead of yellow. Drought, early hard frosts, or storms can spoil the color.

Color peaks in early October; the trees are sometimes deep gold against a blue-sky backdrop, sometimes covered with snow with fog swirling around them for a mystical experience. Be prepared for anything. If you want to be up on Slate Peak at both ends of the day, you may decide to camp out since the roads can be slippery before dawn and after dark. If you do stay overnight, be sure to bring warm clothes and a warm sleeping bag; temperature may get below freezing at night and snow is not uncommon.

Several hikes are especially colorful in early October. Drive up Slate Peak Road to the rest rooms, then walk out on Slate Meadow. You can also follow the Pacific Crest Trail north toward Windy Pass from the Slate Peak parking lot for more larches, meadows, and mountain peaks. For similar delights plus views of a valley and creek below, drive to the end of the road that goes past

From the top of Slate Peak, view hillsides of larches, the only conifer in Washington that turns golden in the fall and drops its needles.

the campground and walk south on the Pacific Crest Trail toward Grasshopper Pass.

Look up now and then; raptors migrate through here in late September and early October.

Food and lodging: Mazama and Winthrop offer all services. Meadows Campground (pit toilets, no water, no trailers) is 2 miles south of the Harts Pass intersection. Rest rooms are on Slate Peak Road. Ballard Campground, 7 miles from Mazama, is the last place trailers can go.

For more information:
Okanogan National Forest
Methow Valley Visitor Center
(509) 996–4000

42

October

Changing Seasons, Passing Through

National wildlife refuges come alive as vocal, migrating birds fill the skies, ponds, and fields; other wildlife actively forage for winter food supplies; and cottonwood and aspen leaves turn a brilliant gold.

Site: National Wildlife Refuges throughout Washington.

Recommended time: National Wildlife Refuge Week is the second week in October.

Minimum time commitment: Half a day plus travel time; two weekends if you want to attend refuge events throughout the state.

What to bring: Binoculars, cameras, sturdy walking shoes or boots. Many refuges waive fees this week; otherwise bring entrance fee, Annual Refuge Pass, or Golden Eagle Passport.

Directions: See below.

The background: In 1995 the Director of the U.S. Fish and Wildlife Service proclaimed the second week in October as National Wildlife Refuge System Week, an annual event "designated to help increase the American public's awareness, appreciation, and support of the National Wildlife Refuge system." The USFWS invites you to visit a national wildlife refuge during this special week, during which refuge staff and Audubon Society volunteers make every effort to "thank the American public for helping conserve these remarkable natural areas."

The fun: Each of the refuges described here holds special activities during NWR Week.

In celebration of National Wildlife Refuge Week, a refuge biologist leads a twilight tour at Columbia National Wildlife Refuge to locations not normally visited by the public.

Eastern Washington

■ *Turnbull NWR,* located in the channeled scablands of eastern Washington. From Cheney drive 4 miles south on Cheney-Plaza Road, turn left on Smith Road at the entrance sign, and drive 2 miles to refuge headquarters. The refuge features rugged scab rock, ponderosa pine, aspen, grasslands, and large wetlands. It supports migratory birds (sixty-three species frequent the refuge) and nesting waterfowl. Take the driving tour early in the morning to see elk, white-tailed deer, and coyotes in upland areas.

During NWR Week, the refuge hosts night hikes on Thursday and Friday—an evening of activities and experiments that help children and adults learn about nocturnal animals (call 509–235–4723 to register). Spokane Audubon Society and the refuge also host a community planting day and enjoy a potluck lunch afterwards.

■ *Columbia NWR,* located in the channeled scablands of the Columbia Basin. From Othello drive 5 miles northwest on McManamon Road, then turn right (north) on Morgan Lake Road into the refuge. A map is available at entrances. The refuge features lakes and arid sagebrush grasslands set among rocky buttes and cliffs. The lakes attract large numbers of migrating waterfowl including tundra swans.

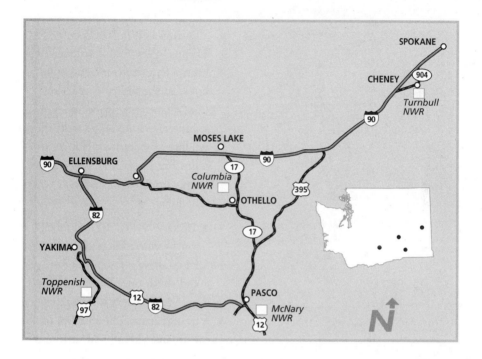

On Thursday and Friday evenings during NWR Week, the refuge offers two-hour bus tours to places in the refuge not open to the public. You will tour areas in the refuge's Marsh Units 1 and 2, making several stops—the last known for its beautiful sunsets. A guide is available to point out and identify wildlife. Buses leave at 4:30 P.M. from Othello High School; call (509) 488–2668 to register.

Request a scenic tour brochure of wildlife areas in the Moses Lake/Othello area at the Central Basin Audubon Society Web site: www.cbas.org/.

■ *Toppenish NWR,* located in the Toppenish Valley south of Yakima. From Toppenish drive south on US 97 approximately 10 miles to the refuge entrance on the west. Wetlands along the creeks are flooded in October to attract thousands of migratory waterfowl, shorebirds, and wading birds. Raptors and marsh birds are also seen. Go before hunting season opens.

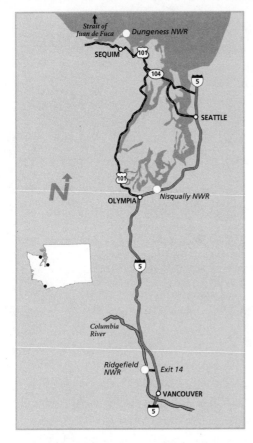

During NWR Week, the Yakima Valley Audubon Society hosts a Saturday-morning open house at the visitor contact station, main refuge parking lot. A volunteer with a scope staffs the wildlife observation platform to point out birds and answer questions. Guided walks are also scheduled.

■ *McNary NWR,* located in arid southeast Washington. From Pasco drive a few miles east and south on US 12, then east on Maple Street to refuge headquarters. The marshes of Burbank Slough and surrounding grasslands and croplands support large numbers of migrating and wintering waterfowl.

One Saturday during NWR Week, McNary NWR staff and volunteers from McNary Environmental Education Center and Lower Columbia Basin Audubon Society provide speakers, walking tours, children's environmental games, a hayride, and displays.

Western Washington

■ *Nisqually NWR,* located on one of the largest undisturbed saltwater estuaries in Washington. From Olympia take I–5 exit 114, turn west under the freeway, then right on Brown Farm Road. The refuge is located where the Nisqually River, McAllister Creek, and Red Salmon Creek meet.

Thousands of ducks, geese, and shorebirds stop here to fatten up and rest during migration; bald eagles, osprey, and other birds of prey perch in trees on the bluffs above the delta.

During NWR Week, Black Hills and Tahoma Audubon societies host bird walks in the refuge. On weekends staff and volunteers assist with bird identification at the twin barns viewing platform.

■ *Dungeness NWR,* located on the world's longest natural sand spit. From Sequim, drive west on US 101, turn north on Kitchen-Dick Road and continue 3 miles to the Dungeness Recreation Area, then drive to the refuge parking lot at road end. Dungeness Spit forms a quiet bay and harbor, gravel beaches, and tideflats. During fall migration the tideflats teem with migrating shorebirds—up to 30,000 waterfowl stop here briefly. The spit is a haul-out for harbor seals to rest and have their pups.

The refuge waives the entrance fee during this week; staff members give out posters, answer questions, and offer bird tours.

■ *Ridgefield NWR,* located on floodplains along the Columbia River. Take I-5 exit 14 to SR 501, drive 3 miles west to Ridgefield, and follow signs to the Carty and River "S" units. These units contain ash, willow, and cottonwood, interspersed with marshes and wet/dry meadows and intermittently flooded by river waters. Basalt outcrops on the Carty Unit form upland knolls above the high-water level with beautiful oak habitat. The refuge holds either a demonstration or a tour during NWR Week each year.

Food and lodging: Nearby cities offer all services.

For more information:

National Wildlife Refuge Week
refuges.fws.gov/general/NWRSWeek.html
National Audubon Society (Washington Office and Chapters)
(360) 786–8020; www.audubon.org/chapter/wa/wa/wastwhere.htm
Individual Refuges
(see Appendices)

43

October

Finding Fungi

The Puget Sound Mycological Society's Annual Wild Mushroom Show is billed as "one of the largest and most complete displays of fresh, wild mushrooms." You will be mesmerized.

Site: Annual Wild Mushroom Show, Seattle

Recommended time: Check with the Puget Sound Mycological Society for exact dates of the show in October or November. It varies slightly each year.

Minimum time commitment: A couple of hours or more.

What to bring: Paper and pen for notes; field guide to mushrooms.

Directions: The Annual Wild Mushroom Show is held either at the Center for Urban Horticulture, just east of the University of Washington ballfields, or at Sand Point Magnuson Park, 7400 Sand Point Way NE.

The background: Yet another source of beauty and delight in nature is fungi, mushrooms, the "fungus among-us"—often overlooked or avoided because of a "mushrooms are poisonous" mindset.

In much of Washington west of the Cascades, October is a favorite month (often into early November) for fungi seekers. Most any moist trail or park will do. You don't have to risk eating them to enjoy finding them. The variety of form and color can be astounding and even cursory information will enrich your view of the natural world.

If you are a beginner at identifying mushrooms, especially if you eventually would like to gather some for eating, it is strongly recommended that you attend the annual mushroom exhibit and then go out with experts for several

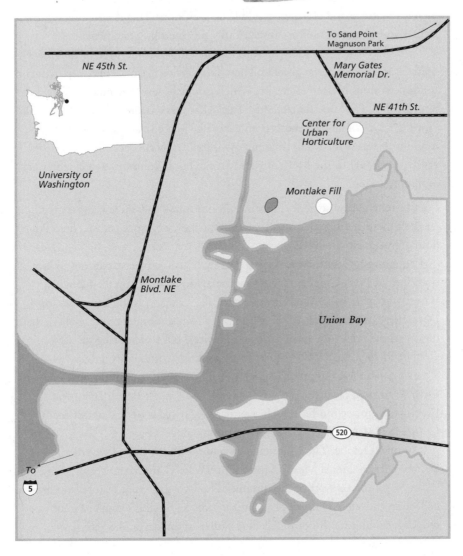

seasons until you are confident of your ability. Field trips with knowledgeable mycologists can be fun. *Note:* Mycologists study mushrooms; mycophiles are fascinated with mushrooms; the Mycological Society is, you guessed it, a group of people organized to study mushrooms.

The fun: The PSMS annual mushroom exhibit will amaze and delight you with the variety of wild mushrooms. It's "mushroom identification 101"—what an opportunity to get started on learning about fascinating fungi! Each specimen is identified and classified as edible or poisonous. There's also a slide show lecture and tasting of mushrooms variously prepared by Seattle chefs.

You may learn that some mushrooms are edible at one stage of their development and poisonous at another. There's one called "alcohol inky cap," which is not poisonous if eaten alone, but which produces severe symptoms if ingested with alcohol. The "questionable stropharia" has fuzzy white stems and tastes like "rotting leaves." The deer mushroom tastes like a radish, and an hallucinogenic mushroom was named "big laughing gymnopilus" by the Japanese because it causes, according to the McKenny and Stuntz book, "unmotivated laughter and foolish behavior."

Next best: Many societies offer mushroom forays to help you get started. Most of these are member organizations, but they welcome guests. Three Puget Sound groups are listed below.

Snohomish County Mycological Society hosts October excursions to locations such as Buck Creek (near Darrington), Goose Creek (up the Chiwawa River Road near Lake Wenatchee), Baker Lake, Camano Island State Park, or Deception Pass State Park. At their Annual Fall Mushroom Show (October), they display to the public the many varieties they have collected during the season. Contact them at (425) 317–9411; www.snonet.org/community/groups/scms/.

The Naturalist Group of The Mountaineers offers mushroom hikes in October to such favorites as the 6.5-mile White Chuck Bench Trail (near Darrington) to see mushrooms, beaver dams, and cedar trees. Contact them at (206) 248–6310, (800) 573–8484; www.mountaineers.org/.

In mid-October The Mountaineers and the Puget Sound Mycological Society host an annual Meany Mushroom Weekend at Crystal Springs Forest Camp, I–90 exit 62 (east of the summit). The two-day event features mushroom collecting and identifying, displays, preparation, a cooking seminar, a gourmet dinner including mushrooms collected earlier in the day, and a Saturday-evening program.

For more information:
Puget Sound Mycological Society
(206) 522–6031 (voice mail); www.psms.org/

Fungus Among-Us

ungi of all kinds are beautiful, colorful, amusing—and a beneficial layer of our environment worthy of at least a casual understanding. There are more than 40,000 species in the Pacific Northwest alone.

Fungi are a cooperative form of life. They do not contain the chlorophyll that green plants use to make food. Rather they must obtain food from outside themselves to survive. Many form partnerships with plants and trees, providing nutrients to each other. This symbiotic association is called "mycorrhizae." These fungi are not just self-serving novelties, they are essential to the survival of all our forest ecosystems. Colonies of these fungi have been declared the largest biomass on earth! Many other fungi are called "saprobic," living on decayed plants and animals, adding to a rich soil layer.

In addition to understanding the unique and fundamental functions of these often ignored organisms, just finding the many fungi is fun to do! Some enthusiasts look at them primarily as a natural art form, admiring the many colors, textures and shapes, top and bottom, inside and out. A series of mushroom photographs look great on a wall; they're interesting to sketch or paint. You can make spore prints for identification or decoration. And many cooks find wild mushrooms to be wonderful additions to their creations.

No matter what the goal, the search is a treasure hunt. Even a beginner may find brilliant yellow or ruffled apricot jelly mushrooms, white spiny puffballs, purple club coral, white, crested coral, orange jelly-belly coral, brilliant red amanitas, white shaggy mane, orange fairy cup, and brown pig's ear.

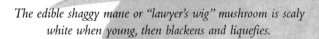

The edible shaggy mane or "lawyer's wig" mushroom is scaly white when young, then blackens and liquefies.

44

Voice of the Wild

The wolf is a symbol of nature untamed, but it is also a subject of fierce and hostile controversy. Take the opportunity this week to learn more about this fascinating and beautiful animal.

Site: Wolf Haven International, Point Defiance Zoo and Aquarium, and other Puget Sound locations.

Recommended time: National Wolf Awareness Week, sponsored by the Defenders of Wildlife, is the third week in October.

Minimum time commitment: A few hours or a day.

What to bring: Camera and binoculars for a really close look at those piercing eyes, entrance fees.

Directions: See below.

The background: It wasn't that long ago that wolf bounties, or cash rewards for dead animals, were still paid in this country. In the Midwest, as recently as the 1960s, one of the duties of some county employees was to pay the bounty for dead wolves brought in, cutting one ear off each hide to avoid payment duplication. Similar efforts across the country nearly exterminated the wolf from the wild.

Today there is a better understanding of the role of predators and a broader appreciation of all wildlife. Wolf reintroduction efforts are currently under way in Yellowstone National Park, the northern Rockies and the southwestern United States—efforts that have never been without passionate arguments on both sides. Olympic National Park has also been identified as a potential reintroduction area for wolves, but the process has just begun. Since

Gray wolves are very shy around people and likely to avoid encounters in the wild.

1996 Defenders of Wildlife, a nonprofit organization, has sponsored a number of events nationwide to "celebrate wolves" the third week in October.

The fun: Wolf Awareness Week events are held throughout the Puget Sound region, and more are being added every year. The Defenders of Wildlife Web site has a complete list.

Wolf Haven International, a wolf breeding and rearing site in Tenino, has specialized guided walking tours of the sanctuary daily throughout Wolf Awareness Week. Tours leave every hour, on the hour. October hours are from 10:00 A.M. to 4:00 P.M. (closed Tuesday). Ask about "howl-in" events. The sanctuary is located 7 miles southeast of I–5 exit 99, on eighty acres of lush forest and Mima Mound fields near Tenino.

Wolf Haven and Defenders of Wildlife host a Wolf Conservation Semi-Symposium the final Saturday of Wolf Awareness Week. Hours are 9:00 A.M. to 5:45 P.M., with a reception and silent auction at night; location varies. This event brings together wolf experts and enthusiasts. Attendees learn issues surrounding wolf recovery in places such as Yellowstone, Northern Rockies, Olympic National Park, and Idaho.

Topics have also included Mexican wolf recovery, rethinking our perception

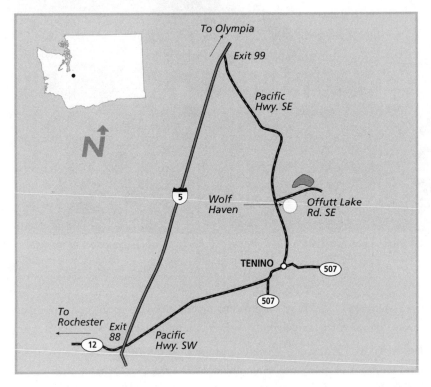

To Olympia

Exit 99

Pacific Hwy. SE

5

Wolf Haven

Offutt Lake Rd. SE

TENINO

507

507

To Rochester

Exit 88

12

Pacific Hwy. SW

N

of wolves, and care for captive wolves. Presenters usually include wolf experts from Defenders of Wildlife, U.S. Fish and Wildlife Service, Wolf Education Recovery Center (WERC), Wolf Haven, and Point Defiance Zoo and Aquarium. A small fee includes Semi-Symposium admission and a Wolf Haven guided tour.

Next best: Visit Point Defiance Zoo and Aquarium to see information displays in the Red Wolf exhibit; Defenders of Wildlife representatives are there to answer questions. The zoo is located at 5400 North Pearl Street, Tacoma, (I–90 exit 132). (See chapter 50 for map). Contact them at (253) 591–5337, or www.pdza.org/ for hours and other information.

Visit Northwest Trek Wildlife Park near Eatonville to see a wolf pack in a large natural-appearing environment with a variety of habitats. During daily wolf feeding, the keeper hides food near the viewing area and lets spectators see wolf hunting and dominance behaviors. Contact them at (360) 832–6117 or (800) 433–8735; www.nwtrek.org/. (See chapter 33 for NW Trek map.)

Look for the Wolf Awareness Week poster and displays of wolf books and literature in libraries all over western Washington.

For more information:
Defenders of Wildlife, Wolf Awareness Week
www.defenders.org/waw/
Wolf Haven International
(360) 264–4695 or (800) 448–9653; www.wolfhaven.org/

Their piercing eyes give wolves a fierce appearance, but they would rather avoid humans than confront them.

45

October

A Flourish of Foliage and Feathers

*Visit the southeastern corner of the state for the annual Fall
Festival of Foliage and Feathers. Experts guide you to see owls,
"champion big trees," and a variety of other birds and wildlife.*

Site: Walla Walla.

Recommended time: The four-day festival is held the last weekend in
October.

Minimum time commitment: As much as you can spare—there are
four jam-packed days of activities for everyone, Thursday through Sunday. If
you can spend only one day, Saturday is usually best.

What to bring: Binoculars for good birding, camera, bird and tree field
guides. Most workshops are free; small charge for each tour.

Directions: Walla Walla is located near the southeast border of our state,
on I–12.

The background: The Downtown Walla Walla Foundation created this
festival to highlight Walla Walla's designation by the city as a bird sanctuary
and its national status as a "Tree City USA." Be sure to include a tour of this
city's officially designated "biggest trees in the state."

The weather is usually pleasant in October and the leaves are gold and
red. You don't have to be athletic or a bird or tree expert—festival tours and
expert guides take care of that for you, encouraging everyone to participate.

The fun: It's tough to choose among so many enticing activities. There are
more than twenty guided tours of wildlife areas, trees and birds—even the
valley's wineries. There is an hour-long urban forest walking tour and a four-

Members of a festival tour stop at Madame Dorion Park on the Columbia River to look for white-throated sparrows.

hour tour of the McNary National Wildlife Refuge where the trails include a wheelchair-accessible walkway. The slough teems with waterfowl—as many as 80,000 Canada geese and 120,000 ducks winter at McNary and many have begun to arrive by now. In the evenings huge numbers of Canada geese fly into the refuge in continuous V-formations, making a raucous honking noise and quite a spectacle.

One unusual and popular activity is an evening trip to search for owls in a cemetery. Possible owl sightings include barn, great-horned, western screech, and maybe even northern saw-whet owls, all are common here. On one birding tour the bus passed an ordinary dirt bank that had lots of holes with white droppings below. It's a significant sign for those in the know. Just after sundown barn owls sit at the entrances getting ready for their nocturnal hunt.

The Natural Area Tour takes you on a walk around the Arthur G. Rempel Nature Trail at Fort Walla Walla (not the paved Recreation Trail nearby). More than eighty-five species of birds and seventeen species of mammals have been identified along the 1.2 miles of trails. Participants on one short walk saw a large flock of magpies roosting in a tree, many songbirds, a

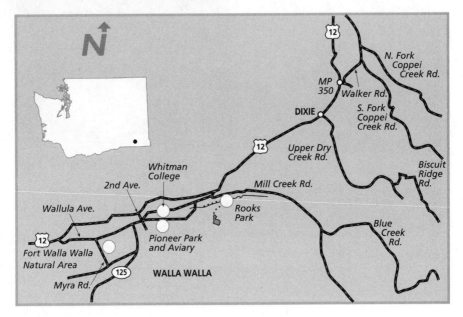

flicker, a great-horned owl, and rabbits.

In addition to the tours and trips, there are numerous workshops, ranging from bird identification to landscaping for wildlife. Special children's activities include making pinecone birdhouses and peanut-butter treats for the birds. Exhibits also include live birds of prey and exotic birds.

Don't miss the Heritage Tree Tour (or self-guided Big Tree walking tour) to see the splendid and colorful record trees throughout the Whitman College campus, Pioneer Park, and various private properties around Walla Walla. Some of the trees are over 110 feet tall (maple, poplar, pecan, London plane, walnut, oak, basswood, locust); some are in brilliant fall color (sweet-gum, maple, ginkgo, honeylocust, osage orange, chokeberry, sumac).

The Washington State Big Tree Program lists record trees throughout Washington. Walla Walla is a certified "Tree City USA"; it has forty-two trees that qualified for inclusion in this list, most of which were planted by farsighted citizens at the turn of the twentieth century. The Pioneer Park and Aviary Tour allows you to see some of these record trees in brilliant fall color, as well as a large variety of waterfowl in the covered ponds and pens of the aviary and the new waterfowl breeding building.

Next best: Several of the lower elevation roads in the foothills of the Blue Mountains east of Walla Walla have beautiful fall color in late October (higher elevations peak earlier in October). Enjoy brilliant yellow cottonwoods and aspen along the creeks, gold and rust foliage against the beige and brown hillsides, and occasional splashes of red and orange. Mill Creek, Biscuit Ridge, and North and South Coppei Creek roads are some of the prettiest.

Tour members board a special trolley in Pioneer Park, home to many record trees, all in colorful October foliage.

Food and lodging: Walla Walla offers all services.

For more information:
Fall Festival of Foliage and Feathers
www.downtownwallawalla.com/Promotions/festivalinformation.htm
Downtown Walla Walla Foundation
(509) 529–8755

46

November

Across the Border and Back

In late fall, schools of herring attract many species of birds to this uniquely located and excellent birding area on Point Roberts.

Site: Point Roberts is northwest of Bellingham, on a thumb-shaped protrusion of land that curls around Boundary Bay. Birch and Samish bays are north and south of Bellingham, respectively.

Recommended time: Early November, however birding is good from mid-October through mid-February.

Minimum time commitment: One day for Point Roberts; a long day or a weekend to visit all the areas south to Samish Bay.

What to bring: Binoculars, spotting scope, field guides, plus identification and proof of vehicle insurance for border crossings (Canadian currency exchange facility is located just a few yards over the border).

Directions: Travel north on I–5 to the U.S.–Canada border crossing at Blaine, then continue 12.4 miles north and west on Highway 99. Take exit 20 (Point Roberts) and drive west on Highway 10 for 4.6 miles; turn left (south) on Highway 17 (Tsawwassen Ferry Road); and in 3.5 miles turn south again on the Point Roberts Road. Drive 2.8 miles to the customs checkpoint, then back into the United States onto Point Roberts. Lighthouse Marine Park and Lily Point are located at the southwest and southeast extremities of the point.

The background: This strange arrangement, a tiny piece of Washington accessible only through Canada, is the result of an error during negotiation of the international boundary in 1872. The trip back and forth across the border is a gentle adventure, and the birding can be excellent.

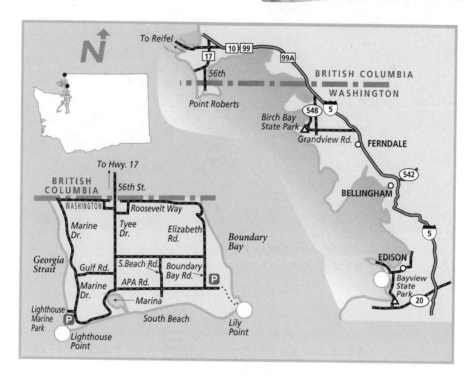

The fun: Get out those binoculars and bird books; the birds are abundant on this trip and easy to see. At Lighthouse Marine Park, walk the trail along the shore for the best views. Herring schools in October and November attract huge flocks of mixed species. At the end of Gulf Street, look for flocks of cormorants sitting on the pilings. Also watch for groups of great blue herons standing in fields; the largest heron colony (Northwest Coast subspecies) in the region is on the west side of Point Roberts.

To reach Lily Point, drive to the east end of APA Road and park near the cemetery. Round the barricade and take the 0.5-mile level trail to the bluff; the steep trail to the beach is just before trail end. Walk along the beach at low tide to see seabirds on Boundary Bay—huge numbers of western grebes and all three scoters in winter, as well as oldsquaws (long-tailed ducks).

*The common loon, here in subdued winter plumage, can be seen
in migration and in winter in Birch and Boundary bays.*

Birds move around a lot, so if they are sparse at these two locations, drive back into Canada and try the Roberts Banks south of the Tsawwassen Ferry. For an extra treat turn west at the Highway 17/10 interchange, drive through Ladner and then 2.3 miles farther west to the turnoff for the George C. Reifel Migratory Bird Sanctuary on Westham Island. The Wrangel Island snow goose population stops off here before heading down to the Skagit Valley (see chapter 5), and early November is a good time to see them. Waterfowl numbers also peak then. Many birds, such as wood ducks, mallards, chickadees, and sandhill cranes, are tame enough to allow you a long, close look.

Next best: To continue your birding drive, or for a shorter day trip, enjoy the seabirds at Birch Bay State Park and the raptors at Samish Flats.

To reach Birch Bay travel back through U.S. Customs at Blaine and then south on I–5 to exit 266, Grandview Road (SR 548). The entrance to Birch Bay State Park is 7 miles west, then 1 mile north on Jackson. Birding is good here through the winter—look for all three scoter species, all three loons, three or four grebe species, harlequin ducks bobbing and feeding in the surf, and many more. Continue north through the park and through the town of Birch Bay to Semiahmoo Marina for more good birding. Bald eagles are common in both locations. We once saw an eagle swoop down and grab a duck from the water and head back to the trees to feed.

To reach Samish Flats, which is about 28 miles south of Bellingham, take I–5 exit 230, Anacortes, and follow SR 20 west for 6.3 miles. Turn right onto Bayview-Edison Road and start looking for raptors—on the wires, in the air, and sometimes on the ground. At 3 miles is the north entrance to the 2.5-mile Padilla Bay Shore Trail, a paved path along the rich Padilla Bay Estuary. At 3.6 miles is Bayview State Park, with beach access and picnic shelters. Stop at the Breazeale Interpretive Center (4.1 miles) for maps and information, free exhibits, an upland trail, and rest rooms.

At 5.8 miles the countryside opens up to an overview of Samish Flats, a spectacular winter raptor area. From mid-October through March you have a good chance of seeing all five falcon species in one afternoon plus the "big four"—bald eagle, northern harrier, and rough-legged and red-tailed hawks. When snowy owls migrate south, this is a good place to see them. Stop here and look at Padilla Bay in the distance; you may see large flocks of wintering dunlin in flight. Great blue herons are common in fields throughout Samish Flats.

Continue north to a "T" intersection at 8.2 miles, watching for raptors all the way. From here a few of the best places to stop and look for raptors and shorebirds are:

■ *West 90 corner* (large parking area 0.7 mile west of the "T").
■ *East 90 corner* (shoulder parking 0.2 mile east of the "T"), the next corner north (0.6 mile), and the Edison parking area on the left just north of the Samish River (1.2 miles).
■ *Farmlands farther east*—at 1.6 miles turn right (south) on Farm-to-Market Road and look for raptors from the side roads (Sunset, Thomas, Field, and Church Roads are some of the best).
■ *D'Arcy Road*—drive west to complete the loop and watch for kestrels on the telephone wires (they nest 0.5-mile east of the Bayview-Edison Road).

Food and lodging: Both United States and Canadian cities along this route offer all services. Birch Bay and Bayview state parks have campsites and rest rooms.

During a chase, peregrine falcons can stoop (plunge steeply downward) at speeds of over 150 mph.

For more information:

Birch Bay and Bay View state parks
www.parks.wa.gov/alphanw.asp
Breazeale Interpretive Center
(360) 428–1558; inlet.geol.sc.edu/PDB/home.html
Pilchuck Audubon Society (weekly raptor field trips)
(425) 252–0926; www.pilchuckaudubon.com/
Skagit Audubon Society
(360) 424–9098; www.fidalgo.net/~audubon/

47

November

Endangered Species, Mating Dance

See endangered Columbian white-tailed deer at their refuge on the Columbia River during this month, the peak of their mating season.

Site: Julia Butler Hansen National Wildlife Refuge for the Columbian White-tailed Deer on the Lower Columbia River, about 30 miles west of I–5.

Recommended time: Rutting season starts in late October and lasts into December; mid-November is the peak—and the best time to see the bucks. Go in late October to combine rut and peak fall color.

Minimum time commitment: At least a half day for the refuge; a day or a weekend for a paddle tour.

What to bring: Binoculars, camera, walking shoes, field guide for birds.

Directions: From I–5 in southern Washington, exit at Kelso or Longview (exit 36 or 39) and drive west on SR 4 along the Columbia River, through Cathlamet. The refuge is west of the Elochoman River; the main viewing area is just past milepost 32.

The background: Wildlife biologists at the refuge advise that the best time to see Columbian white-tailed deer is during the rutting season in November, "when the deer are moving about in their mating dance."

In the 1930s the Columbian white-tailed deer was thought to be extinct. However, cooperative efforts are helping the population to recover. This sub-species is found only along the lower Columbia River near Cathlamet and a few sites in Oregon. The Julia Butler Hansen Refuge provides critical habitat for about 400 deer living on the refuge. Total population along the lower Columbia is only about 800.

Female Columbian white-tailed deer are relatively easy to see at the refuge year-round.

The big floods of several years ago severely reduced the number of deer in the mainland refuge, so measures are being taken to increase numbers. Cows are rotated through the fenced areas to keep the grass short and more nutritious for the deer. Coyote control has resulted in increased fawn survival.

The fun: You almost always see white-tailed does and fawns at the refuge, especially in the early morning and late afternoon, but the bucks are visible only during rut. Their antlers are at their biggest then, and they use them on everything from tree branches to fence posts. Because bucks are less wary during rutting season, you may even see them clashing antlers with each other. For your best chance of seeing them, ask at headquarters where they have been seen lately and sit quietly in that location in the early morning. It may take a while. In mid-November we saw two bucks chasing does early in the morning near headquarters.

Begin the 9.6-mile driving loop through the refuge by stopping at the information kiosks and blinds at the main viewing area near milepost 32. You often see Columbian white-tailed deer and elk from this area. The wetlands here were recently deepened to provide a place where pond weeds can grow and offer nutritious food for the deer in late summer when the grass is not as good. Waterfowl use the ponds in fall and winter.

Head west on SR 4, traveling the loop counterclockwise to spot wildlife from the driver's window. Your car makes an excellent blind for wildlife

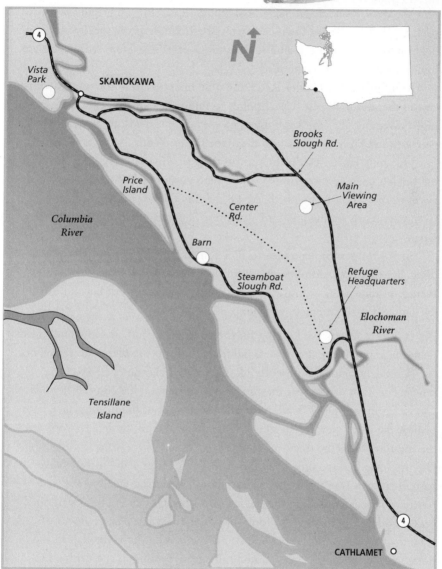

Vista
Park

SKAMOKAWA

Brooks
Slough Rd.

Price
Island

Main
Viewing
Area

Columbia
River

Center
Rd.

Barn

Refuge
Headquarters

Steamboat
Slough Rd.

Elochoman
River

Tensillane
Island

CATHLAMET

observation and photography; use binoculars, spotting scopes, and telephoto lenses.

Turn left on Brooks Slough Road and watch for cormorants and waterfowl in Brooks Slough. Also look for deer in the fields to the south—usually near the trees. Turn left on Steamboat Slough Road (turning right takes you back to the Skamokawa town center on SR 4). Look in the meadows that begin in 0.6 mile; you can almost always find deer here. Does with fawns are sometimes right next to the road.

At 4 miles is the Center Road, the only hiking path in the refuge, which crosses the meadows past several ponds to refuge headquarters. It closes in mid-November after the large flocks of wintering Canada geese arrive so that people won't flush the birds into neighboring farmlands.

One mile farther east is the spur to the Price Island Ferry dock. One piling holds a large nest; see osprey young here in summer. Watch for does and fawns in the brush to the north. At 4.8 miles is a large parking area for Columbia River fishing and bird-watching. The maintenance barn is to the north.

At 5.4 miles is the entrance to Elochoman Slough, a fine place for paddling. For the next 1.5 miles, watch for deer in the fields or near the roads. Refuge headquarters is on the left; the refuge entrance is just beyond. Turn left onto SR 4 to complete your loop.

Next best: As you are looking for the endangered and elusive white-tailed bucks in action, enjoy the other wildlife that inhabit the refuge in November.

A resident herd of Roosevelt elk is always visible somewhere on the refuge. For most of the year they are segregated into a doe and calf herd and a loose group of bulls. Elk are most often seen west of the maintenance barn or near the main viewing area but can be anywhere on the refuge. Look in the meadows near the trees.

In November see short-eared owls in the fields near the maintenance barn, barn owls on early-morning nature walks, and red-tailed hawks and northern harriers searching the fields for rodents, plus all the birds described on the paddle trip below. Also look for white-tailed kites. Large flocks of waterfowl arrive in November and stay all winter. Look for the darker and more rare dusky Canada geese among the geese feeding in the fields and wetlands. Wintering ducks are abundant on the ponds and sloughs, and large groups of tundra swans fly in toward the end of November.

Wildlife viewing by kayak is a special treat. Launching facilities are available at the Cathlamet Mooring Basin, the WDFW boat launch on SR 4, and

Skamokawa Vista Park. As you paddle look for bald eagles and peregrine falcons over Price Island. See western grebes, pied-billed grebes, common loons, double-crested cormorants, and gulls fishing on the Columbia River. They often dive under the water as you approach, so keep a sharp lookout. Paddle up tidal sloughs teeming with buffleheads, scaups, and other ducks; and see a variety of songbirds in the fields on a short after-lunch walk.

Better yet, sign up with the Skamokawa Paddle Center for one of their scheduled weekend tours. These include wildlife and bird viewing by kayak, nature walks, and a stay at the Skamokawa B&B. Brilliant fall color is the attraction at the end of October. Tours in November focus on deer, seals, otters, and birds; late November features tundra swans. Contact them at (888) 920–2777; www.skamokawapaddle.com/.

If you have a group of at least four, the paddle center will arrange a special kayak and walking tour on Tenasillahe Island's 7.5-mile dike. You are likely to see twenty or more of the 200-plus resident white-tailed deer in November, even during the middle of the day.

Food and lodging: Skamokawa Inn B&B, paddle center, and general store are right on the river; camping is available at Skamokawa Vista Park (showers). Cathlamet offers all services.

For more information:

Julia Butler Hansen National Wildlife Refuge for the Columbian White-tailed Deer
(360) 795–3915

48

Wild Sanctuaries in the Big City

Check out Green Lake and four other parks in the greater Seattle area that offer nature walks in fall and winter.

Site: Green Lake and other local parks in Seattle, Bellevue, and Kirkland.

Recommended time: For Green Lake, October through April, first and third Saturday of each month, 8:00 A.M.

Minimum time commitment: Three hours.

What to bring: Walking shoes, warm clothing, binoculars.

Directions: Take I–5 exit 170, drive west on Northeast Ravenna Boulevard, then north on Greenlake Drive N. The east entrance is just north of the Ravenna intersection. Meet on the beach in front of Evans Pool.

The background: Most of these walks are free, two or three hours long, and led by a park naturalist or a knowledgeable volunteer. Guided walks are an easy way to explore and learn more about wildlife and nature in beautiful and varied settings.

The fun: Green Lake is a natural preserve for hundreds of species of trees and plants in the center of a dense urban neighborhood. It draws thousands of people daily to enjoy the water, green space, and numerous birds. Pied-billed grebe expert Martin Mueller, a Green Lake Park Alliance volunteer, leads 2.8-mile winter bird walks around the lake. No sign-up is required, but it is limited to the first fifteen participants, so you may want to get there a little early.

It's a leisurely stroll, with lots of stops to find the male Eurasian wigeon and look at geese, dabbling ducks, buffleheads, goldeneyes, mergansers, pied-

During winter, Eurasian wigeons may occasionally be seen mixed in with flocks of American wigeons. Look for the tawny brown head of the male.

billed and western grebes, and songbirds. Green Lake averages thirty-five to forty species of birds in the winter, but only about fifteen in summer.

A pair of bald eagles established a new nest near Green Lake in 1999—the first in the neighborhood (over sixty pairs of bald eagles nest in the Seattle area). You will usually see several of these regal birds in flight or roosting in the trees. One group also saw a Cooper's hawk chasing a kingfisher. The real treat came at the end of the walk, however, when an unbanded (new to the area), immature peregrine falcon flew in and landed in a tree right in front of Evans Pool. It sat there long enough for everyone who walked by to see this unusual sight through Martin's scope.

Next best in Seattle: These walks require reservations (get directions when you reserve).

■ *Discovery Park* is a 534-acre park situated on Magnolia Bluff overlooking Puget Sound. It provides a sanctuary for wildlife, as well as a place for people to learn about the natural world. Its 2 miles of protected tidal beaches and dramatic cliffs, open meadowlands and forest groves, thickets and streams provide shelter for more than 230 resident and migrant birds.

48a/ Seattle Parks

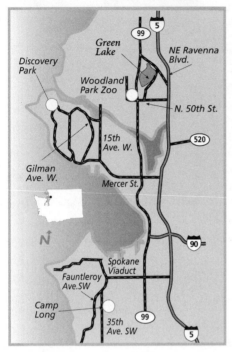

Naturalists lead nature walks on most Saturdays—usually from 2:00 to 3:30 P.M. Depending on the season you may walk the beach to discover migrant birds, walk through the forest to look at fall color, or learn about evergreens. Call (206) 386–4236 for reservations and information.

■ *Camp Long* is a 68-acre park in West Seattle. On several Saturdays each month park naturalists lead free interpretive walks at 2:00 P.M. You may take a family walk through the forest, celebrate the winter solstice, participate in maple sugar tapping, or explore winter plants and animals. On Thursday, join a Camp Long naturalist to explore other South Seattle parks. Call (206) 684–7434 for reservations and information.

Next best on Lake Washington's east side (no reservations):

■ *Lake Hills Greenbelt,* in Bellevue, stretches from Larsen Lake to Phantom Lake. Stop at the Lake Hills Ranger Station on Southeast Sixteenth Street, just west of 148th Avenue SE, to learn about the native vegetation and wildlife of this beautiful wetland corridor. Call (425) 452–7225 for information on guided Saturday nature walks.

■ *Juanita Bay Park,* 114 acres in Kirkland, is home to a vast array of waterfowl as well as beavers, turtles, muskrats, and other birds. Guided nature walks are held on the first Sunday of every month at 1:00 P.M.; meet in the parking lot at 2201 Market Street. A system of boardwalks leads you through wetlands and along the bay. See numerous waterfowl, common snipe, great blue herons, red-tailed hawks, and more. For a real treat head back to the bay as evening approaches to catch the beavers coming out for nighttime activities. Call (425) 828–2237 for information.

■ *Mercer Slough Nature Park,* in Bellevue, is the largest remaining wetland on Lake Washington. Marshes, meadows, and forest provide critical habitat for more than one hundred species of birds, as well as coyotes, beavers, and muskrats. Free ranger-led nature walks resume in January and are held at 11:00 A.M. on Sunday. Walks start at the Winters House Visitor Center, 2102 Bellevue Way SE and explore different parts of the park's 5 miles of trails, depending on the discussion topic, which may cover wetland ecology, wildlife, flora, fauna, or history. Call (425) 452–2752.

For more information:

Seattle Parks and Recreation
(206) 386–1419; www.pan.ci.
seattle.wa.us/seattle/parks/
environment/index.htm
Greenlake
(206) 985–9235

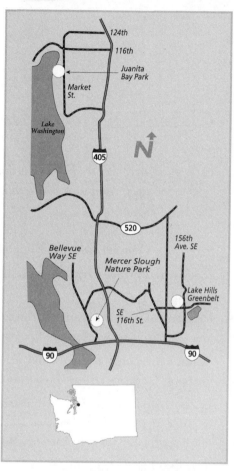

49

November

Champion Trees Measure Up

Let's go see trees this weekend! Not just any trees, but "big trees," "champion trees," measured and certified by the Washington State Big Tree Program.

Site: Lake Quinault, Olympic National Park and National Forest.

Recommended time: Some of the champion trees are accessible year-round.

Minimum time commitment: Half a day plus travel time; or take a long Thanksgiving weekend and enjoy giant trees all along the coast.

What to bring: Camera, binoculars, rain gear, boots, tree field guide, and the book *Champion Trees of Washington State* by Robert Van Pelt.

Directions: From I–5 in Olympia, take exit 104 and drive 48 miles west on SR 8 and US 12 to Aberdeen. Take US 101 west to Hoquiam and then north another 38 miles to Lake Quinault.

The background: How would you like to have "measuring trees" in your job description? Robert Van Pelt does. He is the Washington State Big Tree Program coordinator and research associate at the University of Washington. Part of his job is finding and documenting "champion trees"— trees that are the largest known example of their species. The Big Tree Program is a national program and, as you can imagine, the competition is often intense, but friendly.

An American Forestry Association point system—based on circumference, height, and crown spread—is used to determine a champion tree. The three largest trees in Washington are a western redcedar, a Sitka spruce, and a Douglas-fir; they are all in the rain forest.

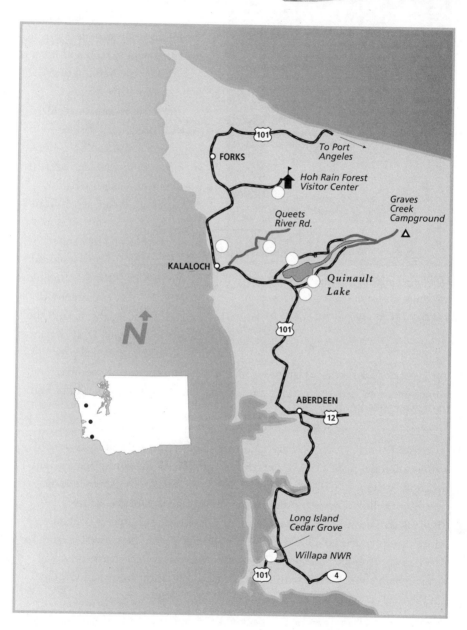

101
FORKS
To Port Angeles
Hoh Rain Forest Visitor Center
Graves Creek Campground
Queets River Rd.
KALALOCH
Quinault Lake
101
N
ABERDEEN
12
Long Island Cedar Grove
Willapa NWR
101
4

Take the Forks logging tour May through September to see the second largest western redcedar tree in the nation (178 feet tall).

The fun: Tracking down champion trees is like a treasure hunt—and you can learn something in the process. Take along a field guide to make sure that the big tree you have found is truly the right species and learn how to identify Washington's most common native trees.

To see awe-inspiring old-growth forest, head for the Olympic Peninsula. The national cochampion western redcedar is located on Lake Quinault's North Shore Road, across from Lake Quinault Resort. It is a moderately steep, 0.25-mile hike from the Chitum trailhead to the tree. Its 20-foot-diameter trunk (63.4 feet circumference) and 159-foot height make it the largest in the state. Truly a giant of a tree! The national park visitor center (closed until mid-June) is several miles up the road; accessible rest rooms are open year-round. Take an easy 0.5-mile loop walk around the lush Maple Glade Rain Forest Trail.

The national co-champion Sitka spruce, 191 feet high and over 58 feet in circumference, grows on Lake Quinault's South Shore Road in an area of cabins 3.2 miles from US 101 (watch for sign). The Rain Forest Nature Trail is 1.3 miles from US 101 on South Shore Road. The lovely 0.5-mile loop winds up Willaby Creek and through a forest of giant Douglas-fir trees (Northwest Forest Pass required). This area has been measured as containing more than 600,000 board feet per acre—another Pacific Northwest record. In 1998 a new national champion Douglas-fir was discovered near here; a trail may be built soon. Check with the national forest visitor information office up the road.

Next best: If you stay for the weekend, visit more giant trees on the peninsula.

Sixteen miles west of Quinault, the Queets River Road turns north off US 101. The largest known Sitka spruce (volume) is located across the road from Queets River Campground. You can see it from the road; there is a short unmarked trail. According to Van Pelt it is "one of the fastest-growing trees on earth, adding as much as 700 cubic feet per year." Or hike 2.6 miles up the Queets River and Klockman Rock Trails to see the second largest Douglas-fir (202 feet tall, 44.5 feet around).

North of Kalaloch turn right (east) off US 101 on a signed gravel road north of milepost 162, and drive 0.3 mile to view the widest western redcedar in Washington. It is a gnarled, hollowed-out tree you can walk inside (64.2 feet in circumference but only 123 feet tall). Farther north on US 101 (south of Forks), turn east on the Hoh River Road and drive 16 miles upriver to see the third-largest Sitka spruce. Visit the Hoh Rain Forest Visitor Center 2.5 miles farther east and hike some of the short, luxuriant rain forest trails nearby.

If you have access to a boat, visit Long Island in the Willapa National Wildlife Refuge, and hike the 2.6-mile trail to the Long Island Cedar Grove. This grove of magnificent old-growth cedars is up to 4,000 years old and has reached full maturity without human interference—a rare terminal forest, and probably the only one on the Pacific Coast.

Food and lodging: Facilities on North Shore and South Shore roads and in Amanda Park offer all services; a few campgrounds are open in November.

For more information:
Olympic National Forest Headquarters
Quinault Visitor Information Office
(360) 288–2525
Olympic National Park Giant Trees
www.northolympic.com/onp/recordtrees.html or
www.nps.gov/olym/invrecord.htm

50

December

Wildlife Parties

December is a busy month! Go see reindeer and other animals at the zoo one morning and still get your cards addressed. Bring your gift list and "adopt a reindeer" for someone special.

Site: Cougar Mountain Zoological Park in Issaquah, east of Seattle, and other zoos.

Recommended time: December.

Minimum time commitment: Take a few hours and enjoy.

What to bring: Warm clothes, entrance fee.

Directions: From either direction on I–90, take Issaquah exit 15. Drive south on Renton-Issaquah Road, then right (west) on Newport Way and left (south) on Southeast Fifty-fourth.

The background: Santa's Reindeer Farm, site of the annual Reindeer Festival, is located permanently at the Cougar Mountain Zoo. It is said that Santa himself selected this site as being easily accessible from the North Pole. Twenty to thirty captive-bred reindeer reside here year-round. They are kept in three large enclosures in December so that you can observe these beautiful animals at close range.

These "reindeer" are a different subspecies of caribou from the ones that have been relocated from Canada to the Selkirk Mountains over the past several years, but they are all in the same family, and these are much easier to see.

The fun: The Reindeer Festival is held at Issaquah's Cougar Mountain

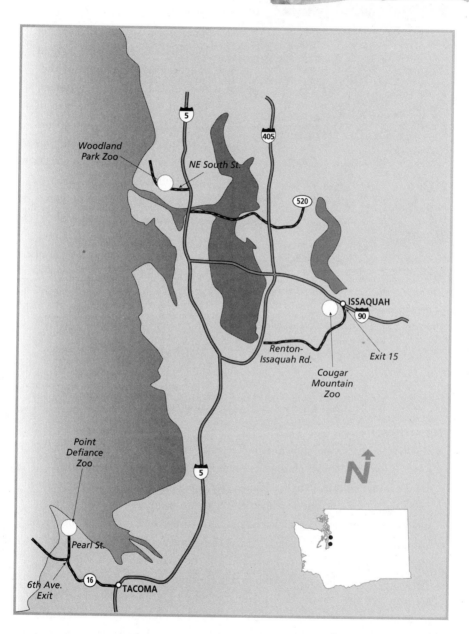

Woodland
Park Zoo

NE South St.

5

405

520

ISSAQUAH

90

Renton-
Issaquah Rd.

Exit 15

Cougar
Mountain
Zoo

Point
Defiance
Zoo

5

N

Pearl St.

6th Ave.
Exit

16

TACOMA

Female caribou are the only females of the deer species that have antlers. They keep them through the winter, thus enabling them to better compete for food.

Zoo nearly the entire month of December on Wednesday through Sunday, plus at least two extra days just before Christmas. The zoo is closed in the winter, but the Reindeer Farm is open mornings and evenings for the festival. It features live reindeer, play areas for the reindeer team, Santa's Sleigh Collection, a run for Santa's takeoffs and landings, the Elves' Workshop, and Santa's very own two-story house.

Evenings, confide to Santa your dearest Christmas wishes and have a picture taken. Santa and his helpers tell visitors about where reindeer live, what they eat, and how to "adopt" a reindeer as a special gift. Sit in Santa's Grand Traveling Sleigh, enjoy music, Christmas lights, and watch Santa's big kittens (beautiful cougars in a large, natural setting) frolic and play.

Next best:

- *Point Defiance Zoo and Aquarium* in Tacoma features "Zoolights," a festive array of lighted displays (more than half a million lights) with a nature theme. Some favorites are the Flame Tree, adorned with 30,000 purple and green lights; the enormous alligator; a "leopard in lights" climbing a tree; and various nursery rhyme characters. Parts of the zoo, including the Arctic Tundra exhibit with polar bears, musk oxen, and Arctic foxes, are open for nighttime viewing. The snack bar and gift shops are also open. Zoolights opens the last Friday in November and continues nightly from 5:00 to 9:00 P.M. through the first Sunday in January; closed December 24 and 25. Call (253) 591–5337 or (253) 591–5268 or visit www.pdza.org/ for directions.
- *Woodland Park Zoological Gardens* in Seattle adds its "Holiday Zoobilee" to holiday attractions the first three weekends in December. While you are

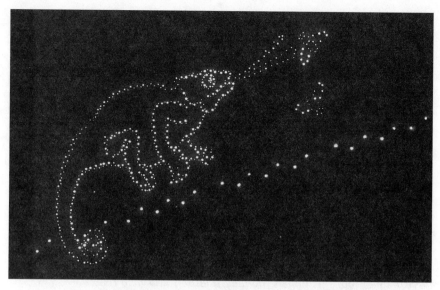

Thousands of people visit the Point Defiance Zoo at night in December just to see the spectacular "zoolights."

there, celebrate winter at the Northern Trail exhibit with the bald eagle, gray wolf, grizzly bear, fisher, river otter, mountain goat, and elk. Call (206) 684–4800 or visit www.zoo.org/zoo_info/plan.htm for directions and event schedule.

For more information:

Cougar Mountain Zoological Park
(425) 391–5508; www.cougarmountainzoo.org/

51

December

Over a Century of Tradition

The National Audubon Society Christmas Bird Count is a nationwide survey of birds that began in 1900 and hasn't missed a year since. Join this birders' holiday tradition and help collect important data.

Site: All over Washington, every Audubon chapter in the state participates in this annual event.

Recommended time: The official Christmas Bird Count (CBC) period always runs December 14 through January 5.

Minimum time commitment: Hardy birders count from midnight to midnight on the designated day (most of the effort is from dawn to dusk) and then share stories over a potluck dinner. Volunteers who can only spend shorter periods of time are also welcome.

What to bring: Binoculars, spotting scopes, bird field guides, maps, clothing to suit the cold weather, snacks, water.

Directions: Contact an Audubon chapter and discuss which group and area to join.

The background: It all began more than one hundred years ago. According to the National Audubon Society, in 1900 ornithologist Frank Chapman was appalled by another holiday tradition at that time, the "side hunt." The team that shot the most birds and other small animals during this hunting event won. As a protest Chapman organized "27 friends in 25 locations" on Christmas Day at the beginning of the twentieth century to count birds, not shoot them.

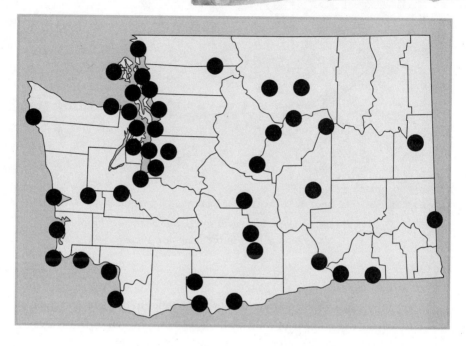

The tradition took off from there and today, bridging into another century, more than 45,000 persons from all fifty states, every Canadian province, the Caribbean, Central and South America, and the Pacific Islands participate in about 1,700 counts. It is, says NAS, the "largest and longest-running wildlife survey ever undertaken." It is exciting that even nonscientists can participate and contribute to an ever-growing body of scientific knowledge.

To get an idea of the amount of data the CBC is supplying, check the Web site sponsored by the Patuxent Wildlife Research Center to see lists and maps of bird populations, distribution, and change over time. The analyses are adjusted so that the data can remain consistently meaningful, even though the birder participation has markedly increased. Just skimming over this data gives you a real sense of how valuable this census is and how good you will feel when you take part.

The fun: Even if you've never done this before, don't be intimidated. Birders of all levels are welcome to join in; experts are mixed with beginners.

*While others look for birds with scopes, this birder uses his camera
to capture birds in the snow near Yakima.*

The sample area for each group is a circle 15 miles in diameter in which all bird species and number of individual birds positively seen or heard are counted. Some groups carpool in caravans, stopping at prescribed intervals to count and retreating to warm vehicles when necessary. Some use the count as a nice excuse to visit a favorite habitat and share the experience with fellow birders. All groups come back to recount their experiences, to share humorous stories of their day, and to debate identifications of unusual birds. It is a day of fellowship, scientific contributions, and fun.

Next best: Sometimes there is simply no time to go anywhere, but you can still watch birds in your own backyard—especially if you provide food to bring them closer. According to the National Audubon Society, "one-third of the adult population of North America dispenses about a billion pounds of birdseed each year as well as tons of suet and gourmet 'seed cakes.'" NAS also reports that limited studies so far do not indicate any problems caused by supplemental feeding, such as altering migration patterns or causing undue dependence on feeders. In other words, feeding birds in your own backyard is pure pleasure for both birds and bird-watchers!

With just a few bird feeders and a good water source, you can attract a large variety of birds (most likely are pine siskins, chickadees, jays, finches, dark-eyed juncos, house sparrows, varied thrushes, and spotted towhees). Add suet to attract downy and hairy woodpeckers, northern flickers, and red-breasted nuthatches. *Landscaping for Wildlife in the Pacific Northwest* by Russell Link, urban wildlife biologist for the state of Washington, is an excellent reference, expecially if you want to further enhance your own personal wildlife habitat with a water source, native plants, trees, and shrubs with berries.

Northern flickers eat more ants than any other North American bird, but also love to eat backyard feeder suet in winter.

Next year, enroll in Project Feeder Watch to regularly report the birds that visit your feeders from November through April. The watch began in 1987, and today nearly 14,000 FeederWatchers contribute information each year.

Another option is to participate in the Great Backyard Bird Count to count birds in your backyard or other area during a few minutes each day for four days, usually in February. For more information on both of these activities, go to www.birdsource.org/.

For more information:
Audubon Society Christmas Bird Count
wa.audubon.org/cbc.htm
Washington Ornithological Society CBC Page
www.wos.org/WACBCs.htm
Patuxent Wildlife Research Center
www.mbr.nbs.gov/cbc/cbcnew.html

52

December

Take Time for Tranquillity

It's time to relax, reflect, and prepare for another year of nature adventures. Travel to resorts in the Columbia River Gorge this weekend and enjoy.

Site: Two Columbia Gorge resorts, both near White Salmon.

Recommended time: If not now, when?

Minimum time commitment: Take as much time as you need or can—a day, a weekend, more.

What to bring: Journal, book, camera, sketch pad, warm and cozy clothes. Do *not* bring laptop, pager, or work-I've-been-meaning-to-do.

Directions: White Salmon is about 65 miles east of Vancouver, just off SR 14.

The background: Washington has many nature retreats, commercial as well as free—in the mountains, on the water, and in the woods—that are ideal settings for relaxing or enjoying outdoor, nature-oriented activities during this winter holiday period.

If you prefer a more rustic winter retreat or need a lower-cost alternative, pick a place, any place, that is really pretty. Take a picnic lunch with a thermos of hot soup, or bring the camp stove and cook up a stir-fry. Take a deep breath, slow down, and really look at your surroundings. Then look at the details—snow on a tree branch, ice glistening in the sun, the way the winter light changes colors in the landscape. Sketch a pattern; take your time with a camera close-up. Breathe.

The fun: It's hard to choose. Will it be a hot mineral bath, walking,

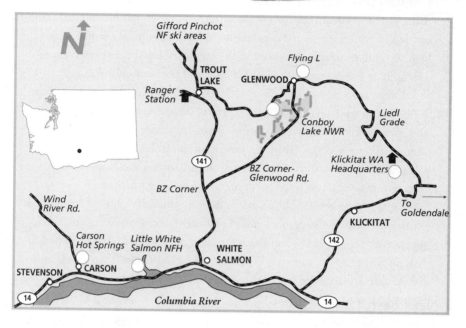

bird-watching, cross-country skiing, kayaking—or maybe a self-indulgent combination.

■ *Carson Mineral Hot Springs Motel and Restaurant:* Located in Carson, on the Columbia River, the historic nine-room hotel was built about 1901. There are two soaking rooms in the bathhouse; each has old, claw-foot tubs for a twenty-minute soak in natural, 110-degree mineral water. Massages are also available—good for what ails you, they say. The twelve cabins are rustic, with no TV or phones. There are two kitchenette suites and one hot tub suite with two bedrooms. The complex includes a restaurant; an RV park is nearby. For reservations call (509) 427–8292 or (800) 607–3678.

Other attractions: Drive scenic SR 14 along the Columbia Gorge. Visit the Little White Salmon National Fish Hatchery east of the Cook-Underwood Road to see salmon year-round in the viewing ponds. Eagles nest nearby and fly in to feast on salmon carcasses; waterfowl are on the

river in winter. If you want to see waterfalls, take a detour to the Oregon
side of the river—they are spectacular.

■ *Flying L Ranch:* A one-hundred-acre retreat at the base of Mount Adams
near Glenwood, it's a popular and busy place, but it doesn't bustle. You can
make the ranch your base for a wide variety of year-round recreational activities, but in winter guests come primarily to cross-country ski or just to relax.
Delicious full breakfasts are served in the ranch cookhouse. For reservations
call (509) 364–3488 or (888) 682–3267; or visit www.mt-adams.com.

Other attractions: The lake at Conboy Lake National Wildlife Refuge
is flooded in mid-December for waterfowl (larger numbers of swans, geese,
and ducks arrive in February during spring migration). Easy cross-country
skiing trails are accessed from the ranch; more challenging trails are in the
Gifford Pinchot National Forest north of the Trout Lake Ranger Station
(See trail map at www.fs.fed.us/gpnf/wrec/d3_ccs.htm#map.)

To see large herds of black-tailed deer by ski, drive about 18 miles east
on the Glenwood-Goldendale Road and down the sharply curving and
spectacular Liedl Grade (deer are often seen on the south-facing slopes).
Ask for directions at Klickitat Wildlife Area headquarters, then cross-country ski across the refuge to see the deer that winter on the refuge.

Next best: The number of nature-oriented resorts in Washington has
greatly increased over the past few years; many have settings that inspire both
adventure and reflection. We list only one in each area, but we urge you to
explore others. When we chose these they were well run, clean, and special in
some way; however, inclusion in this list cannot be considered an endorse-
ment or guarantee.

On-the-Water Resorts

On the Strait of Juan de Fuca west of Sekui is Chito Beach Resort
(360–963–2581; www.olypen.com/chitobch/). The house and three cabins sit
on a peninsula surrounded by beachfront. Walk the beaches, explore tidepools, or enjoy the view of Vancouver Island. See porpoises, river and sea
otters, bald eagles, and seabirds from the resort.

On the central Olympic Coast, Kalaloch Lodge (360–962–2271;
www.visitKalaloch.com) sits on a bluff overlooking the Pacific Ocean.
Choose guest rooms in the lodge or cozy, oceanfront log cabins. Enjoy
beachcombing, tidepools, and wildlife viewing here and at beaches to the
north.

Twenty-seven miles from the coast, on a pristine mountain lake, is ninety-
two-room Lake Quinault Lodge (800–562–6672; www.visitlakequinault.com).

Relax in the main lobby with its grand brick fireplace, or hike the rain forest trails. Winter Elderhostel programs (800–775–3720) are offered at both Lake Quinault and Kalaloch lodges.

Thirty miles up the Columbia River is Skamokawa Inn B&B and the Paddle Center and Estuary Program. Enjoy historic Skamokawa, or take a natural history kayak tour to see the beauty and wildlife in the sloughs of the Columbia River. Contact (888) 920–2777 or www.skamokawapaddle.com for information or reservations.

In the San Juan Islands, northwest of Anacortes, many resorts offer beauty and solitude. On San Juan Island is Lakedale Resort (800–617–2267; www.lakedale. com/). Its cozy upscale log cabins (six people maximum, kitchens)

Nature can transform our spirits at any time of the year.

and lodge overlook Neva Lake and are surrounded by parklands and forest. Look for trumpeter swans on the lake, paddle the quiet waters, or walk the trails.

On Lopez Island, Lopez Farm Cottages (800–440–3556; www.lopez farmcottages.com/) offer small but delightful Scandinavian-style cottages (kitchen, continental breakfast). Enjoy the hot tub set among towering trees, watch the rabbits romp across the meadows, or look for deer in the woodlands.

Orcas Island is home to Doe Bay Resort (360–376–2291; www.doebay. com). It has new and old, always "funky" cabins of all sizes and campsites on the water or in the woods (yurts in summer). Enjoy the hot tubs, sauna, massage, and cafe with natural foods.

Mountain Resorts

The Methow Valley (North Cascades) offers snow activities in a beautiful and peaceful setting. Most resorts offer easy access to the Methow Valley Trail System for cross-country skiing and snowshoeing. We especially enjoyed the lovely Chewuch Inn (800–747–3107; www.chewuchinn.com) in Winthrop—they even arranged a balloon ride.

Several upscale resorts outside Leavenworth (Central Cascades) offer secluded, meditative settings among the snow-covered mountains. Mountain Springs Lodge (800–858–2276; www.mtsprings.com) has been our fall retreat choice for several years. The lodges (soaring timbered ceilings, river-rock fireplaces, and hot tubs) are set in a gorgeous mountain valley.

Mount Rainier Park (South Cascades) is home to the National Park Inn at Longmire, with its spectacular vistas of Mount Rainier. The inn is reminiscent of early-day hostelries with its cozy rooms and stone fireplace. For reservations contact 360–569–2275; www.guestservices.com/rainier/. For guided winter snowshoe tours contact the Longmire Information Center at (360) 569–2211, ext. 3314.

For more information:

Lodging in the Methow
(888) 463–8469; www.winthropwashington.com/accommodations.html
Olympic Peninsula Lodging
www.olympicpeninsula.com/
San Juan Islands Lodging
(360) 468–3663 or (888) 468–3790; www.guidetosanjuans.com/. (Click on "Finding a Place to Stay")

Appendix A:

References and Recommended Reading

Flora (Fungi, Huckleberries, Trees, and Wildflowers)

Alden, Peter, Dennis Paulson, et al. *National Audubon Society Field Guide to the Pacific Northwest*. New York: Alfred A. Knopf, Inc., 1998.

Arora, David. *Mushrooms Demystified, a Comprehensive Guide to the Fleshy Fungi*. Berkeley: Ten Speed Press, 1986.

Arora, David. *All That the Rain Promises and More . . . .* Berkeley: Ten Speed Press, 1991.

Camp, Pamela, Maggie McManus, et al. *Watchable Wildflowers, A Columbia Basin Guide*. Bureau of Land Management: Wenatchee, 1998. (Available from BLM office, 915 Walla Walla, Wenatchee, WA 98801; 509–665–2100).

Churney, Marie and Susan Williams. *Bogs, Meadows, Marshes and Swamps, A Guide to 25 Wetland Sites of Washington State*. Seattle: The Mountaineers, 1996.

Kozloff, Eugene N. *Plants and Animals of the Pacific Northwest*. Seattle: University of Washington Press, 1995.

Little, Elbert L. *Audubon Society Field Guide to North American Trees, Western Region*. New York: Alfred A. Knopf, Inc., 1980.

McKenny, Margaret and Daniel E. Stuntz. *The New Savory Wild Mushroom*. Seattle: University of Washington Press, 1987.

McNulty, Tim. *Olympic National Park: A Natural History Guide*. Boston: Houghton Mifflin Company, 1996.

O'Connor, Georganne and Karen Wieda. *Northwest Arid Lands: An Introduction to the Columbia Basin Shrub-Steppe*. Ohio: Battelle Press, 2000.

Pojar, Jim and Andy Mackinnon. *Plants of the Pacific Northwest Coast*. Redmond: Lone Pine Publishing, 1996.

Spellenberg, Richard. *Audubon Society Field Guide to North American Wildflowers, Western Region*. New York: Alfred A. Knopf, Inc., 1979.

Stroufe, Terry. *Spring and Fall Mushrooms.* Mount Hood National Forest: Northwest Interpretive Association.

Taylor, Ronald J. *Sagebrush Country, A Wildflower Sanctuary.* Montana: Mountain Press Publishing Company, 1992.

Van Pelt, Robert. *Champion Trees of Washington State.* Seattle: University of Washington Press, 1996.

Fauna (Birds, Butterflies, Mammals, Reptiles, and Amphibians)

Adams, Evelyn. *San Juan Island Wildlife.* Seattle: The Mountaineers, 1995.

Angell, Tony and Kenneth C. Balcomb III. *Marine Birds and Mammals of Puget Sound.* Seattle: Puget Sound Books, 1982.

Brown, Herbert A. *Reptiles of Washington and Oregon.* Seattle: Seattle Audubon Society, 1995.

Butler, Robert W. *The Great Blue Heron: A Natural History and Ecology of a Seashore Sentinel.* Vancouver, BC: University of British Columbia, 1997.

Ewing, Susan. *Going Wild in Washington and Oregon.* Anchorage, Seattle, Portland: Alaska Northwest Books, 1993.

Gordon, David G. *The Audubon Society Field Guide to the Bald Eagle.* Seattle: Sasquatch Books, 1991.

Gordon, David G. and Chuck Flattery. *The American Cetacean Society Field Guide to the Orca.* Seattle: Sasquatch Books, 1990.

The Ocean Society Field Guide to the Gray Whale. Seattle: Sasquatch Books, 1989.

La Tourrette, Joe. *Washington Wildlife Viewing Guide.* Helena: Falcon Press, 1992.

La Tourrette, Joe and the National Wildlife Federation. *Wildlife Watcher's Handbook, A Guide to Observing Animals in the Wild.* New York: Henry Holt and Company, 1997.

Leonard, William P. *Amphibians of Washington and Oregon.* Seattle: Seattle Audubon Society, 1993.

Lewis, Mark G. and Fred A. Sharpe. *Birding in the San Juan Islands.* Seattle: The Mountaineers, 1987.

Link, Russell. *Landscaping for Wildlife in the Pacific Northwest.* Seattle: University of Washington Press, 1999.

MacRae, Diann. *Birder's Guide to Washington.* Houston: Gulf Publishing Company, 1995.

Morse, Bob. *A Birder's Guide to Ocean Shores, Washington.* Olympia: R. W. Morse Company, 1999.

Pettingill, Olin Sewall, Jr. *A Guide to Bird Finding West of the Mississippi.* New York: Oxford University Press, 1981.

Sheldon, Ian. *Seashores of the Pacific Northwest.* Renton: Lone Pine Publishing, 1998.

Steelquist, Robert U. *Ferryboat Field Guide to Puget Sound.* Helena: American Geographic Publishing, 1989.

Tilden, J.W. and Arthur C. Smith. *A Field Guide to Western Butterflies.* Boston: Houghton Mifflin Company, 1986.

Wahl, Terence R. and Dennis R. Paulson. *A Guide to Bird Finding in Washington.* Bellingham: T. Wahl, 1994.

Whitaker, John O., Jr. *National Audubon Society Field Guide to North American Mammals.* New York: Alfred A. Knopf, Inc., 1997.

Astronomy, Beachcombing, General Nature, Glaciers, Hikes and Walks, Tidepooling, Volcanoes, and Waterfalls

Davis, James Luther. *Seasonal Guide to the Natural Year, A Month by Month Guide to Natural Events, Oregon, Washington and British Columbia.* Golden: Fulcrum Publishing, 1996.

Landers, Rich and Ida Rowe Dolphin. *100 Hikes in the Inland Northwest.* Seattle: The Mountaineers, 1987.

Mueller, Marge and Ted. *Washington's South Cascades Volcanic Landscapes.* Seattle: The Mountaineers, 1995.

Pich, Walter C. *Beachcombers Guide to the Northwest*. Federal Way, WA: Pich Publishing, 1997.

Plumb, Gregory A. *A Waterfall Lover's Guide to the Pacific Northwest*. Seattle: The Mountaineers, 1998.

Shane, Scott. *Discovering Mount St. Helens, A Guide to the National Volcanic Monument*. Seattle: University of Washington Press, 1985.

Spring, Ira and Harvey Manning. *50 Hikes in Mount Rainier National Park*. Seattle: The Mountaineers, 1978.

Spring, Ira and Harvey Manning. *55 Hikes in Central Washington*. Seattle: The Mountaineers, 1990.

Spring, Ira and Harvey Manning. *100 Hikes in Washington's Glacier Peak Region*. Seattle: The Mountaineers, 1988.

Spring, Ira and Harvey Manning. *101 Hikes in the North Cascades*. Seattle: The Mountaineers, 1979.

Spring, Vicky, Ira Spring and Harvey Manning. *100 Hikes in the Alpine Lakes*. Seattle: The Mountaineers, 1985.

Sterling, E. M. *Best Short Hikes in Washington's South Cascades and Olympics*. Seattle: The Mountaineers, 1995.

Sterling, E. M. *Trips and Trails, 1, Family Camps, Short Hikes and View Roads around the North Cascades*. Seattle: The Mountaineers, 1978.

Washington Atlas and Gazetteer. Maine: DeLorme Mapping Company, 1988.

Wood, Amos L. *Beachcombing for Japanese Floats*. Portland: Binford and Mort Publishing, 1985.

Wood, Amos L. *Beachcombing the Pacific*. West Chester, Pennsylvania: Schiffer Publishing, Ltd., 1987.

Appendix B:

Internet Tips and Nature Subjects Resources

Writing this book would not have been possible without the Internet. We queried chambers of commerce, visitor information centers, regional sites, and many other resources in small towns throughout Washington to find any overlooked seasonal events in their areas. Over 900 Web sites were used to research potential weekends, gather information to plan the trips, check resources we interviewed while on the actual trips, and recheck data in the chapters and appendices.

Web site addresses often change, so you may occasionally need to use a good search engine. If you get a message that your browser is "unable to locate the server," do a search on the name of the organization or subject.

If you get a message "file not found," we suggest starting at the top level in the site address and working down from there (e.g., if you can't find Christmas Bird Count information at www.wos.org/wacbcs.htm, change it to www.wos.org in the Location line of your browser).

The "For more information" section in each chapter of *Washington Nature Weekends* includes resources unique to that chapter. The appendix below has more-general resources. Both phone numbers and Web sites are given for each.

Note: A comprehensive list of Washington State Nature Resources (astronomy, birds, mammals, salmon, wild flowers, trees, mushrooms, etc., plus nature-related local, state, and national government agencies) is located on Sunny Walter's Web site: www.sunnywalter.com.

Nature Subjects Resources

National Audubon Society
Washington State Office, Olympia
    (360) 786–8020; wa.audubon.org/
Individual Washington Audubon Society Chapter information and addresses
    www.audubon.org/chapter/wa/wa/wastwhere.htm
Audubon and Birding Events in Washington State and British Columbia
    www.audubon.org/chapter/wa/wa/events.htm
Washington Native Plant Society (WNPS), Seattle
    (206) 323–3336 or (888) 288–8022; www.wnps.org
Individual WNPS Chapter Web sites
    www.wnps.org/chapters.html

Appendix C:

State and Regional Government Resources

Washington State Accessible Outdoor Recreation Guide
(state parks, wildlife areas, recreation areas, trails, visitor centers, campgrounds)
www.parks.wa.gov/ada-rec/

Washington Department of Fish and Wildlife (WDFW), Olympia
(360) 902–2200; www.wa.gov/wdfw/
Wildlife Areas and Access Points
www.wa.gov/wdfw/lands/wildarea.htm
The Weekender Report
www.wa.gov/wdfw/do/weekendr/weekendr.htm
WDFW Region 1: Eastern Washington, Spokane
(509) 456–4082; www.wa.gov/wdfw/reg/region1.htm
WDFW Region 2: North Central Washington, Ephrata
(509) 754–4624; www.wa.gov/wdfw/reg/region2.htm
WDFW Region 3: South Central Washington, Yakima
(509) 575–2740; www.wa.gov/wdfw/reg/region3.htm
WDFW Region 4: North Puget Sound, Mill Creek
(425) 775–1311; www.wa.gov/wdfw/reg/region4.htm
WDFW Region 5: Southwest Washington, Vancouver
(360) 696–6211; www.wa.gov/wdfw/reg/region5.htm
WDFW Region 6: Coastal Washington, Montesano
(360) 249–4628; www.wa.gov/wdfw/reg/region6.htm
Access Stewardship Decal
(required to park at many wildlife areas and water accesses)
www.wa.gov/wdfw/hab/steward/steward.htm

Washington State Department of Natural Resources (DNR)
Natural Area Preserve Program and Descriptions
(360) 902–1340; www.wa.gov/dnr/htdocs/fr/nhp/wanap.html

Washington State Parks and Recreation Commission
www.parks.wa.gov/
Information Center Line
(800) 233–0321

Individual Washington State Parks Information:
  www.parks.wa.gov/parkinfo.asp
WA State Park Reservations Northwest
  (800) 452–5687; www.parks.wa.gov/reserve.asp

Washington State Department of Community, Trade and Economic Development
Tourism Office
  (360) 753–5600 or (800) 544–1800; www.tourism.wa.gov/

Washington State Accommodations
Hosteling International–American Youth Hostels
  www.hostelweb.com
Internet Lodging Directory: Motels and Hotels in Washington
  www.usa-lodging.com/motels/washington/wacities.htm
Washington Bed & Breakfast Guild
  (800) 647–2918; www.wbbg.com/
Washington RV Park and Campground Directory
  www.gocampingamerica.com/stateassoc/washington/

Washington State Department of Transportation (DOT)
Traveler Information
  wsdot.wa.gov/traveler.htm
Mountain Pass Report
  (800) 695–7623; traffic.wsdot.wa.gov/sno-info/
Washington State Ferries and Vessel Accessibility
  (206) 464–6400 or (888) 808–7977; www.wsdot.wa.gov/ferries/

Appendix D:

U.S. Government Resources

U.S. Department of Agriculture

USDA Forest Service

Pacific Northwest Region, Portland
(503) 808–2971; www.fs.fed.us/r6/
Columbia River Gorge National Scenic Area
(509) 427–2528; www.fs.fed.us/r6/columbia/
Colville National Forest
(509) 684–7000; www.fs.fed.us/r6/colville
Gifford Pinchot National Forest
(360) 891–5000 or (360) 891–5009; www.fs.fed.us/gpnf/
Mount Baker–Snoqualmie National Forest
(425) 775–9702 or (800) 627–0062; www.fs.fed.us/r6/mbs/
Mount St. Helens National Volcanic Monument
(360) 247–3900; www.fs.fed.us/gpnf/mshnvm/
Mount St. Helens Visitor Center, Castle Rock
(360) 274–2100
Coldwater Ridge Visitor Center
(360) 274–2131
Johnston Ridge Observatory
(360) 274–2140
Hoffstadt Bluffs Visitor Center
(800) 752–8439; www.mt-st-helens.com/
Weyerhauser Forest Learning Center
(360) 414–3439; www.weyerhaeuser.com/sthelens/
Okanogan National Forest
(509) 826–3275 or 662–4335; www.fs.fed.us/r6/okanogan/
Olympic National Forest
(360) 956–2402; www.fs.fed.us/r6/olympic/
Wenatchee National Forest
(509) 662–4335; www.fs.fed.us/r6/wenatchee/
Annual Northwest Forest Pass
(required for most national forest trails)
www.fs.fed.us/r6/feedemo/

U.S. Department of Commerce

National Oceanic and Atmospheric Administration (NOAA)
  www.noaa.gov/
Tide Predictions (Oregon/Washington)
  www.co-ops.nos.noaa.gov/tpred2.html#OR

U.S. Naval Observatory
Astronomical Applications Department
(sunrise/set, moonrise/set, eclipses, etc.)
  aa.usno.navy.mil/data/

U.S. Department of the Interior

National Park Service (NPS)
  www.nps.gov/
Lake Chelan National Recreation Area
  http://www.nps.gov/lach/
National Park Service Information Center, Stehekin
  (360) 856–5700, ext. 340
Lake Roosevelt National Recreation Area
  (509) 633–9441; www.nps.gov/laro/
Mount Rainier National Park
  (360) 569–2211 (automated information menu); www.nps.gov/mora/
    Henry M. Jackson Visitor Center
      (360) 569–2211, ext. 2328
    Sunrise Visitor Center
      (360) 569–2211, ext. 2357
    Wilkeson Ranger Station
      (360) 829–5127
North Cascades National Park
  (360) 856–5700; www.nps.gov/noca/
Olympic National Park
  (360) 565–3130; www.nps.gov/olym/
Ross Lake National Recreation Area
  (360) 856–5700; www.nps.gov/rola/
National Parks Pass, Golden Age Passport, or Golden Eagle Passport
  ($15 upgrade that also allows you access to USDA Forest Service, U.S. Fish
  and Wildlife Service, and Bureau of Land Management areas)
  buy.nationalparks.org/

U.S. Fish and Wildlife Service (USFWS)

www.fws.gov/

USFWS Pacific Region

www.r1.fws.gov/

National Wildlife Refuges and National Fish Hatcheries

www.r1.fws.gov/visitor/washington.html

National Wildlife Refuges: Audubon Map

www.audubon.org/campaign/refuge/refuges/washing.html

National Fish Hatcheries

fisheries.fws.gov/region1.htm

Columbia NWR, Othello

(509) 488–2668; www.cbas.org/special/cnwr/

Conboy Lake NWR, Glenwood

(509) 364–3410; www.rl.fws.gov/ridgefield/Conboy.htm

Dungeness NWR, Washington Maritime NWR, Port Angeles

(360) 457–8451; www.dungeness.com/refuge/

Grays Harbor NWR, Hoquiam (360) 753–9467; graysharbor.fws.gov/

Julia Butler Hansen Refuge for Columbian White-tailed Deer, Cathlamet

(360) 795–3915

Little Pend Oreille NWR, Colville

(509) 684–8384

McNary NWR, Burbank

(509) 547–4942; www.rl.fws.gov/mcnwr/McNarypage.htm

    McNary Environmental Education Center

        www.nwr.mcnary.wa.us/

Nisqually NWR, Olympia

(360) 753–9467; nisqually.fws.gov/

Ridgefield NWR, Ridgefield

(360) 887–4106; www.rl.fws.gov/ridgefield/Ridge.htm

Toppenish NWR

(509) 865–2405; www.rl.fws.gov/mcnwr/Toppenpage.htm

Turnbull NWR, Cheney

(509) 235–4723; www.rl.fws.gov/turnbull/turnball.html

Willapa NWR, Ilwaco

(360) 484–3482

Annual Refuge Pass

(refuge entrance is also permitted with the Golden Eagle Passport)

Appendix E:

Best Bets

Best Trips for Families with Young Children

3   Meet Me at the Feeding Station
7   Walk to Cure the Winter Blues
9   Glass Balls and Other Treasures
12 Red Crowns, Gray Cloaks
15 Honor Our Precious Earth
19 Butterflies and Blossoms
25 Celebrating Wildflowers
26 In Search of Spock and Spieden
28 Ebb-Tide Treasures
33 Fascinating Felines and Other Predators
37 Return of the Salmon
45 A Flourish of Foliage and Feathers
48 Wild Sanctuaries in the Big City
50 Wildlife Parties

Easiest Trips

(for the mobility impaired, see also the *Accessible Outdoor Recreation Guide* at www.parks.wa.gov/ada-rec)

1   Adventure on a Long, Long Lake (ferry)
2   Life from the Ferry Lane (ferry, driving tour)
3   Meet Me at the Feeding Station (stationary)
4   Bald Eagles, Surviving and Thriving (stationary)
5   Big White Birds Flock Together (driving tour, stationary)
6   Winter Raptor Central (driving tour)
10 Nature's Mating Game (driving tour)
12 Red Crowns, Gray Cloaks (driving or bus tour)
20 The Big Bang (driving tour)
26 In Search of Spock and Spieden (accessible walk)
41 On the Trail of the Golden Larch (sidebar—driving tour)
43 Fascinating Fungi (show)
47 Endangered Species, Mating Dance (driving tour)
52 Take Time for Tranquillity (retreat)

Best Trips for Rainy Days

Best Trips for Snow

Best Trips for Photographers

29   Ancient Ice (glaciers, wildflowers, mountains)

30   Starry, Starry Night (astrophotography)

32   Secret in the South Cascades (wildflowers, waterfalls, mountains)

33   Fascinating Felines and Other Predators (captive animals)

36   Pelicans in the Potholes (shorebirds, egrets, pelicans)

40   Wooing Wapiti (elk, rain forests)

41   On the Trail of the Golden Larch (fall foliage)

47   Endangered Species, Mating Dance (deer, birds)

49   Champion Trees Measure Up (rain forest, trees)

Best Trips for Walkers or Hikers

7   Walk to Cure the Winter Blue (walk)

8   Cute, Cuddly, and Floats on Its Back (hike)

9   Glass Balls and Other Treasures (walk)

13   Slide Across the Straits (hike)

14   Creepy, Crawly Critters (walk)

16   Let the Blooming Begin (walk)

18   Flyways of the World (walk)

19   Butterflies and Blossoms (walk)

21   Melting Snow, Roaring Water (walk, hike)

23   Walk, Run, Ride, and Work (walk, hike)

27   Flourishing Wildflowers, Newborn Wildlife (walk, hike)

29   Ancient Ice (walk, hike)

32   Secret in the South Cascades (hike)

41   On the Trail of the Golden Larch (hike)

42   Changing Seasons, Passing Through (walk)

43   Fascinating Fungi (walk, hike)

45   A Flourish of Foliage and Feathers (walk)

48   Wild Sanctuaries in the Big City (walk)

49   Champion Trees Measure Up (walk)

Best Trips by Personal Boat

19   Butterflies and Blossoms (kayak/canoe)

23   Walk, Run, Ride, and Work (raft, kayak/canoe)

27   Flourishing Wildflowers, Newborn Wildlife (kayak)

35   Hail the Mighty Waters (raft, kayak/canoe)

36   Pelicans in the Potholes (kayak/canoe)

38   Haul Out at High Tide (kayak/canoe)

47   Endangered Species, Mating Dance (kayak)
52   Take Time for Tranquillity (kayak)

Best Trips by Tour Boat

1   Adventure on a Long, Long Lake (ferry)
2   Life from the Ferry Lane (ferry)
11   Journey of the Giants (charter boat)
13   Slide Across the Straits (charter boat)
15   Honor Our Precious Earth (jet boat)
22   Subtle Blooms and Bold Terrain (jet boat)
24   Feathered Babies (jet boat)
26   In Search of Spock and Spieden (charter boat)
31   Living on the Seas of the World (charter boat)
35   Hail the Mighty Waters (cruise boat)
52   Take Time for Tranquillity (ferry)

Best Bets by Subject

Trips to See Birds and Butterflies

2   Life from the Ferry Lane (seabirds, eagles)
4   Bald Eagles, Surviving and Thriving (eagles)
5   Big White Birds Flock Together (snow geese, swans)
6   Winter Raptor Central (raptors)
10   Nature's Mating Game (herons, swans)
12   Red Crowns, Gray Cloaks (cranes)
13   Slide Across the Straits (raptors, seabirds)
17   Ballet in White and Black (shorebirds)
18   Flyways of the World (songbirds)
19   Butterflies and Blossoms (butterflies)
24   Feathered Babies (osprey, cormorants, eagles)
31   Living on the Seas of the World (pelagic birds)
36   Pelicans in the Potholes (shorebirds, egrets, pelicans)
39   Follow the Leading Lines (raptors)
42   Changing Seasons, Passing Through (waterfowl and more)
45   A Flourish of Foliage and Feathers (waterfowl, songbirds)
46   Across the Border and Back (seabirds)
47   Endangered Species, Mating Dance (waterbirds, raptors)
51   Over a Century of Tradition (bird count)

Trips to See Mammals, Salmon, and Amphibians

1   Adventure on a Long, Long Lake (deer, goats)
2   Life from the Ferry Lane (seals)
3   Meet Me at the Feeding Station (elk, bighorn sheep)
8   Cute, Cuddly, and Floats on Its Back (sea otters)
11   Journey of the Giants (gray whales)
14   Creepy, Crawly Critters (reptiles, amphibians)
20   The Big Bang (elk)
24   Feathered Babies (elk, deer, goats)
26   In Search of Spock and Spieden (orcas)
27   Flourishing Wildflowers, Newborn Wildlife (deer, marmots)
28   Ebb-Tide Treasures (sea life)
31   Living on the Seas of the World (dolphins)
33   Fascinating Felines and Other Predators (captive cats and more)
35   Hail the Mighty Waters (salmon)
37   Return of the Salmon (salmon)
38   Haul Out at High Tide (seals)
40   Wooing Wapiti (elk)
44   Voice of the Wild (captive wolves)
47   Endangered Species, Mating Dance (deer, elk)
50   Wildlife Parties (captive caribou and more)

Trips to See Geology or Astronomy

14   Creepy, Crawly Critters (scablands)
16   Let the Blooming Begin (scablands)
19   Butterflies and Blossoms (mounds)
20   The Big Bang (volcano, cave)
22   Subtle Blooms and Bold Terrain (canyons)
24   Feathered Babies (cave)
29   Ancient Ice (glaciers)
30   Starry, Starry Night (astronomy)
34   A Delectable Feast (cave)
52   Take Time for Tranquillity (gorge)

Trips to See Wildflowers

16   Let the Blooming Begin
18   Flyways of the World
19   Butterflies and Blossoms

Trips to See the Seashore, Ocean, or Inland Straits

Index

About the Authors

Sunny Walter is a professional nature photographer, writer, and former Boeing systems engineer. She was photo editor of *Washington Wildlife* magazine, and currently photographs for Washington State Tourism and environ-

mental organizations, along with designing nature and photo Web sites. Sunny's photos have been published in *Washington, A Journey of Discovery;* two Nature Conservancy books; *Washington Wildlife Viewing Guide; Sunset Magazine; PhotoMedia;* and others. Her interests include hiking, kayaking, and snowshoeing to natural places of great beauty and solitude where wildlife is supreme.

Janet O'Mara is a lifelong writer and editor. She worked for many years for the Washington Department of Fish and Wildlife, the Washington State

Parks and Recreation Commission, and as editor of *Washington Wildlife* magazine. Her interests include bird–watching, camping, hiking, sailing, and sharing the joy of nature with others, especially children.

"*Guerrilla TeleSelling* provides hundreds of ways to make your phone become a powerful weapon to capture the illusive and wary prospect."

—**Lynella Grant**
Author, *The Business Card Book*

"The Guerrilla Team have done it again! They combine great ideas with easy-to-implement strategies to really take advantage of the cyber-world we now live in. This is a winning book with just the right mix of stories and strategies for twenty-first-century success!"

—**Melissa Giovagnoli**
Author, *Make Your Connections Count!*
The Six-Step System to Build Your MegaNetwork

"If you sell anything by phone, this book is *a must read! It will help you sell more, faster!*"

—**Wolf J. Rinke, Ph.D.**
President, Wolf Rinke Associates, Inc., Clarksville, MD
Author, *The 6 Success Strategies for Winning
at Life, Love and Business*

"In this day of fewer being driven faster to do more, with less, *Guerrilla TeleSelling* is a "must read" in your service to your customers! One caution—read it before your competitors do, and hope they never find the Guerrilla tools."

—**Dr. Lyman K. Steil**
President, Communications Development, Inc.,
St. Paul, Minnesota

"This is a terrific book packed with great ideas. Read it now to learn. Keep it close by for frequent reference. I highly recommend it."

—**Nido R. Quebein**
Chairman, Creative Services, Inc., High Point, NC

"At last—a no-stone-unturned warehouse of innovative ideas for tele-marketing staff and management professionals. If differentiation, increasing sales, and working smart matters, this is a must-read, must-do daily guide to being the best in TeleSelling. No pro should be without it. I will give it a five-star recommendation in all of my sales training sessions."

—**Lorna Riley, CSP**
Author, *76 Ways to Build a Straight Referral Business, ASAP*

"This book is a must. For successfully getting through on the phone to overwhelmed people who are sidestepping all your efforts. This book is a must! A MUST! Anyone using the concepts who does not meet with success probably does not feel strong enough about their message."

—**Alan Cimberg**
P ofessional Speaker, Educator, and Motivator

"Finally! A book that "tells it like it is" to all of us who battle with voice mail, gatekeepers, AND the hold button. Thanks again for Guerrilla tactics THAT WORK!"

—**Renee P. Walkup**
President, SalesPEAK, Inc.

"In the best of the Guerrilla tradition, Jay and his partners have done it again. This is a must-read for any telephone salesperson, sales manager, and anyone who does business on the phone."

—**Thomas P. Reilly**
Speaker–Sales Trainer, Sales Motivation Services

"Viva Guerrillas! Multimillion-dollar telemarketing producers already march right to the bank with the breakthroughs they've received from one idea in your book. And this is just one of hundreds of useful and money-generating ideas for TeleSelling professionals. The Guerrilla Group has again struck with ferocious intensity to ensure everyone who reads this book joins the ranks of top producers."

—**Paul R. Scheele**
Author, *Natural Brilliance* and
The PhotoReading Whole Mind Systems